Founding Spirits

Signed by the Author
for

George Washington's
MOUNT VERNON
E S T A T E & G A R D E N S

Founding Spirits

George Washington and the Beginnings of the American Whiskey Industry

Dennis J. Pogue

Harbour Books

1 3 5 7 9 10 8 6 4 2

Library of Congress Control Number: 2011932589

Founding Spirits
George Washington and the Beginnings of the American Whiskey
Industry
Dennis J. Pogue
Includes Bibliographical References

p. cm.
1. George Washington 1758–1799
2. Distilleries – United States
3. American History 1607–1935

I. Pogue, Dennis J., 1952— II. Title.

ISBN 13: 978-0-9835565-0-3 (hardcover : alk. paper)

ISBN 13: 978-0-9835565-1-0 (softcover : alk. paper)

Cover photo of interior of distillery by Russ Flint.
Porthole Portrait of George Washington, 1795 by Rembrandt Peale, 1855–1860.

Edited by Judy Rogers • Cover and Book Design by Emilie Davis

Harbour Books
An imprint of
Mariner Media, Inc.
131 West 21st Street
Buena Vista, VA 24416
Tel: 540-264-0021
www.marinermedia.com

Printed in the United States of America

This book is printed on acid-free paper meeting the
requirements of the American Standard for Permanence of Paper
for Printed Library Materials.

CONTENTS

PREFACE

This book really had its genesis almost 20 years ago. One summer afternoon when I visited George Washington's Gristmill State Park, I noticed that a portion of the lawn was bounded by a large rectangle formed of bricks. A nearby sign indicated that the bricks marked the approximate location of Washington's whiskey distillery. I had known from reading Washington's correspondence that late in his life he had operated a distillery on the property. But until I saw the bricks and the sign, I had never considered the possibility of finding the site and excavating it.

What better way to make Washington more accessible to people who only knew him as the "old man" on the one-dollar bill than to tell his story as a distiller and entrepreneurial businessman? Almost a decade later we had the opportunity to search for the remains of the building, and the sign was as good as its word.

After ten years of excavation, planning, and building, we have erected the replica of Washington's stone still house, and the interest in the site and the story of Washington's distillery has been overwhelming. So much so, that telling the story of the project in book form seemed like the perfect complement, and its appearance caps one of the most rewarding endeavors of my museum career.

* Note: Speech and spelling patterns of the Colonial period were preserved in all quotations with minimal insertions used only for clarification purposes.
* Use of "whiskey" and "whisky" in the text reflects the different spellings of the word that are typically used in the United States and Great Britain, respectively.

ACKNOWLEDGMENTS

I need to thank several individuals and organizations for their assistance in making this book possible. At Mount Vernon, the President and Chief Executive Officer, Jim Rees, and all of the Ladies making up the board of directors were stalwart supporters of the vision to engage the public about the first president's virtually unknown career as a distiller.

The archaeological investigations that revealed and documented the exceptionally well-preserved physical remains of the distillery were at the heart of the effort's success. The excavations and the associated documentary research were led by Mount Vernon's Director of Archaeology, Esther White, ably supported by her assistants, Christy Leeson and Eleanor Breen. Thanks also go to the dozens of other staff, students, interns, and volunteers who worked on the excavation over a period of more than five years. Three talented individuals consulted with me to interpret the archaeological and documentary evidence and develop plans for a faithful recreation of Washington's distillery: Orlando Ridout V, Willie Graham, and John O'Rourke.

The money required to pay for both the research and the reconstruction was provided by the member companies of the Distilled Spirits Council of the United States (DISCUS) and the Wine and Spirits Wholesalers of America. I also want to thank all of the staff of DISCUS and the master distillersand many others in the liquor industry who gave so much of their time and expertise over the years to help us tell the story of Washington's distillery.

Finally, Andy Wolfe and the rest of the team at Mariner Media were a joy to work with, and I thank them for turning my manuscript into a book that gives me great pride.

INTRODUCTION

To the surprise of some, George Washington's association with alcoholic beverages was extensive. In his personal life he was a confirmed social drinker—he consumed ale and beer, cider and brandy, rum and whiskey, and an assortment of wines. He is known to have especially favored the Portuguese Madeira that he imported by the barrel, and which was the strong drink of choice among the members of elite society throughout Anglo-America. Washington offered the wine as an after dinner treat to the many visitors who routinely sought his company in the years following the Revolution, and he delighted in toasting the new nation that he had been so instrumental in founding. As commander in chief of the Continental Army during the war and as the first president of the United States, Washington was involved in many policy decisions relating to alcohol production, its use, and its regulation. General Washington made it clear that alcohol played an important role in the success of the war effort, and on more than one occasion, he lobbied Congress to ensure that the soldiers received their customary ration, which he characterized as "so essential, that it is not to be dispensed with." On the other hand, Washington had few illusions about the detrimental effects of overindulgence. Over the course of his lifetime he was forced to endure the poor performance of valued employees, soldiers, and even their officers, as a consequence of habitual drunkenness and the erratic behavior that ensued.[1]

More knowledgeable students of American history may know about the first president's leading role in suppressing the so-called Whiskey Rebellion. This was an abortive uprising that occurred in 1794, led by disaffected farmers in western Pennsylvania and other frontier regions who were outraged by efforts on the part of the new Federal Government to increase revenues by imposing an excise tax on whiskey. Washington and his Secretary of the Treasury, Alexander Hamilton, were convinced that the revenues generated by the whiskey tax were necessary to promote the economic stability of the nation. But even more important to Washington was affirming the authority of the government to impose the taxes and then to enforce their compliance. So seriously did Washington view the threat caused by the uprising that he personally took command and led almost 13,000 troops into the field to quell the unrest. Thus, for President Washington, this conflict had nothing to do with either the morality or the legality of alcohol production and consumption but rather was a crucial test of the strong central government that he had championed and now led.[2]

What few people know is that only a few years after that event Washington himself embarked on a new career as a producer of alcohol, erecting a stone whiskey distillery near the gristmill at his Mount Vernon estate in northern Virginia. The distillery operated five stills that produced more than 10,000 gallons of rye whiskey in 1799, the last year of Washington's life. Although the still house was destroyed by fire only 15 years later, the extensive plantation financial records, Washington's correspondence, and the accounts of visitors testify to the ambitious scale of the operation, and indicate that it was one of the largest and most profitable whiskey distilleries in the young nation. The unprecedented success of Washington's efforts in this regard make him one of the unsung pioneers in the development of the American whiskey industry.[3]

From naturally modest beginnings in the first decades of the 17th century, the production of alcoholic beverages in America expanded and matured until by the early 1800s it was one of the most important industries in the nation. The production and consumption of brandy was at its height during the first century of settlement, reflecting its traditional prominence in England. Rum was a New World invention, on the other hand, made from distilling molasses (a by-product of making sugar) from the West Indies, and its low cost and ready availability soon meant that it outstripped brandy and all other distilled beverages in popularity. Rum distilleries sprang up along the eastern seaboard beginning in the 1640s, concentrating in cities like Boston that had strong shipping ties to the Caribbean, with the output of the American rum distillers augmenting the vast quantities of the spirit that were imported from the islands. Whiskey was a decidedly less popular beverage than rum throughout the Colonial Era, although it had been made for centuries in the British Isles. But one of the unintended consequences of winning the Revolution was the dramatic increase in the price of Caribbean rum and molasses. The higher prices reduced the American market for rum, which in turn spurred production of cheap whiskey made from local grains to satisfy the demand for a highly alcoholic spirit.[4]

When Washington established his distillery at Mount Vernon in 1797 the American whiskey industry was in the first years of a period of dramatic growth that by 1810 yielded almost 23 million gallons of spirits annually. When combined with rum (almost three million gallons), the value of spirits distilled was $15.5 million, or roughly 8–9 percent of the total estimated value of the country's manufactured products enumerated in that year's census. Even so, the industry continued to be dominated by small-scale operators who produced hundreds, not thousands, of gallons of whiskey each year. With at least 14,191 distilleries spread across 18 states, 2 districts, and 6 territories, average production that year was roughly 1,500 gallons, or less than 15 percent of Washington's distillery's output more than a decade earlier. Over the next quarter-century great strides were made in improving the technology of distilling, with the advent of the steam-heated perpetual still leading to ever-increasing efficiency. As the nation's population grew and as settlement spread to the Great Plains and the West Coast, the whiskey industry responded to the expanding market by increasing production accordingly.[5]

Unlike almost any other major American industry, however, the country's liquor producers faced an entrenched and growing challenge to their very right to exist. Clergymen and reform groups led the anti-liquor movement on the basis of religious, moral, and social concerns, and it constituted a strong force in American life and politics throughout the 19th century. Abrupt swings in the attitudes of the citizenry toward the proper place of alcohol in the fabric of American society finally culminated with the triumph of the prohibition movement when the 18th Amendment to the Constitution was passed by Congress and went into effect in January 1920. Although the law seemed to mark the end to America's long tradition of consumption of alcoholic beverages, only 13 years later the landmark legislation was rejected as a disastrous failure, and the liquor industry was back in business. The enforced hiatus in the legal production of beverage alcohol naturally had a profound effect on the fortunes of individual distillers and brands, but the whiskey industry as a whole rebounded remarkably quickly to its former prominence. Over the intervening decades competition from other types of spirits, growing awareness of the social costs of over-indulgence, and the global reach of market forces and entrepreneurship all have combined to reshape the contours of the industry up to the present.[6]

Given George Washington's iconic status in American history and popular culture, his name and image have been appropriated countless times over the years by a variety of groups and individuals to support their equally divergent agendas. Those on either side of such wide ranging topics as the role America should play in foreign affairs, the nation's treatment of minorities, and the place of religion in American life, all have found a spot for Washington on their team. Not surprisingly, this has extended to the debate over the propriety of alcohol consumption—prohibitionists, teetotalers, liquor advertising agents, lobbyists, and distillers all have enlisted Washington to serve their particular cause.

In the 1840s, Washington's persona was adopted by a short-lived but influential faction of the anti-liquor crusade, who styled themselves as the George Washington Temperance Society. Established in Baltimore in 1840 by a group of reformed tipplers, the motto of the Washingtonians was, "We bear a patriot's honored name, Our country's welfare is our aim." The Washingtonians' goal was to convince their fellow drinkers to sign a pledge of total abstinence from strong drink. Over the next few years the group was remarkably successful in their efforts, with one source estimating that up to 600,000 individuals signed the abstinence pledge. The passionate nature of the Washingtonians' campaign could not be sustained for long, however, and after only a few years their movement lost momentum; by 1847 almost all of the local branches of the group had disbanded. But the efforts of the Washingtonians were not in vain, as they combined with the many other anti-liquor groups that were active in the decades leading up to the Civil War in causing a substantial overall decline in the consumption of alcohol throughout the country.[7]

Almost a century later, Washington literally became the "poster boy" for a sophisticated advertising campaign promoting a venerable whiskey brand, named Mount Vernon Rye. First produced in Baltimore in the 1860s, the "Mount Vernon" referred to on the label was not Washington's home in Virginia, and there is no record of how the brand received its name. But most likely it stemmed from the fact that one of the first monuments honoring George Washington had been erected in the city 30 years after his death, and the upscale neighborhood surrounding the memorial came to be known as Mount Vernon. The distillery and the brand gained considerable notice in 1876 when it was selected to represent the industry at the Centennial Exhibition in Philadelphia, and a working model based on the Mount Vernon distillery in Baltimore was

*George Washington was adopted as the promotional symbol for an
anti-liquor group that was formed in the 1840s, known as the Washington
Temperance Society.*

incorporated into the exposition's agricultural building. The popularity of the brand continued to grow, at least partly due to an aggressive commitment to advertising, which promoted the fact that Mount Vernon Rye won first prizes at four world's fairs (New Orleans 1885, Australia 1887, and Chicago 1893, in addition to Philadelphia). The distillery changed ownership a number of times, but it was in production almost continuously until the onset of Prohibition in 1920. Even then, the company continued to produce "medicinal" whiskey, which was licensed and authorized for sale to private citizens with the prescription of a physician.[8]

It wasn't until after the repeal of Prohibition and the return of legal production of beverage alcohol in 1933 that Mount Vernon Rye took on a closer association with George Washington. This was the golden age of mass-market print advertising, and the re-established liquor industry took full advantage of the many nationally distributed "life style" magazines as a venue to peddle their wares. From that time until the brand finally was discontinued in 1957, Washington "starred" in a series of advertisements for Mount Vernon Rye that appeared in the pages of such glossy mainstream outlets as *Time*, *Life*, and *Esquire*. The anonymous Madison Avenue advertising executives who dreamed up the concept for the campaign certainly did their homework, as they mined Washington's voluminous papers for information to enliven the ads. It started with the discovery that Washington had established a distillery at his Mount Vernon estate in 1797, where he soon made and sold thousands of gallons of rye whiskey. Of special note was the fact that Washington hired a Scotsman, by the name of James Anderson, to operate his distillery, and that Anderson had brought his whiskey making skills with him to America when he migrated from his home country.

One particularly inventive ad that appeared in *Time* on September 30, 1935, used a quotation from a letter that Washington had written in 1797 as its point of departure.

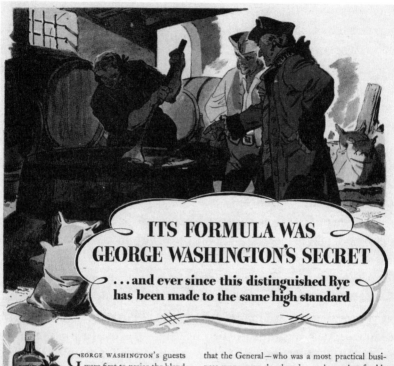

ITS FORMULA WAS GEORGE WASHINGTON'S SECRET

...and ever since this distinguished Rye has been made to the same high standard

GEORGE WASHINGTON'S guests were first to praise the bland richness of the whiskey which today is famed throughout the English-speaking world as Mount Vernon.

But back in 1797 it was the private stock of America's first citizen, whose hospitality was notable for its excellence in all things.

Its formula was a secret between Washington and James Anderson, his chief overseer—at whose suggestion a distillery had been built at Mount Vernon to utilize the bumper rye crops grown on the rich Potomac bottom lands.

Anderson had learned the distiller's art in his native Scotland, and so in time a whiskey was matured that the master of Mount Vernon considered worthy of his house.

So palatable, so rich and mellow was this rye

that the General—who was a most practical business man—soon developed a ready market for his surplus among friends in neighboring states, and even overseas in England.

Washington's heirs continued to make it until nearly a century ago when the distillery was removed to Baltimore—but the original formula is still zealously followed.

It is from this great lineage—this 140 years of accumulated skill—that Mount Vernon Bottled in Bond Straight Rye Whiskey inherits its incomparable excellence.

Mount Vernon
Straight Rye Whiskey—Bottled in Bond
Under U. S. Government supervision

A Good Guide to Good Whiskey

© 1935, The American Medicinal Spirits Corporation, Baltimore, Md.

The Mount Vernon Rye Whiskey brand was marketed widely in the 1930s and 1940s using an imagined association with George Washington and his distillery to illustrate the ad campaign.

Washington wrote to an acquaintance, John Fitzgerald, who operated a rum distillery in nearby Alexandria, asking his advice on the wisdom of accepting Anderson's offer to make whiskey at Mount Vernon. In the letter Washington admitted to Fitzgerald that he knew nothing about making "spirits," and that he was totally dependent on Anderson's avowed expertise. Fitzgerald promptly responded that given Anderson's credentials, the venture was almost assured to be a success. "As to a sale of the whiskey there can be no doubt," Fitzgerald concluded, "if the Quantity was ten times as much as he can make provided it is of a good Quality." More than testifying to Anderson's skills as a distiller, Fitzgerald was alluding to the prodigious quantities of alcohol that were consumed by Americans at the time.[9]

The rest of the rather overwrought copy reads like something issuing from the media offices of any of today's premium spirits producers around the world. First, there was a reference to time honored tradition: "Among the fond recollections of guests at Mount Vernon, after George Washington's retirement to private life, was a superbly mellow rye whiskey" that had been "distilled at Mount Vernon under the skilled hand of James Anderson, the General's chief overseer, who had learned the art in Scotland." This was followed by a nod to the gracious hospitality of the day in allowing others to share the fruits of Anderson's labors. And then there was a little bending of the truth, with the claim that Washington's whiskey was so sought after that it was even exported for sale abroad: "But so excellent was the whiskey, so many begged the privilege of buying a cask or two," that soon Washington's rye "found its way into neighboring states, and even to England." Finally, it concluded with a pledge to maintain a level of quality that presumably would have made the "father of our country" proud: "Mount Vernon Bottled in Bond Straight Rye Whiskey is still produced by the original formula...And that is why you will relish in it today the same magnificent flavor that was the toast of Washington's friends."[10]

After Washington's death in 1799, the distillery passed to
a member of his family and continued to operate until the still
house finally was destroyed by fire in 1814. It never reopened
for business, and the purported connections between the
original and the later products of the Baltimore distillery were
merely fanciful musings aimed at increasing sales to prospective
consumers. The stones making up the walls of the distillery, as
well as the other buildings on the site, were salvaged to form
the foundations for a number of private homes that were built
in the surrounding neighborhood. By 1931 no evidence of the
original structures could be seen, and several tobacco barns and
other farm buildings occupied the pastoral site. An unpaved
local road ran through the property, just as it had more than a
century before, and the surrounding fields still were farmed by
the descendants of a group of Quakers who had purchased the
land in the 1850s.[11]

The situation changed dramatically with the impending
200th anniversary of George Washington's birth in 1732. The
upcoming celebration spurred renewed interest in the site on the
part of Virginia state officials who were seeking an appropriate
means of honoring the first president's memory. After
consulting documentary records and inspecting the tract
to confirm that it was, indeed, the site of Washington's
gristmill and distillery, the state purchased the seven-acre
property. They demolished the modern farm buildings and
began to excavate the site of the mill, which was the first
focus of their attention. The workers soon revealed the stone
foundations of the building, along with remnants of the
raceway that brought water to the mill to power the machinery
that ground the grain. They even found a section of the
wooden water wheel that had been preserved buried several
feet underground in the moist and oxygen-free environment
of the stream bank. Additional excavations uncovered
the foundations of the nearby frame building where the
miller had lived, along with the still house, located about 50
yards away from the other buildings. As reconstructing the

mill was the highest priority, work began on that building in 1932, with both the mill and the miller's cottage completed the following year.[12]

In 1933 officials working for the commonwealth developed an ambitious plan to expand the amenities at the site to include reconstructing Washington's distillery. Given the financial constraints imposed by the ongoing Depression, a shortage of capital undoubtedly was the main reason why the idea was dropped. But discomfort over associating George Washington so closely with alcohol may have been a contributing factor. Even though Prohibition had been overwhelmingly rejected as a costly and destructive failed experiment, in the mid-1930s millions of Americans still viewed alcohol as an evil, and many of them mistakenly claimed Washington as one of their own. Although defeated by the weight of overwhelming public opinion on the legality of alcohol consumption, temperance supporters may well have viewed losing the imagined backing of Washington as a final, unacceptable blow. Linking Washington's name with whiskey in the Mount Vernon Rye magazine ads must have rankled those among the "drys" who saw them, but the idea of the Virginia state government's actually rebuilding a structure identified as Washington's distillery struck a particularly sensitive nerve.

In 1935 the plans to reconstruct the distillery became public, apparently leaked to the Associated Press, who wired the story to its hundreds of subscribers across the country. The news elicited a strong outcry that likely was the final straw dooming the proposed reconstruction project. In response, William Carson, who was the Virginia official in charge of developing the site, wrote what appears to have been a blatantly dissembling letter that was published in a San Antonio, Texas, newspaper called the *Public Opinion*. In his letter Carson denied leaking the news, and went so far as to suggest that the actual site of the distillery may not have been located on the gristmill property after all. This seems to have been an outright lie, as Carson was part of the team planning the new buildings, and there can be no doubt that he knew that the foundation of the distillery had been uncovered there. Equally puzzling is how Carson thought this bit of disinformation would help to calm the media flap. At any rate, the newspaper editor seems to have spoken for many in the anti-liquor camp when he denounced Carson's plan as yet "another infamous lie sent over the country by an element who would drag George Washington's name in the mire," by associating him with alcohol.[13]

Almost 60 years later, officials with the Commonwealth of Virginia approached the Mount Vernon Ladies' Association, the non-profit foundation that operates George Washington's home as a public trust, with a proposal to convey the Gristmill State Park to the Association. Visitation at the mill never reached the levels that had been anticipated by state planners in the 1930s, and the officials hoped that a closer association with the Mount Vernon estate, three miles down the road and with upwards of one million visitors each year, would give the site greater visibility. State officials had made similar offers to the Mount Vernon board of directors many times over the preceding decades, and they always had been politely but firmly rebuffed. The Mount Vernon board had declined the offers in the past out of a belief that operating the mill was beyond the historic mission of the organization. But by 1995 Mount Vernon was in the process of expanding its interpretive programs to include portraying Washington's career as an innovative farm manager and as an entrepreneurial businessman, and the Ladies now viewed operating the mill as a logical complement to those efforts. Since it was known that Washington's distillery had been located near the mill, taking on the property was seen as providing a golden opportunity to learn more about this important element of the plantation economy as well.[14]

In 1997 Mount Vernon took over the park and began to restore the mill so that it would operate as it had in the 18th century. The staff also undertook an archaeological survey of the tract, hoping to relocate the site of the distillery and to find the other smaller buildings, such as a malt house and a cooperage, that are known from documentary sources to have been erected there. Within weeks the archaeologists uncovered conclusive evidence pinpointing the site of the still house, consisting of a cluster of 18th-century domestic items like ceramics, glass, and tobacco pipes, as well as structural remains like nails, mortar, and brick and stone fragments.[15]

From 1999 until 2005, Mount Vernon's archaeologists excavated an area more than 4,500 square feet in extent, and succeeded in tracing the outline of the building's roughly 75- by 33-foot foundation. They also found remnants of brick- and wood-lined drains, scorched soils, and deteriorated bricks marking the locations of the stills, and other evidence for the layout of the distilling operation. Together with the documentary information provided by hundreds of entries in the Mount Vernon plantation records, Washington's correspondence, and other period sources, these findings provided the basis to prepare a remarkably detailed portrait of the building and how it worked. After two years of design and planning, construction of the recreated distillery began in the summer of 2005, with the building completed and opened to visitors in spring 2007.[16]

Far from impugning George Washington's character, the recent effort to document the history of his distillery and present that story to the public is an attempt to further define his persona by examining an aspect of his life and times that largely has been ignored. That Washington was an entrepreneur who bankrolled one of the largest whiskey distilleries in America is undoubtedly a surprise to many, and testifies to the importance of alcohol production and consumption in the early years of the country's history. Visitors to Mount Vernon now are able to observe the full range of agricultural activities that took place at the plantation, including all of the steps required in growing, grinding, and distilling the grain that made its way into the former president's whiskey.

CHAPTER 1

"SPIRITUOUS LIQUORS"

From the perspective provided by the passage of more than 200 years, George Washington might be described as having a "modern" attitude toward alcoholic beverages. He drank a range of "spirituous liquors" (as they were then typically called) both in private and in public, and he went to great pains to supply his family and guests, the soldiers he commanded during two wars, and even his enslaved workers, with appropriate beverages. Yet he also was fully aware of the dangers of drinking to excess, and at different times, he discharged two of his most valued employees because they were unable to control their thirst for strong drink. It was the continued inability of one of these men to curb his drinking that led Washington sadly to observe, "An aching head and trimbling limbs which are the inevitable effects of drinking disincline the hands from work hence begins sloth and that Lestlessness which end in idleness." Nevertheless, Washington remained convinced of the benefits of moderate consumption of alcohol, and late in his life he had no qualms about starting one of the largest and most profitable whiskey distilleries in America.[1]

Beverage alcohol served a variety of purposes in American society during George Washington's day. In an era when the practice of medicine was still rudimentary, drinking alcohol was widely held to be beneficial to health, and doctors routinely prescribed it as a tonic against a host of ailments. Securing dependable sources of potable water had been a challenge throughout much of Western Europe for centuries, and it was a problem that arose in America as well. Ale, beer, hard cider, wine, and distilled spirits all were deemed healthier alternatives to water. As in almost every Western nation, friendly gatherings where liquor was consumed acted as a balm and a bond within all classes of American society. In the North, alcohol often was distributed as a reward to workers, and in the South the practice was extended to enslaved laborers as well as in exchange for performing unusual or especially arduous duties. Finally, as a commodity with a significant market value, the production, distribution, and sale of alcoholic beverages was a major stimulus to commerce and a particular boon to trans-Atlantic trade. In short, alcohol was an integral part of American life, just as it was in Britain, Europe, and most of the rest of the non-Muslim world.[2]

The widespread practice by candidates to dispense liquor at the polls in an attempt to gain the support of voters is one measure of its pervasiveness in early American life. George Washington learned firsthand the consequences of failing to provide such largess. When he first ran for election to the Virginia House of Burgesses in 1755, his campaign was poorly managed, including committing the major oversight of failing to treat the voters to strong drink. As a result, Washington lost the election by the resounding margin of 271 and 270 to 40. Three years later, when he stood a second time for election to the House, Washington employed a different strategy. He purchased large quantities of alcohol and freely distributed it to prospective voters, and this time he won. Washington exhorted his agents not to have "too sparing a hand," and they dutifully gave away 47 gallons of beer, more than 70 gallons of rum punch, 34.5 gallons of wine, 2 gallons of cider, and 3.5 pints of brandy, for which Washington had paid almost £40. If divided equally among the 310 men who cast their ballots for Washington, each man received almost half a gallon of alcoholic beverages. We can only hope that they didn't drink it all in one day.[3]

Washington's account books and correspondence contain many other references to purchasing a variety of liquors. Washington personally preferred Madeira, a sweet wine, and ale and beer, but he also imported large quantities of rum, primarily to serve guests and as rations for his workers. As was his custom in acquiring a wide range of household goods that were not available locally, either in the quality or the quantity that he desired, Washington generally placed his orders with a few favored British suppliers. Most of the beer and porter Washington ordered was brewed in England, but Madeira was a specific type of fortified wine that only came from the Madeira Islands, off the coast of Portugal, and high quality rum was almost exclusively a product of the West Indies. Cider and beer also were made on Washington's plantation, primarily for the use of the workers.

Washington purchased substantial quantities of beer, ale, and porter (a darker variety of the brew) throughout his adult life, using American and English suppliers at different times. Initially he ordered these drinks from England: in 1757 he imported 12 dozen bottles of "fine Porter"; then 139 bottles of beer in 1758; a hogshead of "best Porter" in 1760; one hogshead of "fine old Porter," "1 Groce bottled Porter to be Packd in Shavings," and "2 Casks good strong Beer in Bottles," all in 1761; and so on, throughout the period leading up to the Revolution. Testifying to his ongoing concern for the safety of his shipments, on a number of occasions he specified that the bottles should be packed in wood shavings to guard against breakage. Washington made clear that this precaution was the result of the painful lessons of past experience as he remarked in 1762 that the previous year the bottles had not been packed in that way, and as a consequence they had been "lost."[4]

After the war, Washington decided to replace imported English ale and beer with American brews. Nationalist sentiment seems to have played at least some part in his decision to make the change. In a letter he wrote to the Marquis de Lafayette in 1789, Washington remarked that, "We have already been too

long subject to British prejudices. I use no porter or cheese in
my family, but such as is made in America; both these articles
may now be purchased of an excellent quality." A particular
favorite was the porter Robert Hare brewed in Philadelphia. In
1788 Washington wrote to his friend Clement Biddle requesting
that Biddle secure for him "a gross of Mr. Hairs [Hare's]
best bottled Porter." Two years later, when Washington was
serving the first year of his presidency in New York City, his
secretary, Tobias Lear, tried to acquire more of Hare's tasty
product. "Will you be so good as to desire Mr. Hare to have if
he continues to make the best Porter in Philadelphia 3 gross of
his best put up for Mount Vernon," Lear wrote to an agent in
the city, "as the President means to visit that place in the recess
of Congress and it is probable there will be a large demand for
Porter at that time." Hare's brewery was destroyed by fire later
that year, and Washington seemed to have taken the news to
heart, lamenting that he was sorry "on public as well as private
accts. to hear of Mr. Hares loss." Clement Biddle was able to
find another supplier, however, as he shipped Washington 13
barrels of porter that were received at Mount Vernon in July
the following year.[5]

The Mount Vernon workers brewed beer as well, and the
lack of orders for beer in the financial records for the period
after the Revolution suggests that the product made on
the plantation had largely supplanted the imported variety.
Washington's plantation manager and distant cousin, Lund
Washington, reported to his employer in 1778 that he was in
the process of "making beer" using persimmons, and that he
intended to produce even more the next year. A recipe for "Small
Beer" survives in Washington's papers, which called for boiled
"Bran Hops" and molasses as the main ingredients. This would
have produced a rather flat beverage with low alcohol content,
and it seems highly unlikely that this concoction could have
measured up to the high standards that Washington ascribed
to Hare's porter and to the products of his other suppliers.
Therefore, this home brew may have been valued more for

medicinal purposes than for its taste, and/or it may have been made specifically for the use of the Mount Vernon slaves and other workers.[6]

"Hard," or fermented, cider was a popular beverage throughout Britain's American colonies during the 18th century, with most farmers cultivating their own orchards to ensure they had enough apples to make the beverage themselves. Cider was made at Mount Vernon all during Washington's ownership of the estate, with various entries in the plantation records testifying to its production as well as to its consumption by the Washingtons, their employees, and their slaves. Washington obtained cider from England early on, buying, for example, "12 dozn. Best Herfordshire Cyder in best Mould Bottles, wyred Corks" in 1757, and another 128 bottles of the same the following year. Apparently, however, enough cider routinely was produced at Mount Vernon to meet most of the needs of the plantation.[7]

The Washingtons favored several different types of brandy over the years, including both imported and locally made products. In 1774 Washington bought two kegs of French brandy from a local merchant, the earliest record of his acquiring that particular type of spirit. In 1786 Washington wrote to Lafayette in France lamenting that he was unable to acquire "an anchor of old Peach Brandy" to accompany the barrel of Mrs. Washington's "Virginia Hams" that he was sending as a gift to his old comrade. Interestingly, in 1788 Washington maintained that brandy was a healthier beverage than rum, claiming that wine and brandy from France were not as dangerous to the well-being of the people as the "thousands of Hogsheads of poisonous Rum which are annually consumed in the United States." Possibly Washington's praise of brandy over rum had a political dimension in this instance as his correspondent was the Comte de Moustier, who was then serving as the French ambassador to the United States. Brandy made from peaches and from apples were two of the products of Washington's distillery after it was established in 1797. Records show that 67 gallons of apple and 60 gallons of peach brandy were sent to the Mansion House Farm in October 1799, presumably for the use of the Washington household.[8]

Rum was the most popular distilled spirit in America up until the Revolutionary War, and Washington is known to have imbibed, usually in the form of punch—a concoction of rum, sugar, spices, fruit juices, and water—which was most often made and served by the bowlful. Punch may qualify as one of the first high status "party" drinks in America as it was especially favored when members of the gentry entertained their peers. According to visitors' accounts, punch was served regularly at Mount Vernon, and it probably was a staple at the presidential residences in New York and Philadelphia as well. In 1798 a visitor related that when he arrived unexpectedly at the plantation, Martha Washington "appeared after a few minutes, welcomed us most graciously and had punch served." Punch also was typically offered in taverns and in other more public contexts, such as the polls during elections, 4th of July picnics and other holidays, and the like.[9]

Testifying to its status as a mainstay of fashionable entertaining, in elite homes rum punch was commonly mixed in and then served from large ceramic bowls, the most costly of which were elaborately decorated porcelain vessels imported from China. Washington acquired several bowls of this type over the years. The first recorded purchase was in 1758, when he received "3 punch bowls" from Thomas Knox, of Bristol, England. These bowls probably were made of white salt-glazed stoneware, an English ceramic ware that was fashionable at the time. In 1766 Washington acquired bowls made of more costly "China" (porcelain): a "1 Galln Punch Bowl" and two quart-sized punch bowls with a "Nankn [Nanking] bordr." A surviving highly decorated punch bowl may have been among the items that Martha Washington brought to Mount Vernon after their marriage in 1759. The Chinese porcelain bowl is decorated with painted scenes of birds and flowers that were typical motifs of the mid-18th century. Washington also acquired ladles with which to serve the punch from the bowls, such as the "6 punch Ladles" he received from his London supplier in 1757. An ebony-handled silver punch ladle inscribed with the Washington family crest also survives, which was made circa 1797–99 by a craftsman located in nearby Alexandria, Virginia.[10]

Archaeologists have recovered the remains of other punch bowls, along with a variety of other ceramic and glass vessels that could have been used to store, serve, and consume alcohol, from a trash-filled pit that was located just a few dozen yards to the south of the Mount Vernon kitchen. These include German-, English-, and American-made ceramic mugs, jugs, and pitchers; wine glasses and decanters; and a large number of wine bottles. During this era it was relatively common for wealthy individuals to pay to have the wine bottles that they ordered from abroad marked with seals bearing their name or initials, or even a coat of arms. Although Washington did not indulge in this practice, several seals owned by others were recovered from the midden, testifying to the tradition of bringing bottles of wine along when visiting friends. One seal bears the Fairfax family coat of arms; the Fairfaxes were close friends and near neighbors of the Washingtons, living at Belvoir plantation just a few miles distant. But the seal that was found most often bears the name "John Posey"; Posey owned a plantation, called Rover's Delight, that adjoined the Mount Vernon estate. As it happens, Posey is known to have regularly overindulged in alcohol, which led to his ultimate demise, so it may not be coincidence that more of his bottle seals (four) have been recovered from the excavation than any others. After a long decline in his personal fortunes, marked by increasing indebtedness to Washington, among others, in 1769 Posey finally was forced to sell his holdings at public auction, and Washington purchased a substantial portion of the Rover's Delight tract to add to his estate.[11]

Martha Washington's own recipe for rum punch does not survive, but directions to make another alcoholic concoction have been found written on a sheet of Washington's watermarked paper. This recipe, entitled "To Make Excellent Cherry Bounce," was a mixture of brandy, cherry juice, sugar, and assorted spices. After combining the juice of "well ripened Morello Cherrys" with "old french brandy," sugar, and the spices, the mixture was allowed to ferment and then to stand "for a month or six weeks," before bottling. In September 1784 Washington set out to inspect his properties in western Pennsylvania, which he had not been able to visit since before the beginning of the war nine years before. Among the supplies that he packed were two kegs of West India rum, and canteens filled with Madeira, port, and Cherry Bounce.[12]

Given the many positive references to "old" spirits and wine found in Washington's papers, he no doubt understood that aging in barrels improved the taste of such drinks. In October 1797 he received a gift of "a Dozen Bottles" of aged rum from the architect, William Thornton, who Washington had come to know well from working together on the design of the U.S. Capitol. Four years earlier Washington had been instrumental in selecting Thornton's design for the building, and he later appointed the architect as a commissioner to oversee construction of the federal city. Thornton was a native of the Virgin Islands, and he described the rum he sent to the president as, "The heart of Oak. It is old Spirit that was distill'd upon my own Estate in the Island of Tortola, 28 years ago, and has obtained the deep colour by standing in Oak Casks ever since." Thornton continued, "It is as good as a Tincture of Bark, and would be of no disservice to a Virginia Planter in a Dram Fog." Washington heartily expressed his thanks in a letter that he wrote a few days later, "for the rare and valuable present you have made me. Being the produce of your own Estate renders it more acceptable, and nothing will add more to the go'vt of it, than your coming sometimes to participate in the taste—fog or no fog."[13]

Of all the alcoholic beverages that Washington consumed, Madeira was clearly his favorite. Many visitors noted his fondness for the drink, and how he "loved to chat after dinner with a glass of Madeira in his hand." He was most particular in spelling out his desires for the wine that he ordered regularly from the many British merchant houses where he transacted business over the years. As early as 1759 he ordered a pipe (a cask containing approximately 126 gallons) of the "best Old Wine" from "the best House in Madeira." Subsequent orders generally called for substantial quantities of the drink, ranging up to several hundred gallons at a time, and they usually included the request that the wine be of the highest quality. After Martha Washington's death in 1802, one of the men sent to inventory the contents and assess the value of the estate noted that he found eight pipes of "old Wine"—probably Madeira—believed to be "about to 25 to 30 years old," in the Mansion cellar.[14]

It wasn't only Washington who favored wines from Portugal as they were by far the most popular wines throughout America during much of the 18th century, with the products of France and other European countries commanding a much smaller share of the market. One reason for this marked preference was that Madeira, the most sought-after of the Portuguese wines, improved in quality under the rigors of the trans-Atlantic crossing, unlike most of the others that were adversely affected. The highly charged political climate of the time also was a factor: Portugal was a long-time ally of Great Britain, while warfare with France from 1754 to 1763 made trade between the Americans and the French illegal. Eventually, Franco-American relations warmed considerably when the two nations formed an alliance during the Revolutionary War, and trade opportunities between them naturally increased. Washington ordered 312 bottles each of French Champagne and claret in 1789; in 1793 he purchased 485 bottles, combined, of Champagne and Burgundy. Guests' accounts include several mentions of Champagne being served during dinner at Mount Vernon, and other records indicate that it was found on the table at the president's residence in Philadelphia as well.[15]

On two notable occasions the effervescent quality of Champagne seems to have had a particularly enlivening effect on the spirits of the Washingtons and their dinner guests.

When Richard Henry Lee, who was then serving as president of
Congress, came to dinner at Mount Vernon in 1785, Washington
was eager to extend the evening in the company of his old friend
and comrade-in-arms. The sparkling wine was served, and
another guest noted that "The General with a few glasses of
champagne got quite merry, and being with his intimate friends
laughed and talked a good deal." The young man was well aware
of Washington's reputation as a rather distant host at times,
commenting that "Before strangers [Washington] is generally
very reserved and seldom says a word. I was fortunate in being
in his company with his particular acquaintances." Several years
later a Scottish artist named Archibald Robertson called on the
presidential mansion in Philadelphia to carry out an unusual
errand: delivering a gift from David Stuart Erskine, the Earl
of Buchan, who was an agricultural reformer and an admirer
of Washington. The gift consisted of an oak box "elegantly
mounted with silver," fashioned from the "celebrated oak tree
that sheltered the WASHINGTON of Scotland, the brave and
patriotic Sir William Wallace, after his defeat at the battle of
Falkirk, in the beginning of the fourteenth century." Glasses
of "sparkling champagne" were served at the end of dinner to
help celebrate the happy event, "over which people lingered for
about 45 minutes." At length, Washington and his secretary,
Tobias Lear, exited the room, "leaving the ladies in high glee"—
whether from the intoxicating effects of the Champagne or the
impact of Buchan's gift, cannot be known.[16]

Since wine was among Washington's favorite alcoholic
beverages, it is not surprising that he attempted to grow wine
grapes on his estate. Like many of his fellow Virginians, he was
convinced that the profusion of grapes that were indigenous to
the region practically guaranteed the success of wine making.
"I have long been of opinion from the spontaneous growth of
the vine," he wrote in 1779 to his friend, the Italian physician,
Philip Mazzei, "that the climate and soil in many parts of
Virginia were well fitted for Vineyards and that Wine, sooner
or later would become a valuable article of produce." As early

as 1763, Washington acquired and planted 55 cuttings of the Madeira grape, and more than 20 years later he tried again, receiving several barrels containing more cuttings of the stock. He also experimented with grapes imported from Spain as well as with native varieties. Washington could not know that it was impossible for the imported grapes to survive in America, and all of his attempts at establishing a vineyard ended in failure. The culprit was the grape phylloxera, a tiny aphid that infested the roots of the foreign plants and caused them to sicken and die. It was not until almost a century later that viniculturists discovered that grafting European grape vines onto American root stock was the solution as the resulting plants were resistant to the aphid while retaining their capacity to produce high quality wine.[17]

When Washington placed his first recorded order for Madeira in 1759, he also cautioned that the wine should be "Secur'd from Pilferers." Unfortunately for Washington, he knew only too well about the necessity for taking extra precautions to safeguard the alcohol from theft during its long Atlantic passage. On at least one occasion his shipment had arrived "in bad order" with "The Porter entirely Drank out." On another, Washington complained that "there was a good deal of ullage [loss] indeed—and what I dislikd still more was, a large Tap in the head of the Cask which left me in doubt whether it was done on the Passage (which occasioned the difficiency) or was in the Cask before Shipping of it (as the Sailors, who deliverd it…affirmd)." In these instances, as in many others when he was disappointed in the lackluster manner in which his orders were carried out, Washington felt that his business partners were far from diligent in pursuing his best interests.[18]

Another early example of Washington's feelings of misuse at the hands of his British suppliers occurred in 1761, and again the specific problem at least tangentially involved alcohol. This time Washington ordered a mahogany case designed to hold 16 square bottles, each with a capacity of one gallon, that were intended to store wine and spirits. When he received the

Washington admonished his London agent about the high price he was charged for this 16-bottle liquor chest, complaining that he could have had it made locally at a much lower cost.

case along with the accompanying invoice in the amount of 17 guineas, Washington was appalled. His letter to the supplier, the London merchant Robert Cary and Company, clearly indicates his surprise at what he considered to be the outrageous cost:

> ...another thing occurs which must not escape unnoticed—and that is, A Case bought of Phil Bell at the price of 17 Guineas—Surely, here must be as great a mistake, or as great an Imposition as ever was offerd by a Tradesman. The Case is a plain one, and such as I coud get made in this Country (where work of all kinds is very dear) of the same stuff, and equally as neat for less than four Guineas—is it possible then that 16 Galln Bottles with ground Stoppers can cost 13 Guineas? I think I might safely answer No. I woud have sent it back immediately, but being convinced that there must be some mistake in the Case I have postpond that resolution till you can make a proper enquiry into it. [19]

There is no evidence that the "mistake" was ever rectified, and Washington kept the case and bottles. But it was this type of perceived ill-treatment at the hands of men who Washington viewed as fellow Englishmen that helped ease him along the path toward an eventual break from the Mother Country.

The expensive bottles and accompanying case were just one of many types of specialized vessels and implements that Washington acquired for storing and serving alcoholic beverages. Over the years Washington bought a variety of costly accoutrements, such as decorated wine, punch, ale, and beer glasses; silver cups; cut glass decanters; silver "coolers," used at the table to keep wine chilled on ice; and "frames," also made of silver, complete with caster wheels so that the decanters or bottles could be moved easily around the table. Washington's purchase of all of these unusual and expensive items, and his repetitive instructions to his suppliers that they must, above all, be "neat and fashionable," testifies to his desire to set a table that he deemed appropriate to his self-image and rising position in society.[20]

Ale, beer, brandy, wine, and rum all were imported either in barrels or in bottles, and in the case of certain Spanish wines in large earthen jars. Individual bottles could be brought directly to the table, but it was common to decant wine and rum, at least, into other, more easily handled, vessels; ale, beer, and cider likely were transferred to ceramic jugs or pitchers for serving. In 1757 Washington received "6 Quart Decanters" from his London supplier, and in 1772 he placed an order for "4 Neat and fashe Cut glass Decanters wt. brod Bottms—that they may stand firm on the Table." A dinner guest in 1799 mentioned that he was served ale and beer from "two pint globular decanters on table." In 1763 Washington purchased "4 Enamelled bottle tickets," marked "claret," "port," Madeira," and "Lisbon" to identify the decanted wines.[21]

Washington also purchased sets of specialized glasses from which to drink the beverages, including "2 dozn fine wine glasses Ingraved" and "12 beer Glass Mugs" in 1757; "6 fine wte Enameld Ale Glasses," "18 Wormed and Buttoned punch Glasses," and "24 White enameled Wine" glasses, all in 1761; and six "Neat and fashe" cut beer glasses and "2½ dozn" wine glasses in 1772. However, according to the accounts of visitors to Mount Vernon, Washington seems to have preferred to drink his ale and beer from a silver cup, and he ordered several sets of cups over the years. A pair of surviving silver "camp" cups that are engraved with the Washington crest probably were made for him in 1780 by the Philadelphia silversmith Richard Humphreys.[22]

Soon after Washington was inaugurated as president in 1789, he commissioned Gouverneur Morris, an old friend who was living in London at the time, to acquire a variety of items from English or French craftsmen to help furnish the presidential residence in an appropriately stylish manner. Among the items Washington desired was an elaborate set of "wine coolers," which he described as "handsome and useful coolers for wine at and after dinner...eight double ones (for Madeira and claret wines usually drank at dinner) each of the apertures to be sufficient to contain a pint decanter, with an allowance in the depth of it for ice at bottom so as to raise the neck of the decanter above the cooler." He also ordered "four quadruple coolers" for serving wine after dinner, sized to accommodate either quart decanters or bottles. Each of the coolers also was to feature a handle to facilitate moving them around the table.[23]

Washington was ever mindful of the appearance of his actions, especially once he was cast in the role of representing the new nation in the crucially important and completely novel office of President of the United States. Therefore, although the items in question were both unusual and expensive, he hoped to avoid the appearance of "extravagance" by making the coolers both functional and simple in style. To ensure that Morris understood his meaning, Washington concluded that "One idea however I must impress you with that is in whole or part to avoid extravagance. For extravagance would not comport with my own inclination, nor with the example which ought to be set." Morris was unable to purchase existing coolers matching Washington's description, so he contracted with a London craftsman to execute them according to the president's design. Mindful of Washington's concern about the appearance of extravagance, Morris had the coolers made from less costly silver plate rather than the solid metal. Washington received the coolers in November of that year, and wrote to Morris expressing his thanks for the "elegant" articles.[24]

The next year, Washington acquired two lightweight silver "frames," each accommodating four glass decanters, to substitute for the coolers during the cold weather months. The frames were considerably lighter in weight than the coolers, and along with four caster wheels which were incorporated into the base, they were much easier to pass among the company. Washington enlisted his secretary, Tobias

Lear, in acquiring the pieces, directing that they be made to complement the design of the coolers and crafted in "a handsome fashion."[25]

After Washington left office, he took several of the coolers with him into retirement at Mount Vernon, leaving the rest in Philadelphia. He offered four of the remaining coolers to former members of his Cabinet, "as a token of my friendship and as a remembrancer of it." Those offered the pieces were Washington's Secretary of War James McHenry, Secretary of State Timothy Pickering, Secretary of the Treasury Oliver Wolcott, and Secretary of the Treasury Alexander Hamilton. One each of the four-bottle and two-bottle coolers, and one of the frames, survive in the Mount Vernon collections.[26]

The value of spirits as a commodity is demonstrated in other ways. When Washington had occasion to ship some of his plantation produce to the West Indies, he often directed his agents to seek to acquire rum and other alcohol as acceptable items of exchange. For example, in 1770 Washington transported barrels of herring and hoped to receive, among other things, a hogshead of rum and "a barrel of good spirits" in return. Similarly, in 1772 Washington instructed his agent to sell a shipment of "Superfine Flour" in Barbados and to use the money to purchase "Rum and Sugar from Barbadoes, or any of the Windward Islands." He also expressed interest in acquiring a "Cask of about 50 or 60 Gallns of the best old Spirits especially from Barbadoes." The "old spirits" referred to presumably was aged rum.[27]

In May 1774 Washington dispatched his own ocean-going vessel, the brigantine *Farmer*, to Jamaica carrying a cargo of flour and fish. Among the goods it returned with were three hogsheads (355½ gallons) of "Jamaica rum." Presumably it was some of the rum brought back by the *Farmer* that Washington sold to his overseers, Thomas Bishop (26 gallons) and John Alton (34 gallons), the following year. Washington took advantage of the opportunity afforded by owning his own vessel to serve as a middleman for his neighboring fellow planters, selling

*One of Washington's silver-plated bottle coolers, designed to hold
four glass wine decanters, made in 1789.*

them a variety of imported goods at a respectable profit. After another successful voyage, in 1776, Washington sold three hogsheads of rum, totaling 367½ gallons, to two of his neighbors who lived in Maryland, just across the Potomac from Mount Vernon, at a price that was approximately 20 percent higher than what he had paid.[28]

Another transaction involving alcohol had a more sinister cast to it. Although over time Washington grew increasingly reluctant to sell unwanted or unneeded slaves, on one occasion in 1766 he took the drastic step of dispatching a particularly recalcitrant worker to the West Indies. The slave, named Tom, proved especially difficult to manage, and Washington described him as "both a Rogue and Runaway." Ultimately Washington determined that selling Tom was the best solution for the trouble he caused, and the unfortunate man was put on board a schooner bound for the islands. Washington instructed the ship's captain to sell Tom "for whatever he will fetch," and to use the proceeds to purchase a hogshead of "best Rum," molasses and sweetmeats, and to invest the "residue, much or little, in good old Spirits."[29]

The record of the rum account, entered in the Mount Vernon store book for the year 1787, provides insight into the ways that alcohol was used to encourage and reward the desired behavior of both free and enslaved workers on the plantation. Washington acquired 491 gallons of rum that year, purchased in eight shipments from five merchants; these ranged in volume from a single barrel (31 gallons) to a hogshead containing 125 gallons. Various hired, skilled workers were allotted a daily ration of between two and three pints of rum, for a weekly total of 3⅝ gallons. These individuals included the "German" gardener, Lawson the "Ditcher," the overseers at each of the five farms, and Thomas Green, Washington's talented but ill-disciplined head carpenter.[30]

In addition to the weekly rations, the account indicates that quantities of rum—often as little as a pint or a quart, but sometimes up to several gallons—were distributed on almost a daily basis for a variety of reasons. Most often the alcohol seems to have been given in return for services, either for extra or unusual work in the case of slaves, or as a bonus to outsiders that Washington employed. Among the slaves who received the spirit was Sam, who was given a bottle of rum "for burng the brick kiln," with others allotted to Nat the blacksmith for "burng coal," to "the Carpenters [for] raising the [roof of the] Green Ho[use]" by Mrs. Washington's order, and even to "the people who assisted in getting the cow out of the mire." One pint of rum was earmarked for "the stucco man," the skilled hired craftsman who was in the midst of applying the plaster ornaments in Washington's new, large dining room, presumably as an inducement to him to finish the job.[31]

Each spring immense schools of herring and shad swam up the Potomac River to spawn, providing Washington with a golden money-making opportunity. For the duration of the run, slaves were pressed into service from all parts of the plantation. On these occasions the slaves were expected to work night and day, spreading nets far into the river, hauling in the catch, and gutting, salting, and packing the fish into barrels. In 1772 more than a million herring were caught in this way, with the bulk of the fish put away as rations for the Mount Vernon slaves, and the excess sold for a tidy profit to a local merchant. The rum accounts provide a record of just how much Washington valued the extra effort that this work entailed as "the people at the fishery" were given three gallons of spirits each week between April 3 and May 2, when the run finally was coming to an end. On May 7 a final pint of rum was given "to the people who got the fish out of the boat after night."[32]

Just as the spring fish run required extra labor from the slaves, harvesting the wheat and corn crops was an especially trying time that warranted special considerations. Beginning on June 23, the overseers at the four outlying farms where the crops were grown were given from one to three gallons of rum each week to distribute to the field hands under their charge. This practice lasted until July 16, although smaller quantities of the spirit continued to be distributed for such chores as "cutting the oats at Home," stacking the wheat, and repairing the raceway at the gristmill.[33]

Rum was often provided to the slaves for medicinal purposes as well as for what might be considered humanitarian reasons. On several occasions over the course of the year spirits were distributed to "sick" slaves. Several women received rum to assist them in delivering their babies, including three women "in child bed" during the month of September. Finally, Hercules, the much admired cook who would accompany Washington to New York and Philadelphia during his terms as president, was given three bottles of rum to help him "to bury his wife."[34]

Washington had personal experience with the medicinal side of alcohol use. In the fall of 1757 he suffered for many weeks from an undiagnosed but highly debilitating malady. According to a letter that Washington wrote in November of that year, the rector of his parish, who also practiced medicine, directed him "to drink a Glass or two" of "Mountain, or Canary Wine, every day mixd with Water of Gum Arabic." It isn't recorded whether the rector's prescription proved beneficial or not, but Washington recovered in due course. Washington's belief in the restorative powers of alcohol seems to have continued unabated throughout his life. In 1782 he had the opportunity to minister to an ailing friend, the French nobleman, Marquis de Chastellux, when he arrived at the general's camp suffering "severely from an ague." According to Chastellux, Washington "told me he was sure I had not met with a good glass of wine for some time, an article then very rare, but that my disorder must be frightened away; he made me drink three or four of his silver camp cups of excellent Madeira at noon, and recommended to me to take a generous glass of claret after dinner, a prescription by no means repugnant to my feelings, and which I most religiously followed. I mounted my horse next morning and continued my journey to Massachusetts, without ever experiencing the slightest return of my disorder." With such willing patients and apparently happy results, it is no surprise that practitioners like Washington remained confident in their prescription of spirits as a tonic for so many of life's ailments.[35]

As an aside to the use of alcohol for medicating humans, at least one of Washington's animals appears to have been dosed with brandy. Washington was convinced that mules, the offspring of a horse and an ass, were much more efficient draft animals than horses or oxen, and he expended a great deal of effort to acquire several breeding jacks from the King of Spain. When the first of these animals arrived in November 1785, the shipping invoice included incidental expenses that were accrued over the course of the voyage. Among the charges was, "Cash pd for Brandy to Bathe" the jack's joints, testimony to the common practice of applying alcohol as a topical heat treatment for muscle soreness and joint inflammation.[36]

During the Christmas season, it was customary for family and friends to spend the holiday at Mount Vernon, where the consumption of alcohol doubtless contributed to the festive atmosphere. The slaves also seem to have benefited from the celebratory mood as they usually were given several days' leave from work, and at least occasionally received an allotment of strong drink. On December 24, 1799—incidentally the week following George Washington's funeral—the slaves at the Mansion House Farm were given 30 gallons of whiskey, valued at $17.50, for "a Christmas Dram." When Washington hired a gardener, Philip Bater, in 1787, his contract stipulated that "the said George Washington doth agree to allow him...four Dollars at Christmas, with which he may be drunk 4 days and 4 nights." Bater was to receive an additional "two Dollars at Easter to effect the same purpose; two Dollars also at Whitsontide, to be drunk in two days."[37]

After Washington established his own distillery in 1797, he substituted whiskey for the rum that he had previously provided the slaves and other workers. In the year 1799, several employees drew part of their annual salary in the spirit. These included some of the overseers who directed work at the plantation's outlying farms, as well as the ditcher, James Lawson, the weaver, William Keating, and others. Washington also continued the practice of distributing alcohol to the slaves during periods of particularly intense labor, such as during the wheat harvest. In July, each group of "cradlers" at the four farms, the workers who cut and gathered the grain, was given between 17½ and 22½ gallons of whiskey, presumably to serve both as an incentive and a reward for a job well done.[38]

Over the years, several of Washington's employees developed serious drinking problems, which was one of the predictable consequences in a society where alcohol consumption was such an important part of daily life. In these instances, as he did throughout his life, Washington demonstrated his generally even-handed response to the foibles of others, although his sympathies were often tested. The surprising extent to which Washington was obliged to deal with such failings is reflected in a letter that the president wrote in 1790 to his secretary, Tobias Lear. In the letter, Washington recounted his adventures during a coach trip from his presidential residence in Philadelphia to his Mount Vernon home. "Dunn [a hired driver] has given such proofs of his want of skill in driving, that I find myself under a necessity of looking out for another Coachman," Washington wrote. "Before we got to Elizabeth Town we were obliged to take him from the Coach and put him to the Waggon. This he turned over twice; and this Morning was found much intoxicated." Whether Dunn's driving mishaps were a direct result of his drinking, or the other way around, it is impossible to tell, but Washington's understated tone in recounting the incident suggests that he was only too familiar with this type of behavior.[39]

Thomas Green worked for Washington at Mount Vernon as "Joiner and House-carpenter" from 1783 until 1794. However, over the years, Green's dependability and overall work performance steadily deteriorated, seemingly as a consequence of his increasing drunkenness. After more than a decade of attempting to work through Green's issues with alcohol,

Washington finally was forced to replace the troublesome carpenter. Green's increasing unreliability is recorded in his correspondence with Washington as well as in other papers. In 1788, Green tried to explain his absence by admitting that "I took a little Grog and I found that it hurt me the next day so that I was not fit to do anything." Five years later, Washington's plantation manager, Anthony Whitting, reported to his employer that under the pretext of buying some items for his pregnant wife, Green had asked him for money. According to Whitting, he "put him [Green] off a few days but could not get quit of him untill I had given him two Dollars he went to Town and I believe the most he got was Rum as I saw him very Merry several days later." Soon thereafter Washington wrote to Whitting confiding that he was "apprehensive...that Green never will overcome his propensity to drink," and that this weakness was the cause of his "frequent sicknesses, absences from work, and poverty."[40]

Although Green's continued poor performance would seem to have been ample cause for his dismissal, there was another consideration that deterred Washington from taking that step. Green's wife, Sarah, was the daughter of Thomas Bishop, a veteran of the French and Indian War who had served for many years as Washington's personal servant. Out of respect for this friendship, Washington was unwilling to cut off the financial support for Bishop's daughter and her children, especially since he had little confidence in Green's prospects for finding a similar position elsewhere. In late 1793 Washington's dissatisfaction with Green reached new heights when he found out that the carpenter had elected to make repairs to his own house instead of carrying on the other work that Washington had specified. In a blistering letter to Green, Washington charged that the carpenter was "lost to all sense of shame, and to every feeling that ought to govern an honest man, who sets any store by his character." Nevertheless, Green stayed on, and the next year Washington confided to his plantation manager that, "I am so well satisfied of Thomas Greens unfitness to look after my Carpenters, that nothing but the helpless situation in which you find his family, has prevailed on me to retain him." In the end, Green took matters into his own hands as he abandoned his family and left Mount Vernon forever early in 1794; in four years he was dead. With Washington's assistance, Sarah Green moved to Alexandria, where she tried to support her children by taking in washing and sewing, and by operating a shop. He continued to assist her financially for the rest of his life, and provided her with an annuity of £100 in his will. [41]

As it happens, the manager who reported Green's absenteeism due to drinking, Anthony Whitting, seems to have been plagued by the same affliction. No sooner had he taken over the duties as manager from the previous man in the position, who had died in February 1793, than Whitting's own health began to fail, and he died only a few months later. That Washington held his former manager in high regard at the time of his death is indicated by a letter that he wrote soon afterward, when he mentioned that he hoped to find as a replacement "a man as well qualified for my purposes as the late Mr. Whitting." Apparently Washington heard reports from unnamed parties that changed his mind about the dead man's character, however, and Whitting's alleged overindulgence in alcohol was a leading reason for this change of heart. Six months later when he wrote to his new manager, William Pearce, about the need to set a good example for the workers, Washington cited Whitting's behavior as a case in point, remarking that he had recently learned that the manager was said to have "drank freely—kept bad company at my house and in Alexandria—and was a very debauched person." [42]

William Roberts came to Mount Vernon in 1770 to operate Mount Vernon's gristmill, a vital component of the overall plantation enterprise. Washington had high regard for Roberts's skills as a miller, asserting that he was "inferior to no man…in grinding and keeping a Mill in order," and that he was also an "excellent Cooper and Millwright." Roberts operated the mill as a profitable venture for most of the 15 years he worked at the estate. But Washington also described Roberts as a "madman" when under the influence of alcohol, and unfortunately the miller's addiction worsened over time. In 1785 Washington finally was forced to fire the troublesome Roberts. In a letter that he wrote to one of his business contacts soliciting for a new miller, Washington described his quandary: "My Miller is now become such an intolerable sot...that however unwilling I am to part with an old Servant...I cannot with propriety or common justice to myself bear with him any longer."[43]

Fourteen years later when another miller lost the job in a dispute over wages, Washington appears to have been desperate to fill the position as quickly as possible. Although he made it clear that "honesty sobriety and industry" were the salient characteristics that he was looking for in the new miller, and probably against his better judgment, Washington agreed to rehire Roberts. Washington had been warned that the miller was "such a Sott that he is by No Means fit for business," but his belief that Roberts had "no superior" as a miller seems to have outweighed these concerns. That this was an uncharacteristically bad decision on Washington's part became evident almost immediately. After only three months, James Anderson, Washington's farm manager, found it necessary to settle the miller's accounts and relieved him from his duties.[44]

Washington's experiences in dealing with drunken and undependable employees paled in comparison with what he would be forced to cope with during his periods of service commanding troops during both the French and Indian War and the American Revolution. Appointed as a colonel of the Virginia Regiment at the relatively young age of 23 years, Washington soon learned that keeping up the morale of his men was a major challenge. Distributing alcohol to the troops was a long-standing tradition in the British Army as it was throughout Europe, and the American authorities followed suit. But Washington's command seems to have had more than its share of incidents relating to alcohol abuse. In September 1755 Washington felt compelled to issue an order that "Any

Soldier who is guilty of any breach of the Articles of War, by Swearing, getting Drunk, or using an Obscene Language; shall be severly Punished." This order seems to have had little positive effect, however, as a report soon circulated in Williamsburg that the "greatest Immoralities and Drunkenness have been much countenanced and proper Discipline neglected" in Washington's command. Washington defended his actions to Governor Dinwiddie by maintaining that he had "by Threats and pursuasive means, endeavoured to discountenance Gaming, drinking, swearing, and irregularities of every other kind." Finally, he issued another order making it clear that drunkenness would not be tolerated: "Any Soldier found Drunk, shall immediately receive one hundred lashes; without Benefit of court-martial." Unfortunately, even this clear warning seems to have been regularly disregarded.[45]

Almost 20 years later, Washington again found himself in command of American troops during war, this time in an attempt to win his country's independence from the British Empire rather than working to defend the crown. Once again, alcohol served as an important tool in catering to the desires of the soldiers, and Washington was forced to walk a fine line between tradition and discipline. His numerous official statements on the matter make it clear that Washington viewed the customary liquor ration as an important factor in maintaining the morale of his men. Thus, in August 1777, Washington argued that "It is necessary, there should always be a Sufficient Quantity of Spirits with the Army, to furnish moderate Supplies to the Troops. In many instances, such as when they are marching in Hot or Cold weather—in Camp in Wet—on fatigue or in working parties, it is so essential, that it is not to be dispensed with." In a letter to the president of Congress written in the same month, Washington reiterated that "The benefits arising from the moderate use of strong Liquor have been experienced in All Armies, and are not to be disputed."[46]

Throughout the war Washington was plagued with alcohol-related breaches of conduct, and even dereliction of duty, on the part of his officers as well as his men. Soldiers were convicted of leaving their post and "getting drunk and damning the Officer of the guard," as well as for "getting drunk, when on duty," for which they were punished by receiving at least 30 lashes with a whip on their bare backs. Unfortunately, these were not isolated incidents, and Washington was compelled to inflict increasingly harsh punishments as a deterrent. This included even executing one soldier for "Deserting his post, being drunk, and suffering others to desert to the enemy." Even more troubling was the fact that a number of Washington's officers also were charged with a variety of offenses involving drunkenness. Brigadier General William Maxwell was cited for having commanded his troops while "disguised with liquor in such a manner as to disqualify him in some measure, but not fully, from doing his duty; and that once or twice besides, his spirits were a little elevated with liquor." Maxwell was acquitted, but Major General Adam Stephen, an old colleague of Washington's from the French and Indian War, was not so lucky. Stephen was court-martialed for misbehavior, unofficer-like conduct, and "Drunkenness," and he was dismissed from the army.[47]

Alcohol nevertheless was an integral part of the way of life at camp for Washington as well as for his men. Given the shared trials and dangers, it is no surprise that Washington developed a close relationship with the officers who served on his staff. They habitually dined together, and they routinely drank a variety of alcoholic beverages on those occasions. A list dated August 7, 1776, itemizes the supplies that General Washington withdrew from the commissary just a few days before the start of the Battle of Long Island, New York, and gives some idea of the beverages that were consumed: "1 box Claret, 1 Cag [keg] brandy, 1 box Muscat Wine, 1 basket Cordials, [and] 1 Box Ratafia" (a cordial flavored with fruit kernels or almonds).[48]

In December 1783 the last British soldiers on American soil boarded ship and sailed for home, effectively marking the end of the Revolution. Within a few days Washington gathered the remaining officers of the Continental Army at the well-known tavern of Samuel Fraunces, in New York City, where he bade them an emotional farewell. This parting took on even greater significance for Washington because during the politically unsettled years following the surrender of the British Army at Yorktown in 1781 some of these men may have been on hand to urge the general to take control from Congress and establish a military regime. Washington steadfastly refused, and did everything in his power to ensure that the government of the country that he had worked so hard to establish would be vested in the elected representatives of the American people. After leaving the officers in New York City, Washington traveled to Annapolis, Maryland, where Congress was in session, to formally resign his commission.[49]

Alcohol played a ceremonial part in the final scene marking Washington's long and intimate relationship with his fellow soldiers. According to the first-hand account of Colonel Benjamin Tallmadge, as Washington entered the tavern his "emotions were too strong to be concealed which seemed to be reciprocated by every officer present." After a silence, Washington "filled his glass with wine and turning to the officers said, 'With a heart full of love and gratitude I now take leave of you. I most devoutly wish that your latter days may be as prosperous and happy as your former ones have been glorious and honorable.'" The officers dutifully drank their wine, after which they were led by General Henry Knox, one of Washington's closest comrades-in-arms, to embrace their Commander in Chief, each in turn. By this time, Washington and all of the others in the room were in tears, creating "Such a scene of sorrow and weeping" that Tallmadge "had never before witnessed," and which he never hoped to see again. After recovering their composure, the officers escorted their commander to the waterfront, where he boarded a barge to begin his journey to Annapolis.[50]

It must have caused Washington some discomfort, therefore, when years later he was put in the position of having to expose the demerits of some of the most senior officers when they

*Washington taking leave of the officers of the Continental Army at Fraunces Tavern,
in New York City, on December 4, 1783.*

were under consideration as candidates for positions of high command in the United States Army. Washington's assessments naturally were part of the vetting process leading to selecting the right man for the job. Unfortunately, several of the generals received less than glowing remarks from the president, with many of his concerns relating to their behavior when it came to liquor. Washington described Charles Scott, for example, as "Brave and means well...[but] by report, is addicted to drinking." Washington remembered George Weedon as "rather addicted to ease and pleasure; and no enemy it is said to the bottle." As for Anthony Wayne, Washington found him to be "Open to flattery—vain...[and] Too indulgent to his Officers and Men." However, he could only add that, "Whether sober—or a little addicted to the bottle, I know not."[51]

The now-famous tradition of "Southern hospitality" already had been well established in Virginia by the mid-18th century. In a country with a relatively small population spread over vast areas, making prolonged social visits between households when the opportunity arose became a common practice. In addition, members of the gentry had few attractive options for overnight accommodation during their arduous travels over Virginia's notoriously poor roads. Staying with friends of the family, acquaintances, or even total strangers was generally preferable to resorting to the rough amenities provided by the few available inns.

As a young man Washington experienced the unpredictable results of depending on such varied accommodations. In 1748, at only 16 years of age, Washington participated in one of his first adventures as a member of the "adult" world, when he joined an expedition to the Shenandoah Valley to survey the property of his neighbor and early mentor, George Fairfax. On the fourth night of the trip, the surveyors stayed at the home of an acquaintance named Isaac Pennington, where young Washington learned an important lesson in frontier living. According to his journal, after dinner the party "was Lighted in to a Room and I not being so good a Woodsman as the rest of my Company striped my self very orderly and went in to the Bed as they call'd it when to my surprize I found it to be nothing but a little Straw—Matted together without Sheets of any thing else but only one Thread Bear blanket with double its Weight of Vermin such as Lice and Fleas." After awaking the next morning and cleaning themselves "of the Game we had catched the Night before," the party went about their business. Fortunately, the next night's lodgings were more hospitable as they were treated to "a good Dinner" with "Wine and Rum Punch in Plenty and a good Feather Bed with clean Sheets which was a very agreeable regale." This comment on the availability of wine and rum punch with their dinner is the first reference to alcoholic beverages found in Washington's writings. It isn't known whether the 16-year-old Washington actually drank any of these offerings, but it seems likely that he did.[52]

Washington testified to the common practice of staying in private houses in a letter that he wrote to his mother, Mary Ball Washington, in 1787. In the letter he likened his Mount Vernon home to "a well resorted tavern, as scarcely any strangers who are going from north to south, or from south to north do not spend a day or two at it." Washington made the remark as part of his rationale for why his mother should not come to live with him; both strong-willed and forceful personalities, mother and son seem to have had a strained relationship all during their adult lives. Even so, there is no doubt that Washington was speaking the truth about the volume of visitors to his home. In a letter that Washington wrote to a friend in 1797, he mused that "Unless some one pops in, unexpectedly, Mrs. Washington and myself will do what I believe has not been [done] within the last twenty years by us, that is to set down to dinner by ourselves."[53]

The international fame Washington enjoyed following the stunning victory of the American forces in the Revolutionary War spurred hundreds of admirers from as far away as Poland and France to make pilgrimages to Mount Vernon to meet him. The written accounts made by several of those visitors provide a record of the hospitality that they were afforded when they arrived at the plantation, and they indicate that alcohol played an important role in the gatherings. According to the reports of his dinner companions, Washington habitually "had a silver pint cup or mug of beer, placed by his plate, which he drank while dining." Along with the beer, he usually imbibed two or more glasses of wine. Offering ceremonial toasts was a common practice of the day, and the company typically drank a glass of wine on the occasion. According to the diary of Robert Hunter, the young Scotsman who visited the Washingtons in November of 1785, "The General sent the bottle about pretty freely after dinner, and gave success to the navigation of the Potomac for his toast." According to another visitor a decade later, when he came to Mount Vernon Martha Washington's granddaughter and her husband, Eliza and Thomas Law, also were in residence. During dinner, which consisted of roasted pig, boiled leg of lamb, a variety of side dishes, and puddings and tarts for dessert, the guests "were desired to call for what drink" they chose. General Washington "took a glass of wine," then offered the toast to "All our Friends." After the table was cleared and the ladies had adjourned, the men may have remained to continue their conversation over glasses of Madeira.[54]

Washington ordered that even when he was absent from the plantation visitors should continue to be entertained in a manner befitting their station. It was understood that wine would be served on these occasions, but after learning that guests had drunk more than 50 bottles during a brief span while he was in Philadelphia during the presidency, Washington clarified his desires: "It is not my intention that it [wine] should be given to every one who may incline to make a convenience of the house in traveling or who may be induced to visit it from motives of curiosity," he instructed. He did, however, authorize providing alcohol to his "particular and intimate acquaintances" that might happen to arrive in his absence, or to "the most respectable foreigners" and "persons of distinction (such as members of Congress)." Even so, there was a limit to

Washington's generosity as he made it clear that he preferred that claret be served instead of his much-loved and more costly Madeira.[55]

When Washington was elected as the first chief executive of the United States, he was obliged to consider a great many topics, both momentous and seemingly insignificant, but all without precedent, and the Constitution provided maddeningly little direction on a host of matters. Even such basic details like Washington's official title were left unresolved, and it was only after lengthy consideration that Washington finally decided on "The President," in hopes of imbuing the office with both a sufficient aura of respect and the lack of pretension befitting the leader of the world's first modern republic. Thus it was not surprising that the matter of presidential protocol was left out entirely, and once again Washington was forced to feel his way in determining how the chief executive should interact with other members of the government, foreign dignitaries, and most important of all, with his fellow citizens.[56]

Washington was keenly aware that he needed to establish the dignity of his office while at the same time striking just the right note of humble public service. His solution was to establish a system of formal entertainments where citizens would have the chance to meet him in a carefully controlled setting. These took the form of weekly receptions, or "levees," when "gentlemen" could present their compliments and exchange a few words with the president. Martha Washington also held a weekly levee for ladies and gentlemen, which was a slightly more relaxed gathering, where the president often would circulate and light refreshments were served. In addition to these daytime events, Washington usually hosted a weekly dinner for congressmen, foreign dignitaries, and the like at his home. Compared to the levees, these gatherings were relatively informal, bearing a much greater resemblance to the dinners that the Washingtons had been accustomed to hosting at Mount Vernon. As always, Washington tended to be reserved on these occasions if the attendees were not close acquaintances, but wine was provided in abundance, and the dinner always concluded with a series of toasts.[57]

A significant threat to the stability of the young nation occurred during Washington's presidency, which was directly related to the administration's fiscal policy on whiskey. In order to fund the activities of the federal government, and to help retire the $21 million national debt, largely incurred in fighting the Revolution, Alexander Hamilton, Washington's secretary of the treasury, championed imposing excise taxes on a variety of products, including distilled spirits. The deficit had grown substantially during the intervening years because the government was limited by the conditions of the Articles of Confederation in its ability to raise revenues to support its activities. It was this inherent weakness in the powers of the central government that had induced men like Washington and Hamilton to resolve to establish a strong federal authority in the first place, which was empowered by the new Constitution to run the country and to raise the money needed to do so. After considerable debate and organized attempts on the part of westerners to influence the outcome by submitting anti-excise petitions, Congress acceded to Hamilton and Washington and passed the excise bill in the fall of 1791. Reaction against the measure on the part of the settlers who had recently migrated to the newly available lands west of the Appalachians was immediate and pronounced, and sporadic violence broke out wherever federal agents were dispatched to collect the tax.[58]

Excise taxes were also known as "internal" taxes since the goods that were affected were made domestically rather than imported. Taxes placed on imported goods usually did not significantly affect the general populace since most food and other basic commodities tended to be produced locally. But when the tax was extended to domestic products, the levy was more widely distributed and thus more keenly felt, especially among the lower economic classes. Resistance to such taxes had a long tradition in Great Britain, which is one reason why the American colonists reacted so strongly against a series of tax measures that were imposed on them during the 1760s and 1770s. Parliament justified the excise as necessary to help recoup some of the costs incurred in protecting the American colonies during the French and Indian War. Nevertheless, this brought a predictably strong negative American reaction, with Parliament criticized as violating the unwritten rule against exacting internal taxes during peacetime. The debate over the tax issue escalated and reinforced the growing feelings on the part of many colonists that they were being taken advantage of by their government and their king. From there it was only a series of short steps that brought George Washington and his fellow founders to a conviction of the necessity of American independence. Given this recent history, it is no surprise that many found the decision on the part of the Washington administration to impose excise taxes of their own to be a betrayal of the principles of the Revolution.[59]

Resistance to the whiskey tax was especially strong along the western agrarian frontier as liquor had become particularly important there as a marketable commodity and a steady source of income. One of the benefits of winning the war with Britain was that American farmers were allowed to migrate across the Appalachian Mountains to settle in the rich grain-growing region of western Pennsylvania, Ohio, and Kentucky. These settlers joined with farmers throughout the country to produce bumper crops of corn, rye, barley, wheat, and other grains. Many farmers found that distilling a portion of their crop into spirits was an added financial benefit as alcohol enjoyed a ready market at a high rate of return, was more easily transported than grain, and was not nearly as prone to loss by spoilage. In Washington County, Pennsylvania, alone, there were more than 500 stills, or one for every 10 families, in operation in 1790.[60]

To make matters worse, the tax was widely held to favor the rich at the expense of the common farmer. According to the provisions of the law, producers could comply by paying either nine cents per gallon on the whiskey they actually distilled or a flat rate based on the capacity of their stills. By availing themselves of the second option for payment, this meant that large distillers were at a significant competitive advantage since as their volume of production increased, their tax rate would decline for each gallon they distilled. An added problem for the westerners was that the tax was to be paid in cash, traditionally a scarce commodity in frontier regions.[61]

For western settlers the issue not only revolved around the financial burdens imposed on them by the whiskey tax, but also crystalized the deep misgivings they already felt about their relationship with the new administration. If protecting its citizens is the first and most important test of any government, then as far as the western farmers were concerned, Washington's administration was a failure. The Ohioans in particular had seen little in the way of tangible benefits in return for their allegiance to the distant eastern power, particularly in regard to protection against the depredations of the Indians, who still viewed the Americans as trespassers on their ancestral lands. During the seven-year period after the treaty of peace with Great Britain was signed in 1783, the natives killed, wounded, or took prisoner up to 1,500 settlers in the Ohio Valley and terrorized the entire frontier region. The Federal Government finally responded to local entreaties by dispatching troops to fight the Miami Indians in late 1790. But the force was woefully small and unprepared, and they were soundly defeated in a series of bloody engagements. It wasn't until many years later that the region found comparative peace.[62]

The climax to the conflict over the whiskey excise occurred in western Pennsylvania in 1794, the result of violent opposition to renewed attempts on the part of the government in Philadelphia to collect the tax. Efforts to enforce the excise, and the corresponding local opposition to it, increased steadily in Pennsylvania, but these developments were also echoed as far afield as Massachusetts, Kentucky, Virginia, and almost every other state south of New York. Ironically, the spark leading to open revolt was finally struck in Washington County,

Pennsylvania, which had been named in honor of the first president. The excise inspector there was first abused and then attacked, and several men were killed in the confused fighting that ensued.[63]

To President Washington, this defiance of federal authority struck at the core of his vision of a strong central government and threatened to negate the gains he had struggled so tenaciously to win in instilling loyalty to the concept of the new United States of America. Washington and Hamilton selected Pennsylvania as the appropriate place to enforce their will, and the president called for an army of almost 13,000 soldiers to put down the uprising. Washington himself led the force west to Carlisle, Pennsylvania, the first and presumably the last time that an American president acted in his role as commander in chief to lead U.S. troops in the field. Washington was employing the principle of overwhelming force to put down the rebellion, and the strategy worked perfectly. The rebels dispersed upon the approach of the Army, and further violent resistance to the tax was at an end. Continuing the theme of rapid resolution, few rebels were ever prosecuted for any crime, and Washington even pardoned the two men who were ultimately convicted of treason.[64]

That Washington's forceful steps to bring the so-called whiskey rebels to heel was all about politics and had nothing to do with the morality of making or drinking whiskey is amply demonstrated by the fact that it was during the campaign into western Pennsylvania that Washington is first linked to drinking the spirit. In a letter dated October 9, 1794, the president's secretary remarked to Henry Knox that "As the President will be going...into the Country of Whiskey [Pennsylvania] he proposes to make use of that liquor for his drink." Even so, it is likely that Washington himself would have been surprised if he had been told that less than three years after the Whiskey Rebellion was ended, and only months before he retired from the presidency to return to private life as a farmer, he would authorize his recently hired plantation manager to begin distilling whiskey at his Mount Vernon estate. Within two years Washington's distillery achieved the status as one of the largest producers of whiskey in the country, quite an accomplishment for the 67-year-old former president who freely admitted that he did not have any first-hand knowledge of making alcohol. [65]

CHAPTER 2

MASTER OF MOUNT VERNON

In February of 1798 George Washington carefully reviewed the accounts that his plantation manager and others had kept for his Mount Vernon estate for the previous year. His goal was to assess the profitability of the many related enterprises and, if possible, to arrive at an accounting of his overall financial condition. This was the first time in more than a decade that Washington had attempted such a detailed study, reflecting the fact that he had spent his two terms as president concentrating on the needs of the nation rather than on managing his private affairs. It was particularly important for Washington to know just where he stood financially at this time because he was hoping to find alternate sources of revenue that might be a less strenuous means of making a living than farming and directing the labors of hundreds of enslaved workers. To Washington's relief, the "bottom line" that emerged from his accounting exercise showed a substantial net profit of £898.[1]

When Washington returned from Philadelphia to Mount Vernon after his presidency, his plantation was at its zenith, and it was an expansive and ambitious commercial enterprise. Almost 8,000 acres in extent, and with more than 300 enslaved Africans working and living there, Mount Vernon ranked as one of the largest estates in Virginia. But the level of ambition of Washington's operation can be measured in more ways than by size alone. He was a committed entrepreneur who took considerable risks in exploring new markets and investing in cutting-edge methods and implements, and he was intimately involved in managing all of his related business ventures. Not only did Washington's slaves grow thousands of bushels of wheat, corn, and rye each year, but they also ground the grain in his own mill; starting in 1797 a portion of the grain was converted into whiskey at Washington's new distillery. Both the flour and the spirits were stored in barrels made by Washington's coopers and were sold to merchants in Alexandria, eight miles upriver. Washington marketed the very best of his flour much farther afield, sometimes transported in his own vessels, reaching such distant destinations as the West Indies, England, and Portugal. In this way, Washington exercised more control over all of the steps by which his products were converted into revenue.[2]

Washington's estate in 1798 was different in many important respects from the plantation that he had established more than 40 years earlier. He acquired the 2,000-acre core of the property from the estate of his older half-brother Lawrence in 1754. When he returned to Mount Vernon several years later from a call to public service leading his fellow Virginians in fighting alongside the British in the French and Indian War, he was committed to the life of a tidewater tobacco planter. Tobacco was the economic underpinning of the Colony, and growing it was the primary occupation of virtually every member of the gentry society in which Washington hoped to become a prominent member. When the market was good and the quality of the tobacco was high, healthy profits could be made. But producing tobacco was a labor-intensive occupation requiring large numbers of able-bodied workers to carry out the many tasks that were necessary to cultivate the plants, then to cure the leaves and transform them into a salable crop. It also meant providing housing and food for the enslaved workers, building specialized curing barns and other service buildings, and maintaining a financial safety net to withstand the inevitable down years when either the market price was low or bad weather, disease, or other factors caused a poor crop yield. Thus, a commitment to large-scale tobacco production brought with it a host of other activities and costs, and its pursuit essentially defined the physical character of the plantation.[3]

As early as 1755, Washington made clear his intentions to commit his financial future to tobacco when he shipped his first three hogsheads of the leaf to Great Britain. Four years later, he took another important step along this path when he entered into an agreement with the prestigious London firm of Robert Cary and Company to handle marketing his crop. Once received by his agent, Washington's tobacco was sold to the highest bidder, and after the leaf was processed into cigars and snuff, it could find its way to markets throughout the British Isles and Europe. Cary and Company sold Washington's tobacco on consignment, crediting his account accordingly. Washington then placed orders with the firm to acquire the many manufactured goods that were not readily available in the American Colonies. This type of business arrangement was standard practice for the largest of Virginia's planters as the volatility of the international tobacco market made the security of a long-term business relationship especially attractive. The merchant houses acted as a financial buffer during lean years when the profits on the harvest were lower than expected, as they extended credit to cover Washington's necessary expenses. The merchants did not provide this support out of selfless generosity, however, as they received a high mark-up for their services.[4]

Over time, Washington came to question whether the convenience of the arrangement with his London agents was worth its steep cost, especially given his growing belief that he was receiving poor service in return. The episode in 1761 when Washington felt that he had been charged an outrageous sum for the liquor bottles and their wooden case that he had ordered from London was but one of a growing number of instances when he felt that his business partners were abusing their relationship. As early as 1760 Washington observed that "Tis a custom, with many Shop Keepers and Tradesmen in

London when they know Goods are bespoke for Exportation to palm sometimes old, and sometimes very slight and indifferent Goods upon us taking care at the same time to advance 10, 15 or perhaps 20 prCt [%] upon them." To discourage this practice, Washington took the precaution of advising his agents to avoid informing suppliers that the goods in question were destined for shipment to America.[5]

Even more troubling for Washington was his inability to produce a crop of consistently excellent quality that could demand a correspondingly high price at market. Tobacco takes a particularly heavy toll on the nutrients in the soil, and the relatively infertile Mount Vernon clay was poorly suited to growing the plant. The primitive farming practices of the day only exacerbated the problem. The value of applying fertilizers and of preparing the ground by deep plowing before planting were only poorly understood and seldom practiced. The standard procedure called for a three-year crop rotation where a given field was planted in tobacco and corn in successive years, then left fallow the next growing season. But this approach accomplished little in terms of preserving the fertility of the soils, leading to steadily declining crop yields, and it was only a matter of a few years before the inevitable day when the land was exhausted. The field would have to be abandoned and left to recover its fertility naturally, a process that might take up to 20 years to accomplish, while the planter successively cleared and cultivated other plots in its stead.[6]

While Washington did everything in his power to improve the quality of his tobacco, after almost a decade of dedicated effort it was clear to him that he needed to make a change. As for many of Washington's fellow planters, the columns of numbers on the pages of his meticulously maintained plantation ledgers presented a sobering picture. By 1764 a series of bad harvests and the failure of a number of his debtors to pay him in a timely fashion caused Washington's own debt to Cary and Company to grow to £1,800. After adopting several stop-gap measures in an attempt to reduce his expenditures, Washington foresaw falling even deeper into the red, and in the autumn of 1765 he made plans to forego growing tobacco at Mount Vernon entirely.[7]

But what should he turn to in its stead? In searching for other dependable sources of income, Washington considered various cereal grains, hemp (for making rope), and flax (for cloth). Because of the ready market for wheat and flour that could be found both at home and abroad, however, Washington ultimately selected that grain as his new cash crop. At the same time he continued to grow corn as the primary ration for the Mount Vernon workers as well as to feed his animals. Instead of consigning his crop to merchants in London, Washington now sold his wheat in nearby Alexandria, or wherever the best price could be found. The plantation records indicate just how rapidly he ramped up production: from 257 bushels in 1764 to 2,331 bushels in 1766, and 6,241 bushels in 1769. Washington's commitment to wheat cultivation is reflected in a comment that he made in 1774: "The whole of my force is in a manner confind to the growth of Wheat and Manufacturing of it into flour."[8]

When Washington determined to abandon tobacco, it meant that he was departing from the path that Virginia's landed gentry had followed with great success for more than a century. Switching from one cash crop to another in turn dictated a host of other changes. These ranged from reconfiguring the fields, replacing outmoded barns and other buildings, and reorganizing how the enslaved field hands worked and were supervised to establishing new trade networks and adding a variety of plantation crafts aimed at reducing unnecessary expenditures. But the most important result of all was that by embracing the new economic system Washington did not tie himself to a specific market or to the dictates of creditors. Now he had the independence and flexibility to react to changing circumstances.[9]

Another benefit of growing wheat instead of tobacco was that the grain could be planted, cultivated, and processed with the aid of animal power instead of depending on manual labor.

The fact that all of the many steps required in growing tobacco had to be performed by hand is what encouraged Chesapeake planters to invest in slave labor in the first place, and Washington had acted accordingly. By 1765 at least 55 adult enslaved workers were living at Mount Vernon. After switching to grain Washington suddenly found himself with more field hands than he needed to grow his crops, and he immediately began to explore other moneymaking activities to which he could devote the excess labor. The most important of these pursuits were spinning and weaving cloth, blacksmithing, and harvesting fish from the nearby Potomac River, but he attempted a number of other commercial ventures over the years with varying degrees of success.[10]

Almost all of these activities had the added benefit of helping to rein in Washington's expenditures by reducing the need to purchase food and certain supplies and services from outsiders. By training his workers to manufacture the fabric for their clothes and to make and repair their shoes and by growing corn, raising hogs, and expanding the fishery to supply most of the food needs of his slaves, these costs were reduced accordingly. Similarly, the various enslaved skilled workers—such as the blacksmiths, carpenters, masons, coopers, and other craftsmen—were capable of carrying out most of the tasks required to erect and maintain the buildings; to repair harrows, plows, and other farm implements; to fabricate barrels needed to transport goods; and even to build a seaworthy schooner.

The blacksmith shop was an important element of the plantation economy from the earliest days of Washington's ownership of Mount Vernon. For a number of years it was a steady source of income as Washington's smiths performed work for the residents of the surrounding "neighborhood," along with supplying the many needs of the plantation. Between 1755 and 1799 a total of 134 individuals, most of whom lived within a five-mile radius of the Mansion, were listed in the smith accounts as having patronized the shop. Most of the wide range of tasks the smiths performed qualified as standard fare for an 18th-century country smithy: repairing farm and domestic implements, making horseshoes and shoeing horses, and fabricating such varied objects as nails, keys, axes, and plows. As time passed and the Mount Vernon plantation expanded dramatically in size and complexity, the support needed from the smiths increased accordingly, and the opportunities to carry on outside work declined.[11]

The first references to the Mount Vernon shop were in January 1755, when Washington purchased a set of blacksmith's tools: a bellows, vices, tongs, files, hammers, an anvil, and the like. The shop itself may have been completed by the following April when Washington paid a workman to build the chimney. In 1768 the first shop appears to have been replaced by a new and apparently larger building, which survived until after Washington's death in 1799. Archaeological excavations carried out at the site of the building beginning in the 1930s succeeded in revealing the brick base of the forge and portions of the foundation, indicating that the structure was roughly 25- by 16-feet in dimension. The excavators also found abundant physical evidence for the activities of the smiths, including production waste such as slag and ash; coal and charcoal; scraps of iron and copper; fragments of hammers, chisels, and other tools; and even pieces of plows and other agricultural and domestic implements.[12]

Over the years Washington employed both hired white journeymen and his own slaves as blacksmiths. The first smith to be identified in the records was Peter, a slave who worked at Mount Vernon for 10 years starting in 1760. For most of this period Peter was assisted by two young enslaved men, named Nat and George, and presumably it was part of Peter's job to school these men in the craft. If so, this arrangement does not seem to have succeeded as Nat was indentured for three years starting in March 1770 to another smith in the county "to learn the Art and Trade of Blacksmiths." Peter's whereabouts after 1770 are unknown as his name is missing from the plantation documents, and in September of that year Washington hired a

"Dutch" smith by the name of Dominicus Gubner to operate the shop. Gubner was paid at the rate of £32 per year, and he continued in the position for the next three years. Finally, when Nat completed his indenture in 1773, Gubner's contract was not renewed and the slave returned to become Washington's lead blacksmith. For the next 25 years, Nat partnered with George, the other slave who had assisted Peter and then Gubner, in operating the Mount Vernon shop.[13]

Washington's sometimes stormy dealings with Nat and George over the years shed some light on the inherent conflict marking the relationship between masters and slaves. In January of 1788 Washington responded to an offer made by a friend to provide him with a blacksmith by characterizing his own smiths as "tho' not very neat workmen, [they] answer all my purposes in making farm utensils, etc., in a plain way." Two years later he sounded less satisfied with their performance, complaining that "my bungling smiths, has lamed one of the Horses that draw the Waggon in Shoeing him." Finally, in 1792 Washington observed that "the Smiths…I take to be two very idle fellows," and the next year he discreetly began to search for replacements, seeking "a compleat Blacksmith" who must also be "an honest, sober, and Industrious man." He apparently was unable to find such a paragon, and Nat and George stayed on as the Mount Vernon smiths for the remainder of Washington's lifetime. The smiths' side of the story is undocumented, of course, but their apparent lack of motivation in carrying out their duties may well have been related to their enslaved condition.[14]

As the plantation expanded almost four-fold in size (from roughly 2,000 to almost 8,000 acres) between 1754 and 1786, the work of the Mount Vernon shop came to be almost exclusively devoted to its support. The increase in the number and type of agricultural implements, the exploding population of draft animals, and the more specialized nature of the ironwork required at the gristmill and later at the distillery monopolized more and more of the smiths' time. The number of outside individuals who patronized the Mount Vernon smiths declined accordingly, and the shop ceased to be a significant source of revenue. According to the plantation accounts for 1797, the total expenses for the year were £94.16.6, including purchasing three shipments of steel and iron, totaling almost £85, and a new bellows, vice, and sledge hammer for £8.8. Total income was £129.9.4, yielding a net "profit" of £34.12.9. With a single exception, the income was derived from tasks carried out on the plantation and debited against the various farms, the mill, the distillery, and to the carpenters. As this was an accounting of internal transactions, Washington therefore did not realize a profit in the strict sense, as he had earlier when the shop had a clientele that extended beyond the plantation itself.[15]

Making cloth was the first of several new crafts that Washington initiated. By January 1767 six women (five black slaves and one white indentured servant) were employed in spinning and weaving under the direction of a hired supervisor, Thomas Davis. In the first year, Davis and his crew wove slightly more than 1,500 yards of linen, wool, and cotton cloth of various sorts, valued at £51.11.1. The second year, production increased to 815 yards of linen and 1,355 yards of woolen linsey and cotton, valued at £54.3.4; revenues for the following two years were £53.10.1 and £44.11.0. Some of the material was used on the plantation, with the remainder sold to Washington's neighbors. One customer was John Dulan, who in May of 1767 purchased 23½ yards of plaid cloth and 9 yards of "bird eye Linn[e]n" for a total of £1.14.3. Dulan paid his bill with a combination of cash and trade, supplying Washington with chickens and eggs to make up the difference. As with the blacksmith shop, over time the cloth made by Washington's slaves served more to satisfy the needs of workers on the plantation than as a source of revenue; by 1797 the actual cost of the spinning operation amounted to a net loss of £51.2.[16]

The Potomac River shoreline that stretched along almost 10 miles of Mount Vernon's eastern boundary provided Washington with another highly profitable commercial

opportunity. By catching a portion of the millions of shad and
herring that passed the plantation each year during their spring
migration to spawn, Washington sought to supplement the
food supplies for his slaves, while at the same time providing
an additional source of income. Washington's fishing operation
consisted of spreading a long seine net out into the channel
to catch the fish, then hauling them ashore where they were
gutted, cleaned, and packed into barrels. A small boat powered
by two men using oars, rowed out into the stream following
a semi-circular path. The seine, as much as 450 feet long and
with lead weights attached to one edge and corks tied to the
opposite side, was paid out over the stern as the vessel traveled
in its arc. Hauling lines, or ropes up to 1,500 feet in length, were
attached to either end of the net, which the boat brought back
to other workers waiting on shore. The fishermen hauled in on
the lines, causing the net to close and trap the fish. Once the
net reached the shallows, the workers waded into the water to
retrieve the catch in bushel baskets, and the fish were salted and
packed into barrels to be preserved. If carefully handled, the
fish could remain edible for as long as a year.[17]

In this way Washington's slaves caught more than one
million herring and more than 10,000 shad in the spring of
1772. A portion of the catch was distributed to the slaves as
rations while the balance was sold to local merchants. In that
year Washington sold the excess to the Alexandria merchant
firm, Robert Adam and Company, in return for £184. The sale
of fish continued to be an important source of ready money
throughout Washington's lifetime, with the profits from the
fishery listed as just over £165 in the year 1797.[18]

During the years leading up to the outbreak of the
Revolution, Washington owned at least two oceangoing vessels,
which he used to transport his grain, flour, fish, and other
products to Alexandria and more distant markets. The first
vessel, a schooner, was built by Washington's carpenters under
the direction of a local craftsman named John Askew. The first
record of boat building is an entry in Washington's diary from

September 15, 1765, when he recorded that the carpenters had worked 82 days "on my Schooner." The carpenters continued working on the vessel for the rest of September and seem to have finished the job by mid-October. In December Washington paid another craftsman to install the rigging, and it was launched in February. The schooner embarked on a variety of voyages: transporting lumber to Mount Vernon from a local saw mill, delivering a cargo of 1,403 bushels of wheat to a merchant in Alexandria, and the like. In 1769 the vessel may have made its first voyage to the West Indies when it delivered a shipment of herring to the island of Antigua. The following year, Washington invested in sheathing the bottom of the schooner with copper plates to protect it from the shipworms that were a major nuisance in southern waters. Without the protection of the copper, the worms could bore through the stout oak hull in a matter of months. The documentary records are silent on the whereabouts of the schooner after 1770, and Washington seems to have given up any aspirations he may have had for a career in shipping.[19]

In 1774 Washington found himself owning another trading vessel almost against his will. Two years earlier the brig *Fairfax* docked at Mount Vernon, and Washington arranged to ship barrels of his flour on its return voyage to the West Indies. As was the common practice, the ship's captain, Daniel Jenifer Adams of Charles County, Maryland, was empowered to sell the flour on Washington's behalf to the highest bidder. But instead of returning to Virginia after selling the cargo, Adams apparently used Washington's money to purchase the vessel, and then proceeded to sail and transport goods among the islands without paying Washington what he was due. Washington resorted to obtaining a court order to have the brig returned and his account settled, but Adams was not able to pay his debts, and the vessel accordingly was advertised for sale. No buyers came forward, however, and Washington himself "was compelld to buy it" against his own inclination, as he "had no desire of being concernd in Shipping."[20]

Over the next two years the vessel, renamed the *Farmer*, was used to transport Washington's cargoes of flour, corn, and fish to ports in the West Indies as well as to Portugal. In May 1774 the *Farmer* carried a shipment of flour and fish to Jamaica, while just over a year later, the vessel delivered 4,000 bushels of corn to Lisbon, returning with 3,000 bushels of salt. Washington received a tidy profit from reselling rum and other commodities brought back on the return voyages, but he also incurred a variety of expenses as a cost of doing business. These included paying the wages and expenses for the captain and crew and fees to pilots and harbor masters, as well as purchasing ropes, sails, masts, and many other ship sundries. In the end, Washington may have determined that the profits to be made in owning the vessel simply did not outweigh the trouble in overseeing the many necessary details, especially given the multitude of other demands on his time, and in April 1775 he sold the *Farmer*. Washington did not give up on ship owning entirely, however, as he purchased shares in two other vessels, the brig *Becky* and the ship *George Washington*, which made a number of successful trading voyages between 1776 and 1779.[21]

When Washington returned home at the conclusion of the Revolutionary War after an eight-and-a-half-year absence, he found that his estate was in dire need of his attention. Just before the outbreak of the conflict in 1775, Washington had embarked on a carefully considered plan to expand the Mansion, replace the associated outbuildings, and reorganize the surrounding gardens and grounds. He already had enlarged and improved the Mount Vernon Mansion—a one-and-one-half-story frame house originally built by his father, Augustine, in 1735—when he returned to Mount Vernon in 1758 after his service in the French and Indian War. His goals for the second round of improvements were considerably more ambitious, however, as he chose to emulate the then currently fashionable English architectural and landscape models in completely redesigning his estate. In Washington's stead, his plantation manager, Lund Washington, had attempted to carry out his employer's designs, but much remained to be accomplished.[22]

The new design called for essentially doubling the size of the Mansion with the addition of matching wings to the north and south facades, as well as attaching a distinctive and unusual double-height porch running the entire 94-foot-length of the east front. Two superimposed pediments above the main door, a prominent cupola topped by a weathervane centered on the roof, a three-part "Venetian" window set in the wall of the largest room in the north wing of the house, and a variety of other stylistic details were incorporated into the new design to attain Washington's goal of creating a cohesive and fashionable appearance. Both the overall design and most of its specific elements were based on the tenets of Anglo-Palladian architecture, the fashionable style of the day that ultimately derived from the buildings of classical Greece and Rome. Washington served as his own architect, guided by a variety of models, both in the form of published English sources and extant structures that he saw in his travels.[23]

At the same time that Washington remade the Mansion and the supporting structures according to neoclassical precedents, he reconfigured the surrounding gardens and grounds with reference to the ideas of picturesque (or naturalistic) landscape design espoused by a number of prominent English authors. Washington's 1,000-volume library contained the influential book *New Principles of Gardening* by Batty Langley, which served him as a particularly important source of inspiration. The essence of picturesque design was to develop spaces and vistas that served to heighten the aesthetic qualities of the site, and which were meant to be "natural" in appearance even though they were man-made contrivances. A broad bowling green bounded by a serpentine walkway, trees and shrubs planted in carefully arranged groves and "wildernesses," and "Ha-ha" walls that partitioned the landscape but which were built in such a way that they did not act as a visual barrier were all English-inspired elements of the design. The surrounding landscape, therefore, was envisioned as complementing the Mansion and the other buildings in forming a cohesive and fashionable ensemble.[24]

After returning to Mount Vernon in December 1783, Washington almost immediately set about completing the aborted building campaign that his plantation manager had attempted to carry on in his absence. This entailed plastering, painting, and furnishing the interior of the new north wing of his house, which was to accommodate an elaborately decorated dining room. Even more work was required to complete the landscape plan: reconfiguring the two main gardens and relocating two small service buildings to fit the new design; changing the route of the entrance to the Mansion to accommodate the bowling green; and building a two-story brick greenhouse to serve as a focal point for the formal upper garden. It took almost four years to complete all of these projects, but at the same time this work was going on, Washington began to lay the groundwork for an even more ambitious effort to reorganize the agricultural underpinnings of the estate.[25]

The well-tended farms that Washington remembered from the days before he left home to lead the Army appeared very different to him after his return. He remarked in a letter he wrote to a friend in November 1785: "I never ride to my plantations without seeing something which makes me regret having [continued] so long in the ruinous mode of farming, which we are in." Characteristically, Washington did not act hastily, searching out the best advice then available in hopes of finding alternatives to the traditional approaches to farming that he found so unsatisfying. Washington soon found what he sought as he embraced a new system of agriculture that had been developed over the preceding decades by a group of innovative agronomists in England and Scotland. This movement was led by the gentleman farmer and author Arthur Young, who was widely regarded by his contemporaries as the leading agricultural thinker of his time.[26]

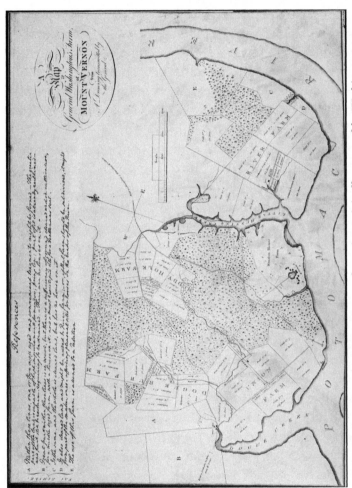

Map of the 8,000-acre Mount Vernon plantation, originally prepared by Washington, 1793.

Washington's initial contact with Young came in 1785 through an intermediary, George Fairfax, an old friend then living in England. Washington wrote to Fairfax seeking advice in finding a new plantation manager as his previous employee Lund Washington had just left after 12 years of service to start farming on his own. Washington specified that the candidate must know all of the best farming methods then current in England, closing with the hope that he should be, "above all, Midas like, one who can convert every thing he touches into manure, as the first transmutation towards Gold." Fairfax passed Washington's request along to Young, and the two men soon struck up a spirited correspondence that lasted until Washington's death. After receiving Young's cordial first letter—which included a gift of several copies of his influential journal, *Annals of Agriculture*—Washington responded with enthusiastic thanks, and also expressed his intention to rededicate himself to the life of a farmer. "Agriculture has ever been amongst the most favourite amusements of my life," Washington wrote, "though I never possessed much skill in the art, and nine years total inattention to it, has added nothing to a knowledge which is best understood from practice, but with the means you have been so obliging as to furnish me, I shall return to it (though rather late in the day) with hope and confidence."[27]

Young's "system" was known as the "new husbandry," and it called for a number of related measures primarily aimed at safeguarding soil fertility. According to this plan, crops were rotated over a longer period—six or seven years—fertilizer was extensively employed, and the fields were assiduously prepared for planting. The draft animals that provided the power to plow the fields, and to plant, cultivate, and process the grain, also supplied an important by-product in the form of manure that could be used as fertilizer. Finally, Young advocated rigorous field testing as the only way to assess objectively the effectiveness of his and others' ideas. Washington strongly endorsed this approach, remarking in his first letter to the

Englishman that "of the many volumes which have been written on this subject [agriculture] few of them are founded on experimental knowledge," and they "are verbose, contradictory, and bewildering."[28]

That Washington had a long-term commitment to empirically testing ways to improve his crop yields is indicated by an experiment that he conducted in 1760 when he set out to assess the relative values of several different types of fertilizers. According to the entries in his diary, Washington divided a box into 10 compartments, into which he placed soil and seeds, then applied different materials that he hoped might possess nutrient enriching properties. These included horse, sheep, and cow dung, sand and clay, "marle" (probably either clay mixed with lime or fossil shell), creek mud, and "black mould" (also from a creek bed). After watering the seeds and carefully monitoring the results over a period of two weeks, Washington concluded that the plants in the box containing the black mould performed the best.[29]

Given his background as a committed and detail-oriented farmer, it is no surprise that Washington found Young's ideas to be provocative. But there was another, even more telling reason why Washington embraced this system so completely: he was convinced that the new nation that he was instrumental in founding was dependent on agriculture for its long-term success. Washington expressed his championing spirit in an April 1788 letter to his fellow farmer Samuel Chamberline of Talbot County, Maryland: "Every improvement in husbandry should be gratefully received and peculiarly fostered in this Country, not only as promoting the interest and lessening the labor of the farmer, but as advancing our respectability in a national point of view; for, in the present State of America, our welfare and prosperity depend upon the cultivation of our lands and turning the produce of them to best advantage." Washington further demonstrated his support for agricultural innovation during his presidency when he repeatedly called for the creation of a National Board of Agriculture. Congress failed to act on his proposals, however, and it was not until 1862 when President Abraham Lincoln established the Department of Agriculture that a federally-funded entity was finally created to support Washington's vision.[30]

Washington realized that most farmers could not afford to take risks since the cost of failure might mean starvation. In lieu of a government agency to take the lead, Washington understood that it would be up to wealthy farmers like him to shoulder the burden, as they had the resources to withstand the occasional setbacks that were almost guaranteed by this approach. Washington spelled out his commitment to this program in a letter to his fellow agricultural innovator John Beale Bordley of Maryland in 1788. Washington observed that "Experiments must be made—and the practice (of such of them as are useful) must be introduced by Gentlemen who have leisure and abilities to devise and wherewithal to hazard something. The common farmer will not depart from the *old* road 'till the *new* one is made so plain and easy that he is sure it cannot be mistaken"[31]

Armed with the advice provided by Young and others, in 1786 Washington began to implement a variety of measures that, taken together, once again served to reinvent his farms. They included drawing up several rotation plans, and he finally adopted a seven-year scheme that gave him two crops of wheat and a half crop each of corn and potatoes during that span. He reorganized each of the four outlying farms into more efficient entities, complete with centrally located service yards, new barns and other specialized buildings, fields laid out to match the crop rotation scheme, and changes to the way his overseers managed the work of the field hands. Finally, Washington experimented with a variety of crops, including those provided as seed by Young and others, and developed new designs for plows and other implements based on published sources.[32]

A number of structures that Washington built at Mount Vernon during this period not only demonstrate his willingness to embrace new ideas but also testify to his fortitude in expending valuable resources to develop the infrastructure to accommodate them. Washington reconfigured and supplemented the existing building stock with new structures designed to handle a broader array of crops. He set about erecting three major new barn complexes that together would service the four outlying farms. Washington probably originally intended to build three similar, English-style grain barns, rectangular buildings with central threshing floors flanked by mows on either side for storing straw and hay. Two of the barn complexes followed the general lines of the English model, but the third structure was to take on a unique form that marks it as one of the most unusual buildings in American agriculture.

This remarkable 16-sided barn was built at the Dogue Run farm in 1792–95, and it was designed for the specific purpose of separating kernels of wheat from straw. At Mount Vernon and throughout the Chesapeake region in the 18th century, wheat was either threshed by hand, using a flail, or it was "treaded out" by horses. In the latter case, the harvested wheat was laid out in a wide circle and horses trotted over it, with the impact of their hooves separating the grain from the stalk. The treading had to be conducted outdoors, however, which meant that the success of the process was dependent upon good weather. In addition, even though horses performed the actual treading, it was still a labor-intensive procedure, as workers had to separate and gather the treaded grain by hand, and the resulting product often required extensive cleaning. Washington's new barn was an attempt to solve these problems by moving the treading inside a building specially designed to accommodate it. The 16-sided footprint meant that horses could walk unimpeded in a circle, and slotted floor boards allowed the grain to fall through the spaces to the storage bins below. In addition to allowing the treading to occur at any time of the year, safe from inclement weather, the building acted as a secure, lockable storage facility.[33]

The barn's shape was an unusual feature to be found in an agricultural building, although polygonal structures per se were

not unheard of in 18th-century Virginia. The majority of those
that survive are small round or eight-sided support structures
like garden houses, dairies, and privies that are features most
often found within ambitiously designed landscapes. At Mount
Vernon, two privies and two seed houses that are incorporated
into the formal gardens, along with the cupola on the roof
of the Mansion, all are octagonal. Polygonal shapes also
were used in military architecture, like the octagonal powder
magazines in Williamsburg and Charleston, South Carolina,
and any number of coastal fortifications. Most of the non-
military structures owed their geometric shapes to aesthetic
concerns, although some, especially ice houses, were designed
with specific functions in mind. The Dogue Run barn's
16-sided footprint was similarly inspired, as Washington
designed the building to be as round as feasible to accommodate
the circular path taken by the horses when treading out the
grain.[34]

The character of the flooring upon which the horses trod
on the grain may have been an even more innovative design
feature. The oak floorboards were cut 2½ inches square, and
they were nailed in place with a gap between them so that
when the heads of grain were separated from the straw they
could fall through to the granary below. Although the evidence
is far from conclusive, there are no known examples of a
similar floor in use before Washington's, and thus the slotted
floor may have been his own invention. Supporting this
interpretation is the fact that Washington was compelled
to perform a series of empirical tests to determine the most
efficient width of the gap between the boards. Washington's
directions to his farm manager, William Pearce, are typically
detailed and reflect his commitment to trial and error in
solving this type of problem. The question was to find the
happy balance between spacing that was too wide, which
would allow the straw to work its way into the space and
choke off the passage of the grain, and too narrow, or prone
to jamming. Washington directed that the floor boards be laid

in sections of varying gaps and then tested; in due course, a spacing of 1½ inches between the boards was determined to work best.[35]

Depending on the outcome of his experiment with the barn at Dogue Run, it seems that Washington planned to build at least one more treading barn. He did not follow up on this intention, however, and the decision probably related to his ongoing interest in yet another technological innovation. Within two years of completing the treading barn, Washington paid a mechanic named William Booker to travel to Mount Vernon to construct a portable threshing machine. In addition to providing greater flexibility, a portable thresher also was much less expensive to build and maintain than barns like the one at Dogue Run. For years Washington had been following closely the progress of a number of inventors who had been trying to perfect such a device. In 1787 Washington read in Young's *Annals* about a threshing machine that had been developed by a man named William Winlaw. Washington asked Young for his candid assessment of the machine's capabilities, clearly signaling his interest in acquiring a copy depending on Young's positive review. The Englishman's appraisal was mixed, however, and Washington decided against pursuing it. A few years later while in New York during his presidency, Washington had the opportunity to observe for himself a machine built according to Winlaw's design at work. He concluded that "Upon the whole it appears to be an easier, more expeditious and much cleaner way of getting out Grain," but because of its complexity, he was concerned that his slaves would not be able to operate it. By 1797 Washington apparently was convinced that Booker's thresher was sufficiently reliable and user-friendly to warrant a trial. Portable threshers were used to process grain in concert with the treading barn at Dogue Run during the remaining two years of his life.[36]

The other barns Washington built were more traditional in their function and layout, but the process by which he arrived at the design for the structure erected at Union Farm further demonstrates his innovative approach to such matters. In 1786 Washington purchased the last parcel of land that he needed to enable him to expand an existing farm, renamed "Union Farm" because it was a result of combining existing fields with the newly acquired tract. He immediately began to reorganize the layout of the farm, including relocating the quarters for the enslaved field hands who were assigned to work there under the direction of a hired overseer and building a new brick barn and an associated farmyard. In November of that year, Washington wrote to Young asking his advice on the design of a barn suitable for a farm of 500 acres in size. Young responded by providing a detailed plan for the proposed building, complete with a threshing floor, storage bays, and a yard and sheds to accommodate livestock. Washington began construction in the fall of 1787, and a year later the new barn was nearing completion. In a letter he wrote to Young in December 1788, Washington stated that "It is constructed somewhat according to the plan you had the goodness to send me: but with some additions. It is now, I believe, the largest and most convenient one in this Country."[37]

Back at the Mansion House Farm, Washington erected another unusual structure: a "stercorary," or "dung repository," which was an open-sided building designed for composting manure and other organic materials. In 1787 Washington completed the stercorary, located just a few hundred feet south of the Mansion, and it may be the earliest example in the country of a structure erected specifically for the purpose. It featured a recessed cobble-stoned floor, 31 by 12 feet in dimension, which acted like a mixing bowl where Washington directed that "trash, of every sort and kind about the house, and in holes and corners" be deposited, along with animal manure and other organic waste. It was open on all four sides to allow air to circulate and to facilitate loading and unloading. The manure was allowed to cure until it was ready to be used as fertilizer in the surrounding gardens and orchards. An acquaintance of Washington's and a fellow member of the

Philadelphia Society for Promoting Agriculture named Richard Peters published a design for a remarkably similar structure in the *Memoirs* of the society in 1808. Archaeologists have excavated the site of the building and found structural remains—including the largely intact cobblestone floor—that testify to the striking resemblance between the two designs. This naturally raises the question of whether Peters and Washington had conferred on the topic during one of their meetings.[38]

Throughout the 45 years that Washington operated Mount Vernon, raising livestock was an important and sometimes profitable contributor to his plantation economy. As at almost every other large plantation of the period in the region, the meat from slaughtering cattle, swine, and sheep, as well as their milk, wool, and hides, contributed to the bottom line either as savings on otherwise needed expenditures or as revenue from selling the surplus to neighbors and other markets. Horses, oxen, and, later on, mules supplied the raw power needed to work the fields as well as to haul grain, tobacco, and other cargoes; horses provided the primary means of overland transportation. With the decision to switch from tobacco to grain farming, the role of livestock expanded accordingly, while Washington's commitment to a more rigorous system of husbandry in the 1780s extended to a series of efforts to improve the management of his stock. These ranged from upgrading basic procedures like improving the pens used when fattening the cattle and swine, and feeding them on the nutrient-rich slops from the whiskey distillery, to culling and breeding to improve the bloodlines of his herds and flocks, and acquiring champion jackasses from Spain to sire a breed of superior draft animals.[39]

The traditional method of managing swine in 18th-century Virginia was to allow the animals to run free in the woodlands for most of the year, to forage on acorns and other forest mast. Typically they would be herded together in the autumn and penned for fattening before slaughtering. In December 1785, for example, Washington slaughtered 128 hogs (pigs weighing more than 140 pounds), yielding 17,385 pounds of pork. Approximately 2,300 pounds of the meat were distributed to Washington's five overseers and managers, with the remaining 15,000 pounds reserved for the use of his "family." One of the widely advertised benefits of operating a distillery was the value of the leftover slops for feeding livestock, and when Washington approved of establishing a whiskey distillery at the gristmill in 1797, the focus on hog raising was shifted to that site. Over a three-month period in the fall of 1798 the carpenters built wooden sheds and pens to contain both swine and cattle, and they erected troughs to transport the slops to the pens for feed. The sheds were substantial structures— supported by hewn cedar posts, with oak plank walls and floors, and covered with shingle roofs—measuring up to 90-feet long and 12-feet wide.[40]

As with swine, Washington enlarged his flock of sheep over the years and explored ways to improve their quality. While pigs were sufficiently hardy to live on their own foraging in the woodlands for much of the year, sheep required considerably more care and attention to prosper, not in the least being protection from wolves and other predators. As a consequence, substantial flocks of the animals were a rarity at 18th-century Virginia plantations. As early as 1758 Washington's flock totaled roughly 100 animals, which appears to have been an unusually large number for the period. The plantation records indicate that each year Washington carefully selected the best specimens to be kept as rams and ewes for breeding purposes while the others were culled for meat. After the Revolution Washington sought to purchase lambs to replenish his flock, and he made inquiries in Britain to acquire what he hoped were superior animals. Robert Bakewell, a well-known breeder from Leicestershire, was credited with developing a breed of sheep that would fatten at an earlier age while yielding less waste when they were butchered. British law precluded exporting Bakewell's sheep, but Washington eventually was able to acquire lambs that had been descended from the breeder's animals. According to the livestock inventories, by 1785 the sheep population had increased to 283 animals; 14 years later it more than doubled again to 640.[41]

In addition to their meat, sheep provided another valuable commodity in the form of wool. As Washington expanded his spinning enterprise in the late 1760s, the output of wool from his own flocks took on greater significance in supplying his needs and reducing his expenditures accordingly. When touring several northern states during his first term as president, Washington observed firsthand the success of the New England farmers in expanding their wool production, which in turn supported the burgeoning regional textile industry. In 1789 Washington sought to promote the same success in Virginia as he wrote to the governor championing inducements to farmers to increase their flocks. In 1794 Washington bragged that a sample of wool from his own Mount Vernon sheep that he had sent to England several years earlier had been judged "to be equal in quality to the Kentish Wool." For Washington, who always looked to England as the standard of quality against which American products should be measured, this news was gratifying indeed.[42]

Washington maintained a herd of cattle at Mount Vernon, not only to supply meat, hides, and milk but also to plow the fields and perform other heavy-duty occupations. Oxen (castrated males) were used as draft animals up until the age of eight years, after which they were set out to pasture to fatten and then were slaughtered for meat. In 1785 a total of 26 draft oxen were included in the livestock inventory, along with 310 other cattle: 75 steers, 101 cows, 61 heifers, 58 calves, 9 "Beeves fatting," and 2 mature and 4 young bulls. Washington was particularly interested in obtaining well-bred bulls in hopes of improving the quality of his stock. He suffered a number of setbacks in this regard, however, as few of the animals seem to have performed to his expectations. In 1775 the plantation manager, Lund Washington, wrote to his employer informing him that "Our bull has lately given a Specimen of his mischievous disposition" as he apparently gored and killed one of the wagon horses. In 1797 Washington succeeded in acquiring "a young bull of the breed of Mr. Bakewell" from Edward Lloyd, of Talbot County, Maryland. In 1798 a visitor remarked upon seeing "a superb bull," which he stated had cost Washington "some two hundred dollar," but only a few months later Washington complained that "it is to be regretted that I should derive so little advantage from a Bull, the sole inducement to buy which, was to improve my breed of Cattle; for I do not find that he has served more than a few Cows which have occasionally been here."[43]

Washington's first priority was to make use of the milk from his cows for his own purposes on the plantation. A dairy had been set up relatively early on at the Mansion House Farm by Washington's older brother Lawrence as a "Dairy" building is listed in the inventory of his estate that was taken in 1753. Washington referred to the dairy in his diary in 1760, and dairying may have taken on more prominence at that time as a result of his marriage to Martha Custis the previous year as it was a task that was typically put under the supervision of the lady of the house. This enterprise was moderately successful in supplying the needs of the household, especially milk, but Washington still often found it necessary to buy cheese and butter to keep up with the demand. Washington was particularly fond of English cheeses as he placed many orders with his London agents for cheddar, Cheshire, and Gloucester. By 1789, however, he wrote to the Marquis de Lafayette that he had decided to promote American cheese production, and that locally made cheeses were available of "excellent quality."[44]

By the late 1780s Washington viewed the growth of Alexandria and the plans to build the Federal City just a few miles north of his estate as an opportunity to make a profit by providing the inhabitants with dairy products. In 1788 he ordered a dairy building to be constructed at his River Farm, and in 1794 he authorized the same at two of the other farms "to see if the Milk at each could not be turned to some account."

By 1797 there were indications that Washington's hopes for these ventures were coming to pass as the dairy at Union Farm earned a respectable profit of £30.12.3, offering butter for sale as well as supplying the Washington household, and produced at least 239 pounds of cheese. But only two years later, the promising start seems to have lost momentum as Washington complained to his plantation manager, James Anderson, that "It is hoped, and will be expected, that more effectual measures will be pursued to make butter another year; for it is almost beyond belief, that from 101 Cows actually reported on a late enumeration of the Cattle, that I am obliged to *buy butter* for the use of my family."[45]

When at Mount Vernon, Washington inspected the farms almost daily from horseback. He also rode to the hounds as often as several times a week during the 1760s and 1770s and then again for several years after he returned from the Revolution. No less an authority than Thomas Jefferson offered his opinion that Washington was "the best horseman of his age." The livestock list that was compiled in 1785 included two riding horses, Nelson and Blueskin, honored veterans who had served ably as Washington's mounts during the late war. It also included an Arabian stallion named Magnolio, which Washington attempted to race. Magnolio failed to live up to his owner's expectations on the race track, however, and in 1788 Washington traded him to his friend and sometime business partner Richard Henry Lee in exchange for 5,000 acres of land in the Kentucky territory. Both commodities bore some uncertainty as the quality of the land could not readily be determined just as Magnolio's track record was mixed, but both men seemed to think that they came out ahead on the deal. In addition to the riding horses, 21 draft animals were devoted to pulling the Washingtons' coach, the hack, the wagon, and the carts, while 47 more were employed in plowing, for a total of 130 animals in all. By 1797 Washington had acquired a stallion, named Traveler, who brought in another £9.17 in stud fees.[46]

Washington had become convinced that mules, the sterile offspring of an ass and a horse, worked longer and harder, ate less, and were easier to train than draft horses. In 1785–86 he finally succeeded in acquiring several champion jacks and she-asses from Spain and Malta for the purpose of breeding. The livestock inventories that were made in 1785 and 1799 provide conclusive evidence to indicate the expanding role of mules at Mount Vernon. There were 130 horses and no mules on the estate at the earlier date, but 14 years later the number of horses had plummeted to 36 while the mule population had risen to 57. The number of working oxen also declined dramatically—from 26 in 1785 to none in 1799—having been replaced by the 42 working mules recorded in the latter year. In 1797 Washington also received the considerable sum of £56 in fees in exchange for the labors of his jacks in the form of reproductive services as the animals toured the region to mate with the mares of Washington's fellow farmers. If all worked according to plan, Washington hoped that the animals would be the source of "a race of extraordinary goodness that will stock the Country." In this vision, as in so many others, Washington proved prescient as mules became the mainstay of Southern agriculture over the next 150 years. According to the United States census of 1880 the population of mules had increased to approximately two million.[47]

To take full advantage of the potential commercial benefits of wheat production, in 1770–71 Washington replaced his severely deteriorated gristmill with a larger and more efficient structure. A gristmill that may have been built as early as the 1730s by their father, Augustine, was included as part of the 2,000-acre plantation that George Washington inherited in 1754 after the death of his older half-brother Lawrence. The mill was in a dilapidated condition as early as 1760, however, when Washington noted in his diary that it took 55 minutes to grind one bushel of corn. A local millwright carried out extensive repairs to the building in 1764, but in 1769 Washington finally resolved to build a new mill, to be located on the opposite side of Dogue Run and about a half-mile downstream from the previous site. From February 1770, when Washington selected the new location with the help of John Ballendine, the owner of nearby Occoquan Mills, he spent a year erecting the building and digging the millrace (a channel to carry the water that was needed to turn the mill wheel). Workers harvested much of the wood that was needed from Washington's land and neighboring parcels; large river rocks were floated down from the falls of the Potomac to serve as the foundation for the building, while the stone for the walls was quarried locally.[48]

Washington's mill used the force of a stream of water that was channeled into the building to turn a large wooden wheel, 16 feet in diameter. The power generated by the wheel, rotating between four and eight revolutions per minute, was transferred by a series of gears to run two sets of millstones. Each set consisted of a pair of large (four to five feet in diameter) circular stones, one superimposed and suspended over the other; it was between the grooved surfaces (known as furrows) of these stones that the grain was ground. The upper, or "runner" stone, turned at more than 100 revolutions per minute, while the lower, or "bed" stone, remained stationary. The grain was fed through a hole in the upper stone and trickled down to make contact with the sharpened furrows carved into each surface. The furrows were cut in such a way that in concert they pulverized the grain and converted it into meal. Once it was cleaned, sorted, and dried, the wheat meal (now considered flour) was ready to be sold. The less needy corn meal was simply sieved to separate the final product from the fragments of outer hull to complete the process.[49]

The new mill was intended to grind the grain of neighboring farmers as well as that grown at Mount Vernon, and the two sets of millstones enabled it to produce different grades of product. The millstones included a pair made from a type of fresh water quartz called "buhr" that was imported from France and was capable of producing high quality flour for the merchant trade. The French stones were the best in the world as they were especially hard and could hold the sharp cutting edge needed to produce the finest grade of flour. Washington acquired his set of French stones in December of 1771; they were four-feet-four inches in diameter and cost £38, almost double the price (£20) that he paid a local supplier the previous November for a pair of stones of lesser quality. As was customary, the miller collected a toll of one-eighth of the product ground for others. The merchant trade, on the other hand, was entirely a commercial arrangement with the mill owner purchasing grain from other farmers to grind in addition to his own.[50]

Any sense of elation that Washington may have felt upon completing the new mill was short-lived: on January 27, 1771, Washington noted that he had received "News of part of my Mill Wall's falling in." This problem apparently was at least temporarily remedied, but less than four months later his plantation manager, Lund, wrote to him reporting, "our Mill is once more in a bad way, the Wall between the water Pit and Cog pit, is falling down, which has occasioned the Floor with the W[eigh]t of Flour on it to settle down about 3 inches." Once again, the necessary temporary repairs were made to allow the mill to resume grinding. But it was not until the following September that hired masons were able to shore up the sinking wall and stabilize the building.[51]

Providing a dependable source of water to power the mill also proved to be a greater challenge than Washington probably anticipated. The race was essentially a trench, roughly seven- or eight-feet deep and six-feet wide, that had to be dug by hand for a distance of more than a mile. The purpose of the race was to divert water from Dogue Run along a course that would allow gravity to bring it to the mill. In places where the elevation of the ground dipped, the bed of the race had to be raised with wooden posts and planks. The arduous job of digging the race began on April 26, 1770 and continued for about a year, with Washington employing many hands to try to speed up the process. He even offered the workers an incentive of 18 shillings in payment per rod (about 16 feet) of trench that was excavated "if they woud be brisk and stick to it." Apparently even this inducement was not sufficient, however, and soon Washington turned to additional Mount Vernon slaves to assist in digging the waterway. The race was finally completed in April 1771, but keeping it cleaned out and in good repair was a regular chore. Already by the following year the millrace had silted in to the point where it required six slaves two months time to clean it out so that the mill could grind.[52]

During the summer of 1771 carpenters were hired to build a house for the miller, and on August 10, Washington noted in his diary that he had "Raised a House at the Mill for the Miller to live in." Later that month the chimney was erected, and the walls were plastered on September 10. Archaeological excavations carried out at the site in 1931 revealed that the house was located about a hundred feet from the mill. According to an insurance document from 1803, the cottage was 24 by 16 feet in dimension, and in a letter from 1785, Washington mentioned that there was "a small kitchen convenient thereto" and that the garden was "properly paled in." In addition to his wages of £80 per year, the first miller to work at the new mill, William Roberts, and his family were allowed to live in the cottage at no charge. He also had the privilege of feeding a cow and raising fowl at Washington's expense. In return, Roberts agreed to oversee the work of the coopers as well as to manage all of the business of the mill, and even to act as millwright in carrying out any normal repairs to the machinery that were required.[53]

According to the 1803 insurance document, the mill was built of stone, two and one-half stories high, 32 by 46 feet in dimension. In a letter from 1783, Washington provided a relatively detailed description of the complex as it appeared at that time. He stated that there were "two pair of Stones, one pair of which are French-burr, employed in the merchant business. The Mill house is of Stone, large and commodious, the dwelling house, which is convenient, is within thirty yards of it; and has a garden enclosed adjoining. A Coopers Shop is

also near, and the whole convenient to tide water." The earliest
detailed map of the area, Washington's plan of the Mount
Vernon "Five Farms" from 1793, shows three structures on
the property, presumably the mill, the miller's cottage, and the
cooperage.[54]

By 1791 the mill was in need of substantial repairs.
Washington went far beyond carrying out the required
maintenance, however, as he was one of the first to pay to
install a series of improvements that had been developed and
patented the previous year by Oliver Evans of Delaware. In
Washington's day the technology that was available to carry
out the mandatory step of grinding grain into edible meal
had changed little over the previous 2,000 years. Although the
power generated by the waterdriven wheel turned the stones
to grind the grain, a good deal of manual labor was needed to
handle the heavy sacks of grain and then to transport, clean,
and package the meal and flour. By the time Washington built
his gristmill some slight advancements had been made in the
technology, but his mill still used essentially the same overall
design as those described thousands of years earlier in the texts
of Roman authors.[55]

Evans's designs transformed a traditional mill into an
automated machine, with each step in the milling process
united and powered by the force of the water wheel. The grain
was transported throughout the building by means of a system
of drives, elevators, and chutes. Wheat could be taken from a
wagon or the hold of a vessel, then be cleaned, ground between
the millstones, dried and cooled, sifted, and delivered to barrels
ready for packing. All of these steps were possible without the
intervention of a human operator, except as adjustments to the
machinery became necessary. These revolutionary innovations
made milling much less labor intensive and more efficient and
thus more cost effective. In the fall of 1791 the millwright,
William Ball, installed the automated system in Washington's
mill under the direction of Oliver Evans's brother, Evan
Evans.[56]

In addition to linking the machines to clean the grain and then to sort the meal after it was ground, Evans invented a totally new device to solve an age-old problem. Flour is extremely sensitive to temperature and humidity, and is particularly prone to spoilage as a result of excessive moisture. The "hopper boy" that Evans invented automatically spread out the meal on the floor to cool and dry and then diverted it to another device to be sorted and packed into barrels for shipping. Previously this time-consuming chore had been the responsibility of one of the workers (usually a boy) assigned to the mill, spreading and turning the meal with a rake. Once dried, the worker had to shovel the meal back into the bags and carry them downstairs to the bolter to be sorted. As testimony to the novelty of the device, it was one of the main features that a foreign visitor to Washington's mill commented on in 1798: "An American machine invented by Evans (who has published a work on mills) for the aeration of the flour is very ingenious."[57]

Even after the automated system was added, however, the operation of the mill continued to give Washington cause for concern. The basic problem appears to have been an insufficient volume of water provided by the original race excavated almost 20 years before. Washington reasoned that digging new sections of the race to increase the water flow would be more efficient than attempting to repair the old channel. But even when the race was in good repair, in dry weather the creek from which the flow was diverted simply did not have the capacity to operate the machinery. Therefore, as part of the planned upgrade, Washington intended to turn "such streams into his Mill-Race as will keep her going at all times." The work again progressed slowly, however, and the new race was not completed until the winter of 1796–97, almost three years after the project began.[58]

Given the limitations of the available technology, Washington's mill could only convert a portion of the grain into flour of the highest grade. The best flour had the smallest particle size and was relatively free of bran—the residue of the outer hull of the grain; the lower grades were called "middlings" and "shipstuff." Between September 1776 and October 1777 the mill produced 2,016 bushels of flour, 10,968 bushels of middlings, and 3,034 bushels of shipstuff. In 1771 Washington sold a large batch of product, with the flour bringing 20 percent more per barrel than the middlings and 30 percent more than what he received for the shipstuff. The significant difference between the prices paid for flour versus the lesser products would have served as a strong incentive to improve the overall quality.[59]

After installing the Evans system in 1791, Washington's mill appears to have produced a much higher proportion of finer grade flour than before. This included what was called "superfine" flour, that was more pure and even more finely ground. According to the plantation ledger for the years 1799–1800, Washington's superfine flour generally sold for between $8.00 and $9.00 per barrel, while his "flour" sold for between $7.50 and $8.00. On at least one occasion Washington sold 12 barrels of middlings for $6.66 each, while the shipstuff commanded a much lower price, at only about $1.50 per barrel.[60]

Washington naturally was keen to make the most of the new improvements, urging his miller at the time, Joseph Davenport, to run the mill "Nights, as well in the day, as all Merchant Mills do," when the supply of grain and water allowed. He also instructed Davenport to perform an experiment, whereby he was to measure and weigh 100 bushels of wheat, before and after it was ground, as well as carefully record the quantity of the different grades of flour that were produced. In this way, Washington hoped to determine whether it was more profitable to sell the wheat as flour or as unprocessed grain. Apparently it took Davenport an inordinate length of time, nearly two months, to conduct the experiment, which caused Washington to question whether Davenport was "too lazy to give the necessary attention to the business which is entrusted to him."[61]

Davenport was one of a long line of millers who worked for Washington over a period of more than four decades. Millers in general occupied an important yet somewhat tenuous position in American society. As one measure of their elevated status, they were excluded from military service because of the vital importance of their work to the community. But in contrast with this seeming indication of respect, millers often were viewed with mistrust as well. Possibly because it was difficult for customers to oversee and check their work, millers were frequently accused of taking more than their allotted share of the flour and meal that they ground, of packing barrels loosely, and of mixing qualities of flour to their benefit. The skepticism that Washington often displayed toward the performance of his millers seems to have conformed with the general attitudes of the day.[62]

Davenport, the miller, died suddenly in January 1796, possibly from a heart attack as he complained of suffering chest pains just a few days prior to his death. In his letter informing Washington of Davenport's untimely passing, the farm manager, William Pearce, made the rather laconic comment that he died "at a time when we had a good head of Water and was Giting on with Grinding our wheat." After the miller's death, Pearce assigned his own son to the mill to help Davenport's former assistant, the slave named Ben, until a suitable replacement could be found. By the following August another miller, Patrick Callahan, had been hired. Washington's opinion of Callahan's work habits seems to have been no higher than Davenport's, as he described Callahan as "though tolerably knowing as a Miller he is an indolent man." Washington's dissatisfaction with Callahan only increased over time, and came to a head when the miller apparently asked for an increase in pay. The discord generated by this dispute over payment may have led to Callahan's only staying on the job for another year, as he left Mount Vernon in August 1799.[63]

With Callahan's departure, Washington rehired his former miller, William Roberts, an experiment that failed almost immediately due to Roberts's undiminished penchant for abusing alcohol. Therefore, the enslaved African-American miller's assistant, Ben, who had served in the mill for many years, probably oversaw its operation during the last months leading up to Washington's death in December 1799. In 1792 Washington appears to have been describing Ben when he mentioned "a smart young negro man who acts as an Assistant in the mill, in which business he has been employed for several years, and of course may be calculated upon as understanding the common and ordinary business of a mill." It is likely that Ben could read and write and perform the arithmetic necessary to carry out the business end of the operation. Besides working in the mill, Ben assisted in the cooperage and spent many hours repairing and cleaning the millrace.[64]

Eleven men were listed as working at the gristmill property in the census of the Mount Vernon slaves that Washington compiled in 1799. These included Ben and another young slave, Forrester, who worked in the mill, and nine others who were employed in the cooperage or in the distillery. Originally a separate building located near the mill, the cooperage was adapted to serve as the first distillery in 1797. With the addition of the distillery the demand for barrels to store and transport alcohol, in addition to those already needed for flour and fish, seems to have outstripped the coopers' ability to keep up. The farm ledger records that large numbers of barrels were acquired each year in trade from various customers. Normally the coopers were placed under the supervision of the miller, but after the distillery was established, the farm manager, Anderson, likely took on greater responsibility in their supervision.[65]

Although Washington's experience with his millers was often a cause for complaint, and the mill continued to suffer from a lack of water in the summer months and from a long string of accidents like the collapse of the wheel pit walls, the mill was a highly profitable venture. As early as June 1771 Washington sold 128,000 pounds (426 barrels) of flour to an Alexandria merchant, and the very next month another 200 barrels of his flour were shipped to Jamaica. In 1797, the mill trailed only three of the farms and the fishery in profitability, accounting for £117 of net revenue. For the 12-month period between October 1797 and the following November, the mill ground more than 5,000 bushels (roughly 275,000 pounds) of wheat into flour, valued at £2,289. Several thousand bushels of corn and rye were ground as well, which was used internally as both a food product and as the main ingredients in the whiskey made at the distillery that Washington established that year.[66]

As important as all of these ventures were in terms of Washington's overall financial plans, throughout his life he was fixated on acquiring the most valuable commodity of all— land. Among the Virginia gentry the quest to accumulate large tracts of western land was a particularly popular strategy, although actually profiting from increasing land values could be much more difficult to accomplish than was supposed. For an ambitious young man like George Washington, operating without great family resources and left fatherless at a young age, cashing in on land speculation must have had enormous appeal. Washington spelled out the prospects for finding success in a letter he wrote to his neighbor, John Posey, in 1767: "An enterprizing Man with very little Money may lay the foundation of a Noble estate in the New Settlements upon Monongahela [a river in Pennsylvania]…for proof of which only look to Frederick, and see what Fortunes were made by the Hite's and first takers up of those Lands: Nay how the greatest Estates we have in this Colony were made; Was it not by taking up and purchasing at very low rates the rich back Lands which were thought nothing of in those days, but are now the most valuable Lands we possess?"[67]

Washington's ability to acquire frontier land was aided immeasurably by the years he spent and the experience he gained during his early career as a land surveyor. Upon the untimely death of his father in 1743, Washington's inheritance in property and slaves was simply inadequate to launch him on a career as a successful tobacco planter. Thus, at an early age

Washington was forced to cast about for another way of making a living. Surveying was a relatively lucrative occupation, and its practitioners held a place of honor in society as well, on a level with doctors, lawyers, and clergymen. In addition to the fees that they collected for their services, frontier surveyors also benefited from the opportunity to acquire choice parcels of land for their own. After taking lessons in surveying at the age of 15, Washington acquired the tools of his trade and he apprenticed for several months under the eye of a local professional. The next year he was appointed to the position of surveyor for the newly formed county of Culpeper. This was a remarkable achievement for one so young, and Washington's selection undoubtedly was largely due to the support of the powerful Fairfax family, long-time friends of the Washingtons and in-laws of his older brother, Lawrence. During the three years that George Washington was a practicing professional surveyor, he made at least 190 surveys, earning him the considerable sum of approximately £400. Equally important was that he was able to purchase more than 2,100 acres of prime land, all located in the fertile lower Shenandoah Valley. [68]

After the fall of 1752 Washington gave up surveying for profit as the prospects for continued success in the profession began to diminish along with the supply of unclaimed, desirable lands. Instead, he once again used family connections to obtain a commission from the governor of Virginia to serve as adjutant of the militia, at an annual salary of £100. Washington was quite interested in pursuing a lifelong career in the military, and he must have viewed this appointment as the first step along that path. Unfortunately, he was ultimately unsuccessful in obtaining what he wanted most, a commission in the British Army; he did not have the resources, either in money or political connections, that were needed to achieve his goal. Nevertheless, the experience Washington gained from serving alongside the British and commanding Virginia forces during the French and Indian War would pay him many unanticipated dividends over the course of his life. Chief among these was the preparation it afforded for his later role as commander in chief of the Continental Army during the Revolution. But it also led directly to his acquiring tens of thousands of additional acres of land as his reward for his wartime service to the Colony, which would become part of the foundation for his financial success.[69]

In 1754 Virginia's royal governor, Robert Dinwiddie, issued a proclamation setting aside some 200,000 acres of land to be awarded as bounties to soldiers and officers who volunteered to serve during the war. A variety of legal issues relating to the bounty lands arose over the years, and it was not until almost 20 years later that it was determined exactly which lands were eligible to be claimed. Nevertheless, Washington eventually succeeded in securing more than 20,000 acres of bounty land located in the Great Kanawha River Valley, near where the Kanawha empties into the Ohio River. In addition to the lands to which he was entitled as a consequence of his own service, Washington acquired title to bounties that were due other veterans. For example, in 1770 Washington purchased a warrant for 3,000 acres of bounty land from his friend, neighbor, and fellow veteran, John Posey. When added to the other parcels that he had acquired earlier and to those he purchased over the years in other parts of Virginia, and in Pennsylvania, Ohio, Kentucky, Maryland, and New York, the total acreage of western lands that Washington owned exceeded 50,000.[70]

Washington was confident that the value of his frontier holdings would naturally increase over time as American farmers migrated westward looking for fertile land to settle. In actuality, Washington reaped little profit from most of his western tracts as the density of settlement in these areas remained sparse during his lifetime. The property that he owned in the Shenandoah Valley, on the other hand, did prove valuable as the area experienced a significant growth in population following the close of the French and Indian War. Washington's preferred strategy was to enter into long-term lease agreements with tenant farmers, who were responsible for making any improvements and paid an annual rent that was collected by his agents. When Washington was fortunate to employ dependable men in that capacity, the system worked reasonably well; in the years following the Revolution, Washington received rents totaling approximately £170 annually from his properties in Berkeley and Frederick counties. But undependable agents, the disruptions caused by the Revolution and conflict with Native Americans, disputes over land titles, and settlers squatting on Washington's land and refusing to pay him his due combined to reduce the revenues that he might reasonably have expected to receive.[71]

The great distances involved made it difficult for Washington to manage his western land closely, a fact that he alluded to in 1794 when he wrote to an acquaintance "that landed property at a distance from the Proprietor, is attended with more plague than profit." When he recorded those gloomy words, Washington may have been thinking specifically about the many problems he had encountered in managing one particular tract, known as "Washington's Bottom," located in Fayette County in western Pennsylvania. Washington began in 1767 to acquire the parcels that eventually made up the 1,600-acre property, and he first visited the area in the fall of 1770 during his initial trip to inspect his western holdings. Two years later, Washington entered into a partnership with Gilbert Simpson, Jr., the son of one of his long-time tenants at Mount Vernon, to farm the property on his behalf. Simpson soon proved himself to be a lackluster farmer and an even worse manager, and over the next decade the enterprise failed to repay Washington's investment in a variety of improvements, including building a gristmill at the cost of more than £1,200. Washington's involvement in the Revolutionary War had made it impossible for him to do much about the problems at Washington's Bottom, but one of the first items on the long list of issues for him to address after his return was to sever his relationship with Simpson and attempt to recoup as much of his investment as possible.[72]

Upon his arrival at Washington's Bottom in September 1784, Washington found the property in woeful condition. All of the buildings were in disrepair, the fields that had been cleared ranged widely in quality, the fruit trees had been killed by the previous winter's severe weather, and, most distressing of all, the mill was dilapidated and in poor working order. Washington had been led to believe that the mill was one of the "finest" to be found west of the mountains, and his disappointment in its sad condition therefore must have been acute. Washington concluded his report by succinctly summing up the scant prospects of his receiving any return on his substantial expenditures: "In a word, little rent, or good is to be expected from the present aspect of her."[73]

In 1787 Washington rented a portion of the Washington's Bottom property to a war veteran named Israel Shreve, but this event simply initiated another round of painful financial dealings. In 1795 Shreve purchased the tract on credit, but even though he soon sold parts of the property to others, for several years in a row he failed to send Washington the agreed upon payments. At long last Washington felt compelled to bring suit to collect the debt, but he soon relented. Washington was moved by a letter that he received from Shreve that made a pathetic plea to postpone the inevitable. After listing a variety of extenuating circumstances, Shreve concluded by throwing himself on his old commander's mercy: "I have known your Excellency Several times repreave Crimanals who had forfeited their lives and restore them again to be Citizens I have a good Wife and Several dear Little Children Round me who has Committed no fault to merit So greavious a turn in Life If your Excellency Could Condisend to pass by this grevious punishment it would be hundreds to my advantage and perhaps not one cent to your Disadvantage." Washington agreed to withdraw his suit, but Shreve's health already was failing, and he died the following year without paying Washington the money he was owed.[74]

When Washington traveled to Washington's Bottom in 1784 to inspect the property and end his failed business relationship with Gilbert Simpson, it was only one leg of an extensive tour that he planned to inspect his western properties and to scout out possible routes for trade to the Ohio country. Washington had heard more bad news pertaining to a substantial tract that he owned along Miller's Run in western Pennsylvania, this time in the form of serious challenges to his ownership. Washington had experienced difficulties with squatters settling on his property in the years before the Revolution, but his agents had been generally successful in defending his rights. Over the course of the war years the number of unlawful settlers undoubtedly had increased, and Washington was eager to re-establish his claims and collect the revenues that were his due. But what Washington found when he arrived was even more disturbing than he could have imagined as there were as many as 14 households firmly planted on his land, and with scant interest in leaving.[75]

In addition to the usual problems encountered in attempting to manage affairs from a distance, Washington was faced with a strong cultural bias in favor of those actually occupying property, at the expense of the lawful but absent owners. At heart was the attitude held by frontiersmen, as well as by some officials, that any occupation of the land was preferable to leaving it vacant and unimproved. As a consequence, the efforts to clear the property, to erect dwellings and other buildings, to plant orchards and to grow crops, was viewed by many as a more valid claim to ownership than the mere possession of a patent. Thus, while the men who had settled on Washington's Miller's Run property probably realized that they were violating his ownership rights, they may well have expected him to make concessions that would lead to an agreement that was beneficial to both parties. Washington arranged a meeting with his unlawful tenants, who were a closely knit group of Scots-Irishmen and fellow members of the Associate Presbyterian Church. All were men of some consequence in the community, although Washington took a different view, derogatorily describing them as "willful and obstinate sinners." The settlers offered to purchase the land in question if Washington offered moderate terms, but he declined to sell the parcels, preferring to enter into long-term lease agreements instead. In their turn, the settlers refused what Washington considered to be a non-negotiable offer, and the meeting broke up with angry words and hurt feelings.[76]

Washington was determined to succeed, and he immediately took the appropriate steps to protect his rights. He enlisted the county sheriff to serve eviction notices on the squatters, and he engaged a local lawyer, Thomas Smith, to bring suit against them in court. Over the next two years, Washington worked diligently to compile the necessary documentary evidence in support of his claim to the land, and he strategized with his lawyer to develop the strongest case possible. Finally, in October 1786 Washington's suit was heard in a circuit session held in Washington County, presided over by Thomas McKean, a Pennsylvania Supreme Court justice. Although Washington had hoped to participate in the trial, a brief illness prevented him from attending. To Washington's relief, the judge ruled in his favor in every case, upholding his title to the land and leaving it to him to dictate the terms of settlement. In his moment of victory and with his rights defended, Washington could afford to be generous in his demands, concluding that:

> Altho' the present occupants have little right to look to me for indulgences, and were told not to expect them; yet, as they are now in my power, it is neither my wish nor intention to distress them further than the recovery of my property from their usurpation, must unavoidably involve them in. They may therefore become Tenants upon terms equitable between man and man, or purchasers.[77]

While the complicated business of dealing with the squatters on his Miller's Run property diverted his attention for a time, Washington soon returned to another topic that was even more interesting to him than sorting out the tangled legal and management issues relating to his frontier lands. After many false starts and in the face of considerable obstacles, Washington hoped to reinvigorate the scheme to build a canal to skirt the falls of the Potomac that would be the first step in creating a network of transportation links between the East Coast and the interior of the continent. Over the next two weeks Washington explored the western Virginia and Pennsylvania backcountry, scouting first-hand the lay of the land and the character of the rivers and streams, and interviewing surveyors, traders, and others who had the local knowledge he sought. At the end of the journey, Washington's enthusiasm for the scheme was more pronounced than ever as he concluded that all of the important streams could be rendered navigable, and that easy portage routes could be cleared to connect the rivers where necessary. As a consequence, it would be possible to transport cargoes from as far west as the Ohio River valley to his own home port of Alexandria, just a few miles to the north of Mount Vernon.[78]

Washington had been involved in the planning for such a canal since 1754 when he first explored the inland waters of the Potomac and concluded that the river was the "more convenient least expensive and I may further say by much the most expeditious way" to the Ohio Country. But it would be many years before any progress was made in realizing this vision. Given the joint control of the river by the colonies of Virginia and Maryland, any navigation scheme had to be sanctioned by both governments. In 1772 Washington and others succeeded in persuading the Virginia General Assembly to pass an act opening navigation of the Potomac as far as Fort Cumberland, more than 100 miles upriver, but a similar act was defeated in the Maryland assembly. The onset of the Revolution effectively ended any hopes of pursuing the canal for the duration of the war, but after returning from his western trip in the fall of 1784, Washington turned his attentions to resuscitating the idea. Leveraging the considerable influence he had gained from his war exploits, Washington succeeded in getting the needed navigation bills passed simultaneously in the Virginia and Maryland assemblies, which together created the Potomac River Company. With Washington as the company's first president, over the next several years sporadic progress was made in clearing both major and minor obstructions to navigation, including the most daunting of all—blasting a channel through the rock to bypass the Great Falls, just above Georgetown. Finally, the Maryland legislature stepped in to provide the support to complete building the locks and canals necessary to skirt the falls, and the system opened in February 1802. Although Washington's overly ambitious hopes of establishing a trade route linking the port of Alexandria with the vast areas within the Potomac and Ohio River drainages were never realized, the canal did succeed in facilitating local river traffic.[79]

As the Potomac Canal would bring more settlers to the western regions where he owned thousands of acres of prime real estate, Washington had a vested interest in its success. At the same time, he was certain that transforming the Potomac River into a major artery for trade with the interior would be a boon to the economy of Virginia. But as with his commitment to exploring advancements in agriculture, Washington's vision for the expansion of the West turned from an initially narrow personal pursuit of profits to something much broader. In short, Washington was concerned that the settlers who were free to migrate west of the Appalachians after the Revolution would find little reason to remain linked with the new United States. Writing from his study at Mount Vernon in the fall of 1784, Washington clearly saw the peril: "For what ties let me ask, should we have upon those people, and how entirely unconnected shall we be with them, if the Spaniards on their right, or Great Britain on their left, instead of throwing stumbling blocks in their way as they now do, should envite their trade and seek alliances with them?" Opening roads and canals into the interior to carry trade and to facilitate communication, Washington hoped, would serve to bind "the Middle States with the Country immediately back of them," and keep alive his vision of the United States as a continental empire.[80]

The effort to promote the Potomac Canal led to another development that in the long run would have considerably greater significance for the nation than simply opening the river to navigation. The question of legal control over the river had been a long-standing point of contention between the colonies of Virginia and Maryland. Maryland's original grant from the Crown established its boundary at the southern shore of the Potomac, but Virginians also were given the right to free navigation and use of the stream. It was this jurisdictional uncertainty that had forced Washington to seek authorization in both assemblies for his canal company, and for the scheme to have any chance of success, an agreement would have to be worked out to both parties' satisfaction. A preliminary meeting had met with limited success, but the following conference, held in March 1785 at Washington's Mount Vernon estate, led to an agreement that addressed a variety of topics relating to tolls, tariffs, responsibilities for protecting the river, and more. So successful was the outcome that it spurred the participants to plan yet another meeting, this time to include representatives from all 13 states, to explore other ways to improve interstate cooperation.

While that meeting, held in Annapolis in September 1786, was poorly attended and quickly broke up due to the lack of a quorum, the organizers tried again the following year. This time, all of the states eventually sent their representatives to Philadelphia, and the ultimate outcome was the new Constitution of the United States, the document that finally made clear that the nation Washington had been so instrumental in founding would be a truly united republic and not a collection of loosely confederated sovereign states.[81]

The Potomac Canal Company was not the first attempt that Washington was involved with that aimed to open up the Virginia frontier to commercial interests. Beginning in 1763, Washington joined with several of his peers to acquire and develop the area known as the Great Dismal Swamp, an enormous tract of 900 square miles in extent, consisting of boggy and heavily-forested land straddling the Virginia-North Carolina border. Although the timber resources had long been recognized as a potential source of wealth, Washington and his partners had a much more ambitious goal: they hoped to drain and clear the area in order to open the rich land for farming. The 12 partners petitioned the Virginia council and received a patent to 40,000 acres of the unclaimed land, and the Dismal Swamp Company was born. Each of the shareholders was expected to provide capital, especially in the form of enslaved workers, to support the enterprise. In 1764 Washington sent his share of workers, 5 adult slaves, to join with almost 50 others to begin the arduous work of draining the swamp.[82]

Over the next decade Washington remained one of the strongest proponents of the Dismal Swamp scheme, devoting considerable attention to managing the operation along with supplying a constant stream of cash and other resources. But draining the swamp eventually proved beyond the capability of the company to accomplish, and the focus shifted instead to harvesting the timber for shingles, barrel staves, ship masts, and the like. At the same time, the partners embarked on a second venture, to build a series of canals to connect the swamp with the Elisabeth and Nansemond Rivers, and thus to establish a trading link to the Atlantic Coast. Once again, even though Washington and the others provided more money and slaves, progress on the canals was extremely slow. It was not until both the Virginia and North Carolina assemblies passed acts to support the canals that the resources needed for success became available, and the canals finally were completed many years later. However, by that time Washington had passed from the scene. In 1795 he had sold his share of the company to Henry Lee. But as so often happened when Washington attempted to trade his frontier lands for much needed cash, Lee was unable to pay his debt, and the property reverted to Washington's estate in 1809.[83]

Even considering Washington's dedication to building up his personal wealth through farming, land speculation, and the rest, it is fair to say that his financial success was aided immeasurably by an infusion of capital from the estate of Martha Washington's first husband, Daniel Parke Custis. When Custis died unexpectedly in 1757, he left his widow and their two small children, Jacky and Patsy, in a very secure financial position. Custis's estate was appraised at more than £30,000, an enormous sum in mid-18th-century America. Martha Custis and the two children shared the estate equally, and thus upon their marriage Washington took possession of the £10,000 that was due his bride. Since the children were underage he was charged with managing their financial affairs as well. Although Washington already had begun to expend significant sums to enlarge Mount Vernon before marrying Martha Custis in January 1759, it was the addition of the money from the estate that put the household on a solid financial footing, and allowed him to acquire even more adjoining land. Many years later, when Patsy Custis died suddenly from a particularly violent epileptic seizure, Washington took possession of the remaining portion of her share of the estate. This windfall, in part, allowed him to embark on another campaign to expand the Mount Vernon mansion that he initiated in 1775.[84]

One measure of Washington's success as a businessman is provided by considering the value of his property in the year of his death. When he prepared his will in 1799, Washington himself estimated the worth of his estate at $530,000. This was a considerable sum at a time when a yeoman farmer or a skilled craftsman might expect to earn little more than one or two hundred dollars per year. Based on accepting Washington's estimate at face value, some recent writers have even argued that he was one of the wealthiest men in American history. This assessment is highly exaggerated, but there is no doubt that during his lifetime Washington was one of Virginia's richest men. According to one study of the 100 wealthiest property owners in the state in the decade of the 1780s, Washington ranked securely in the top 10.[85]

Notwithstanding the fact that Washington was a wealthy man, for most of his life he seems to have fallen into the category of "land rich, cash poor." He suffered from the age-old problem facing farmers everywhere, and anyone else whose business requires investment in expensive capital improvements. These expenditures tied up a great deal of money, while revenue-making opportunities were limited due to the constraints of a credit-based agricultural economy that depended on long-distance trade with England. Switching from tobacco to grain production mitigated the problem somewhat, but on many occasions Washington found himself short of ready cash. For example, in 1789 when the newly elected president set off to New York for his inauguration, Washington did not have the money to finance his journey, and he was forced to borrow £100 at 6 percent interest from an Alexandria bank.[86]

In addition to calculations of raw wealth, it is informative to compare the scale and extent of Washington's entrepreneurial enterprises with those of his peers. Like the vast majority of the members of the 18th-century Virginia elite, Washington's wealth derived from a focus on land and slaves, first to grow tobacco and later wheat as cash crops to serve the trans-Atlantic economy. But diversifying to guard against market downturns in agricultural products by investing in a variety of related activities was a common strategy for most of Virginia's successful planter-businessmen. The range of crafts and industries that Washington engaged in at Mount Vernon generally fell within the norm for a plantation of its size. Blacksmithing, cloth making, shoemaking, livestock raising, and dairying, all were commonly associated with farming, and were a means of making the plantation more self-sufficient in addition to producing revenue. Some of Washington's related ventures were more unusual, like his enthusiasm for mules as a more efficient type of draft animal. For those plantation owners whose property adjoined a stream that was part of the migratory fish run, fishing in the spring each year represented a potentially lucrative venture, and Washington naturally took full advantage of the opportunity.[87]

When Washington made the transition to wheat cultivation after 1765, he found expanded commercial opportunities in milling and shipping his grain and flour, which he first capitalized on by building a more efficient gristmill and later by installing the Evans automated milling system. Mill-owning was one of the most common activities that planter-businessmen of the day engaged in. But Washington's investment in the Evans improvements in 1791, along with his earlier decision to abandon tobacco, are instances where he was well ahead of the curve in comparison with most of his peers. The decision to erect a distillery at Mount Vernon in 1797, on the other hand, was not noteworthy in itself as hundreds of other Virginia farmers had embarked on whiskey making as a natural complement to their farming operations. It was the large scale of Washington's distillery, thanks to the expertise and business sense of his Scottish farm manager, that was exceptional.[88]

Many of Washington's peers were heavily involved in trading, either as shipowners or as merchants supplying imported goods to their circle of neighbors and business partners. According to one study, in 1786 up to 25 percent of Virginia's most successful planters either owned a tavern or a store, were partners in a mercantile firm, or provided merchant services out of their home plantations. Another 8 of the 65 men included in the sample participated in shipping or shipbuilding. Washington's engagement as a merchant trader was limited to the few years in the 1770s when he owned all or part of several vessels that he used to transport his commodities to the West Indies and elsewhere, and to bring back goods—particularly rum—that he sold to selected customers.[89]

Where Washington differed dramatically from his fellow Virginia farmer-entrepreneurs, however, was in his paramount role in public affairs, and in his willingness to harness his personal interests to the cause of a strong American nation. Washington's writings are filled with clear statements about his hopes for the future of his country and his fears that they may not come to pass. In a letter that Washington wrote to one of his aides in 1793, he gave full voice to his vision for the future: "If we are permitted to improve without interruption, the great advantages which nature and circumstances have placed within our reach—many years will not revolve before we may be ranked not only among the most respectable, but among the happiest people on this globe." It was his commitment to this vision—and his fear of the competing forces of political factions, regional conflicts, and the intrigues of foreign nations—that led Washington to accept the role as first president of the United States, at a time when he most ardently wished to spend the rest of his days in retirement at Mount Vernon. This was just the last in a long line of decisions where he subordinated his personal desires to public service. In more mundane settings, Washington had shown similar leadership in championing improved agricultural practices, encouraging western settlement, and adopting state-of-the-art techniques like portable threshing machines and Evans's automated milling machinery, all of which fall into the same pattern of transcending personal gains to further national aims.[90]

During the last years of his life, Washington addressed yet another compelling personal matter that also held significance for the future of the nation: the fate of the hundreds of enslaved African-Americans whose labors had served as the engine for much of his financial success. Washington hoped to divest himself of much of his hard-won property to be able to raise sufficient cash to manumit the entire community of Mount Vernon slaves. Although ostensibly a private concern, Washington knew that everything he might say or do in this matter would be of national interest, and he hoped once again to act as a model for his countrymen to follow. Unfortunately for the Mount Vernon slaves, for the nation, and for Washington, he wasn't fully successful in this effort, and only a portion of the enslaved community could be freed. Washington's will carried a powerful statement in opposition to the institution of slavery, nonetheless, but in this case the example of the "Father of His Country" seems to have had little impact on those he hoped to lead.[91]

Over the course of his lifetime, Washington's attitudes toward slavery underwent a marked transformation. From his initial unquestioning support for slavery as an economic institution and a wholehearted commitment to it as the source of his personal prosperity, he grew increasingly frustrated at dealing with its inherent inefficiencies. This change of heart is evident at least by 1778, when he remarked that "every day [I] long more and more to get clear of [Negroes]." When Washington reinvented his plantation with wheat as its cash crop, he pointed Mount Vernon along the path to economic success for the time being. But try as he might to develop new industries and occupations to employ all of his slaves, he possessed many more unskilled laborers than he would ever need. At the same time that Washington came to view slavery as a failing economic system, for humanitarian reasons he made the decision to discontinue selling them: "The advantages from the sale of my Negroes, I have very little doubt of," he wrote in 1779, but "my scruples arise from a reluctance in offering these people at public vendue [auction]." Fifteen years later Washington expressed his opinion on the topic even more clearly, remarking, "Were it not then, that I am principled agt [against] selling Negroes, as you would Cattle in the market, I would not, in twelve months from this date, be possessed of one as a slave."[92]

Washington faced an unusual and increasingly difficult challenge when it came to formulating a plan to manumit the Mount Vernon slaves. Over the years, many of his slaves had intermarried with those individuals who came to Mount Vernon as the property of the estate of Martha Washington's first husband, Daniel Parke Custis. Under Virginia law, the

Washingtons had rights to the labor of the "dower slaves," but they could not be freed without paying restitution to the estate for the benefit of the surviving heirs. Washington elected to honor the marital status of the Mount Vernon slaves, even though unions among the enslaved had no legal standing in Virginia. He followed through on this conviction by consistently working to keep the families from being separated, even when doing so would have been in his own financial best interest, as he repeatedly declined to sell unneeded slaves if it meant that family members would be dispersed. In a 1786 letter, Washington emphasized his unwillingness to carry out any such transactions, stating that "it is... against my inclination...to hurt the feelings of those unhappy people by a separation of man and wife, or of families." In another letter he wrote years later, Washington summed up his overall predicament with his usual insight and precision: "It is demonstratively clear, that on this Estate [Mount Vernon] I have more working Negroes by a full moiety, than can be employed to any advantage in the farming System... To sell the overplus I cannot, because I am principled against this kind of traffic in the human species. To hire them out, is almost as bad, because they could not be disposed of in families to any advantage, and to disperse the families I have an aversion."[93]

From his position as presiding officer over the Constitutional Convention in 1787, Washington had a ringside seat from which to observe the deep political divisions in the assembly over the question of slavery. The sectional conflicts that had arisen during the war over the enlistment of free blacks and slaves, the differing approaches taken by the individual states in regulating slavery within their borders, and the conflict over repeated attempts to restrict the international slave trade all served as precursors to the even more highly charged debates that were to come in the convention hall in Philadelphia. For Washington, the adoption of a constitution that would unify the nation behind a strong central government was the paramount goal. From this perspective, slavery was a topic fraught with peril, and one for which a compromise solution was the best that could be achieved.[94]

During the last years of his second presidential administration, Washington began to formulate plans for putting his personal affairs in order against the day when he would again retire to private life. A prime objective was to ease the strain of overseeing his vast estate by selling or renting the bulk of his property. One idea was to interest progressive English farmers who might be induced to migrate to America to take over cultivating the Mount Vernon farms. For Washington this plan represented the answer to so many of his most heartfelt desires. Not only would he be free of the toil and aggravation of overseeing the day-to-day plantation operations, he would also escape the frustrations of trying to adapt a system of slave labor to his innovative vision of Mount Vernon's future. And perhaps best of all, Washington would presumably experience the satisfaction of finally witnessing firsthand the benefits of the many innovative farming practices that for years he had been trying to implement. Unfortunately, the one Englishman who expressed an interest in acquiring a portion of the estate was disappointed in the quality of the soil and declined Washington's offer.[95]

For Washington the land scheme took on even greater significance because it was integral to his plan to manumit the Mount Vernon slaves. Since the Custis (or "dower") slaves could not be freed without paying compensation to the heirs, this meant that he needed to raise upwards of £6,000. As the total profit Washington received from all of his plantation operations for the year 1797 was calculated at £898, this represented an enormous sum. The first indication of Washington's ambitious plan is contained in a series of letters he exchanged in 1794 with his secretary and close friend, Tobias Lear, and with the English agronomist, Arthur Young. As Washington portrayed it to his correspondents, the plan consisted of two interrelated parts: selling his thousands of acres of western lands and selling or renting the four outlying Mount Vernon farms. By divesting himself of most of his acreage, he would no longer require large numbers of field hands, which would allow him to set free the 123 slaves that he owned. With the profits from the land sales, Washington hoped to be able to buy the 153 dower slaves from the Custis estate, in order to set them free as well. Thus, he would overcome the problem of breaking up the intermarried families, since all of the slaves could be freed at the same time.[96]

Washington's apparent willingness to sell off thousands of acres of land to finance his manumission scheme indicates that he had come full circle in respect to the status of the Mount Vernon slaves. Much of Washington's initial ambivalence toward holding fellow human beings in bondage was due to financial considerations, but this plan suggests that his moral concerns were now paramount. Freeing all of the Mount Vernon slaves, even at great cost, had become the highest priority, and Washington was apparently willing to suffer a major reduction to his personal fortune to accomplish it. Just how far Washington had traveled on his path from unabashed slave master was made clear in the letter he wrote to Lear in 1794. Washington outlined the benefits that he hoped would result from the change, which included reducing his expenses to the point where he could support himself through occupations less onerous than farming. He elaborated further in an aside marked "private." "I have another motive," he wrote, that "is indeed more powerful than all the rest, namely to liberate a certain species of property which I possess, very repugnantly to my own feelings; but which imperious necessity compels."[97]

These plans came to nothing, however, as Washington received only a few serious inquiries in response to the advertisements to sell his western lands, and no English farmers stepped forward who were willing to rent or purchase the Mount Vernon farms. Given the fact that large tracts of cheap unclaimed land were still available in western Pennsylvania, in Kentucky, and in Ohio, enabling immigrants to settle them at little cost, the market for undeveloped property remained poor. It is not surprising, therefore, that Washington could not find anyone willing to pay him his asking price, and as a consequence nothing came of his plan to free the dower slaves. Although he never seems to have expressed his thoughts on the topic in writing, Washington's disappointment must have been acute. When it came time to write out his last will and testament, Washington therefore was left with the unpleasant task of devising a final solution for the future of Mount Vernon's slaves; one that could not achieve his stated goal of preserving the slave families.[98]

In the end Washington arrived at a compromise, stipulating that the 123 slaves he owned were to be freed, but only after his death and that of his wife, Martha. All the careful planning was needed to avoid witnessing the "painful sensations" that were sure to result from the enforced separation of the intertwined families. Clearly uncomfortable with the knowledge that the freedom of so many depended on her own death, Martha Washington elected to accelerate implementation of this clause of the will. In due course the slaves were manumitted on January 1, 1801, little more than a year after her husband's death and almost 18 months before her own. While there is no record of the reactions of the Mount Vernon slaves to this event, either on the part of those freed or those who remained in bondage, it must have been the cause of much sadness as well as joy.[99]

While the final act of these dramatic events was yet to play out, in 1797 Washington considered both the satisfaction and the cares that would attend his return to Mount Vernon, and he was particularly receptive to any scheme that would increase revenues without requiring any additional effort on his part. It was against this backdrop of a lifetime of devotion to estate building and his recent failure to convert a portion of this capital to enable him to free all of the Mount Vernon slaves that the Scotsman James Anderson entered Washington's life. In late 1796 Washington hired Anderson to serve as his plantation manager, a position that carried the responsibility to oversee all of the many activities related to the farming operations, as well as the various crafts, the fishery, and the rest. The Scotsman almost immediately wrote to his new employer, who was still in Philadelphia serving out the last months of his second presidential term, with a scheme to establish a whiskey distillery. Given Washington's circumstances, Anderson's proposal found a willing listener, and he wanted to learn more about it.[100]

MOUNT VERNON ESTATE ACCOUNTS FOR THE YEAR 1797[101]
(Tabulated February 2, 1798)

Balances to:	Dogue Run Farm £	397.11.2
	Union Farm	529.10
	River Farm	234.4.11
	Mill	117.7.9
	Smith's Shop	34.12
	Distillery	83.13
	Jacks	56
	Traveller	9.17
	Shoemaker	28.17.1
	Fishery	165.12.$^{3/4}$
	Negro hires	969
	Total Credits	£2,617
Charges:	Mansion House	[£1,466]
	Muddy Hole	[60]
	Spinning	[51]
	James Anderson (salary)	[140]
	TOTAL DEBITS	[£1,717]
	NET PROFIT	£ 898

CHAPTER 3

"A PRETTY CONSIDERABLE DISTILLERY"

When James Anderson wrote to George Washington in January 1797 proposing that producing whiskey made from corn and rye grown on the plantation would be a profitable complement to his milling business, it is doubtful whether either man had any idea just how successful the enterprise would turn out to be. By 1799, the last year of Washington's life, his distillery was one of the largest of its kind in the entire country. By almost any measure—the size of the building (2,250 square feet), the number (5) and capacity (616 gallons) of stills in operation, or the volume of alcohol produced (approximately 10,500 gallons)—Washington's distillery far exceeded all but a few of the thousands of others that had sprung up across the nation. But much more important to Washington was that the distillery lived up to Anderson's promise of financial reward; the combined profits ($1,858) from selling the whiskey and the livestock fattened with the spirits byproducts outstripped any of Mount Vernon's other revenue centers. Although not all went precisely according to plan—Washington soon was forced to enter the market to purchase grain from other farmers to keep up with the spiraling demand—the Scotsman's performance was as good as his word.[1]

In the summer of 1796, Washington was entering the final months of his second term as president of the United States, and he probably was counting the days until he could begin his final retirement at his beloved home, Mount Vernon. Running the ambitious agricultural operation that he had built up over the years was not an easy task, however, and he always had depended on a hired manager to oversee the daily activities of his hundreds of workers. The current manager, William Pearce, had only worked for Washington since 1793, but he already had informed his employer that because of a series of ailments, he was planning to retire at the end of the year. Washington's expectations for his successor were characteristically high, as he made clear in a letter to Anderson after he had expressed interest in the job. According to Washington, "Besides being sober, and a man of integrity, he must possess a great deal of activity and firmness, to make the under Overseers do their duty strictly," and he "must be a man of foresight and arrangement; to combine and carry matters on to advantage; and he must not have these things to learn after he comes to me." Crucially, "He must be a farmer bred, and understand it in all its parts."[2]

Anderson came to his job as Washington's plantation manager after a long and varied career farming his own lands or managing the estates of others, both in Scotland and in America. In one of the letters Anderson wrote to his prospective employer that summer, he provided details on his life and past employment "in the Farmer's business," with particular attention given to the many skills he possessed that he thought were pertinent to the position in question. Most important for the present purpose, Anderson reassured Washington that he was well-versed in all of "the practical parts of Farming in Britain, conjoined with six Years experience in this Country where Soil, and Climate make some alleviations necessary." Born and raised on his father's farm near the village of Inverkeithing, 40 miles north of Edinburgh, Anderson began his career at the age of 21 by apprenticing for two years with "a Gentleman, Famous in Farming." Anderson then was hired to supervise a neighboring estate, which he managed for several years, before he acquired a farm of his own. According to his letter to Washington, Anderson "farmed on my own account" for 19 years, "18 of which I was also largely in the Grain line, And had several manufacturing Mills." The primary market for

Anderson's grain was the expanding Scottish whisky industry, and especially the distilling conglomerate owned by the Stein and Haig families, whose five distilleries together controlled almost 50 percent of the production of Scottish whisky by 1788.[3]

Unfortunately for the Steins and the Haigs, and for the growing number of farmers like Anderson who supplied them with the barley that was the principal ingredient of their spirit, the Scottish whisky industry was dealt a grievous blow in 1788. Early in that year the English Parliament passed an act aimed at reducing competition from Scottish whisky by effectively excluding Scotland's distillers from exporting their product to England for one year. This resulted in the loss of sales for roughly 880,000 gallons of spirit (the volume shipped in the year 1786), and drove the Steins, Haigs, and many other Scottish distilling firms, along with their creditors and suppliers, into bankruptcy. With the support of a few important backers, within a few years the largest whisky producers were able to rebound and regain a significant share of the market, but the immediate impact on their grain suppliers was devastating. In Anderson's words, it was after "the failure of a Sett of Distillers in 1788" that he "nearly lost all, And many more were ruined," and this calamity was the spur three years later for him to migrate to America with his family to begin life anew.[4]

After moving to Virginia in 1791, Anderson first tried his hand at grain farming on rented land before returning to his earlier career as an estate manager. At the time that he applied for the job managing Mount Vernon, he was employed supervising a smaller but still substantial farm of 1,700 acres, called Salvington. The property was owned by Cary Selden, whose mother was the sister of John Mercer of Marlborough, located near Fredericksburg, just 40 miles south of Mount Vernon, and a family and a property that Washington knew well. In addition to supervising the crops and the livestock, Anderson operated a distillery for Selden, which he claimed "turns to good account." Although Anderson registered no specific complaints about working for Selden, he must have seen the chance to join Washington and to manage a much larger enterprise as a major improvement in his fortunes.[5]

After exchanging letters during the late summer of 1796, Anderson and Washington met at Mount Vernon on 6 October, when they agreed to the terms of the Scotsman's employment. For an annual salary of £140 and other considerations such as the use of a house located south of the Mansion near the ferry, Anderson agreed to Washington's many requirements, and he began his duties on 1 January, 1797. It didn't take Anderson long to lobby his new boss with the idea of establishing a distillery at Mount Vernon. Washington wrote from Philadelphia to his manager on 8 January giving him at least conditional permission to proceed. "I consent to your commencing a distillery, and approve of your purchasing the Still, and entering of it," Washington wrote, "And I shall not object to your converting part of the Coopers shop at the Mill to this operation." Washington expressed some concern about situating the distillery at the mill, however, commenting that "idlers (of which, and bad people there are many around it) under pretence of coming there with grist could not be restrained from visiting the Distillery, nor probably from tempting the Distiller, nay more robbing the Still; as the Mill would always afford a pretext for coming to that place." Nevertheless, Washington conceded that the mill was the perfect site for the new venture, given the "necessity of water passing thro[ugh] the Distillery," along with the ready access to grain and barrels, and its convenience in proximity to roads and a navigable stream.[6]

At first the distillery used two stills and was set up in the existing cooper's shop that had been converted for the purpose, and it was immediately successful. During the week of 22 February, 1797, Anderson produced the first 80 gallons of whiskey and stored it in the cellar of his house at the ferry for safekeeping. Over the course of the year, the distillery produced more than 600 gallons of whiskey and realized a profit of £83.

By June, Anderson was so convinced of the success of the venture that he wrote to Washington with a detailed proposal for enlarging the operation. The plantation manager envisioned a stone structure that could comfortably house five stills, along with a malt house, and a kiln to prepare malted barley, the third main ingredient in the whiskey mash bill along with corn and rye. Anderson estimated that purchasing three additional stills, a copper boiler, and a quantity of wooden mash tubs would amount to $640. The cost of erecting the buildings was not included in his estimate, as Anderson anticipated that much of the work would be carried out by Washington's enslaved masons and carpenters.[7]

Before Washington would agree to build the new still house, he solicited the advice of a knowledgeable friend, John Fitzgerald, who operated a sizeable rum distillery in nearby Alexandria. Washington was candid in confiding to Fitzgerald that "The thing [distilling] is new to me, in toto," but that Anderson's "experience in this country, and in Europe," inclined him to accept the proposal. In response to Washington's query about the potential success of the expanded whiskey distillery, Fitzgerald replied, "As I have no doubt but Mr. Anderson understands the Distillation of Spirit from Grain I cannot hesitate in my opinion that it might be carried on to great advantage on your Estate...as to a Sale of the Whisky there can be no doubt if the Quantity was ten times as much as he can make provided it is of good Quality." With this very positive endorsement in hand, Washington agreed to Anderson's plan, writing to him in June that "from your knowledge of it and from the confidence you have in the profit to be derived from the establishment, I am disposed to enter upon one."[8]

Preparations to construct the new distillery began in earnest during the first week of October 1797, as the various workmen began to produce the many necessary building materials ("hewing of timber for the still house"). By the next week work had begun on site, as the Mount Vernon masons were busily engaged in digging the trench in which to set the foundation.

Then in a remarkably brief span of only eight weeks, they laid the stone footings, raised the walls, and continued to prepare wood for the roof framing and for the interior furnishings. In short order the roof structure was in place, the shingles were nailed on, and the frames for the doors and windows were installed. By January the project had progressed to the point where the brick chimneys were rising and the floor was laid, and wagons were hauling the new stills from town. During the month of February, the focus was almost exclusively on interior work, including building partitions, hanging doors, plastering, and painting. The distilling equipment was installed by the end of the month, with the stills and the "boiler" in place, the worm tubs for condensing the spirit into alcohol at the ready, and troughs to direct water throughout the building under construction.[9]

On March 2, 1798, Washington wrote to his friend, Samuel Davidson, of Georgetown, remarking that, "I have erected a pretty considerable Distillery at my Mill (about 3 Miles from this place)." He also mentioned that James Anderson's eldest son, John, who was 21 years old when the distillery opened, "resides thereat, and carries it on." The younger Anderson appears to have been involved with the distillery almost from the beginning, as he was paid £12 for three months of work in the fall of 1797, and in January 1799 he received $66 in payment for his services as a distiller for the previous 11 months. In the letter to Davidson, Washington also expressed his desire to hire an assistant to Anderson, and he offered Davidson's nephew the job in return for $100 in annual salary and lodging at the distillery. Davidson's nephew did not accept the offer, but a number of young men served in that capacity over the next several years.[10]

As the distilling operation had expanded considerably, the demand it placed on the Mount Vernon grain supply increased accordingly. In fact, the quantities required seemed quickly to have exceeded the capacity of the Mount Vernon farms to keep up, and Washington soon entered into agreements to purchase

This artist's rendering of the gristmill and distillery property as it may have appeared in 1799 is based on a combination of archaeological findings and documentary evidence; clockwise from top is the miller's cottage, distillery, animal sheds, malt house, wharf, cooperage, and gristmill.

IMAGE: ORIGINAL ART WORK BY LEE A. BOYNTON

corn and rye from various sources. On June 26, 1798, George Washington wrote to his nephew, William A. Washington, agreeing to purchase 500 barrels of corn annually, at the Alexandria market price. Washington also agreed to accept grain in payment for whiskey, suggesting to his nephew that "if you should want *more*, or any of your neighbors want *any*, it would be convenient, and always in my power, to supply you—and for grain, wheat, Rye or Indian Corn in exchange." In October 1799, Washington wrote to his nephew again to reiterate his interest in purchasing more of his grain. The letter also provides some insight into the success of the distillery as Washington warned that "Two hundred gallons of Whiskey will be ready this day for your call, and the sooner it is taken the better, as the demand for this article (in these parts) is brisk."[11]

When combined with the cost of erecting and outfitting the new still house, the additional and apparently unexpected expense of purchasing grain caused Washington to call on his agents to redouble their efforts in collecting his rents and other debts due him. In a letter to one agent, Robert Lewis, Washington provided a candid assessment of the situation that suggests that he already may have been entertaining second thoughts about the whiskey making scheme. "I have been induced, by the experience and advice of my Manager, Mr Anderson—to erect a large Distillery at my Mill; and have supplied it with five Stills, Boilers—&ca which, with the (Stone) House, has cost me a considerable Sum already, but I find these expenditures are but a small part of the advances I must make before I shall receive any return for them, having all my Grain yet to buy to carry on the business," Washington complained. As a consequence, he entreated Lewis "to exert yourself in the collection of my Rents, and that you would let me know, upon the best data you can form an opinion, what dependence I may place on you—not only as to the amount of the sum, but also as to the period of its payment, that I may regulate matters accordingly."[12]

Another issue arose that was even more troubling to Washington, as it came to his attention that James Anderson was considering leaving Mount Vernon to take another job when his first year's contract for services expired on December 31. In a letter to the potential employer, Washington lamented that Anderson has "run me into a very considerable expence (contrary I may say to my intention, or wishes) in erecting a Distillery which I shall not know what well to do with," if the Scotsman were to leave. Anderson finally declined the contending job offer and he remained at Mount Vernon as the plantation manager for the remainder of Washington's life.[13]

According to the ledgers of the plantation accounts, Anderson was as good as his word when it came to the profits of the distillery. With the new still house up and running, production approached 4,400 gallons of alcohol in 1798, mostly whiskey with a small quantity of brandy, and generated a profit of £344. By the next year, production more than doubled to roughly 10,500 gallons, valued at $7,674. According to the accounts, 57 individuals purchased the alcohol, paying an average of 60 cents per gallon for "common" whiskey, that had been twice distilled, and almost one dollar per gallon for higher quality whiskey that had been distilled up to four times. The distillery also continued to produce a few hundred gallons of apple and peach flavored brandies. In addition to alcohol, livestock in the form of pigs and cattle, and vinegar were sold. The total profit from the sale of all alcohol and related produce totaled $1,858 (roughly £600) in 1799.[14]

Washington's customers sometimes paid for their liquor solely with cash, but more often they traded a wide range of commodities as well. The most common item offered as barter was grain, primarily corn and rye that was then used to help satisfy the raw material needs of the distillery. Even though Washington's coopers supplied large numbers of barrels that were needed to store and transport flour, whiskey, and fish, apparently they were unable to keep up with the demand as several customers exchanged barrels of all sizes for alcohol. A

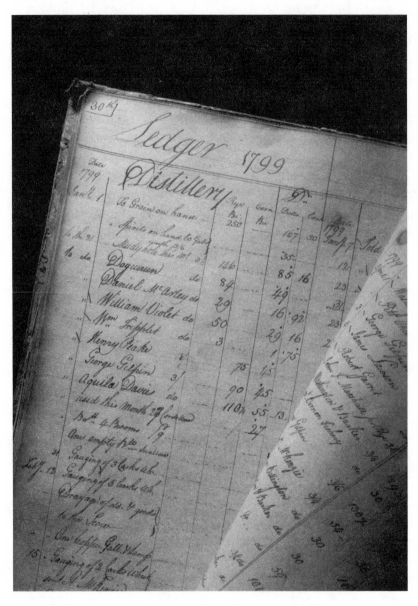

Two ledgers containing the plantation financial accounts covering the first several years when the distillery was in operation provide detailed information on the types and volumes of spirits produced as well as the names of the purchasers and the prices that they paid.

variety of other goods that were accepted in payment included foodstuffs such as salt, butter, molasses, and oysters, as well as candles, tar, and "soal (sole) leather." Others paid for their purchases by performing specialized services, including gauging (measuring the volume of) barrels and hauling freight.[15]

The landowners in the vicinity of Mount Vernon provided a ready market for much of the product of the distillery, and included among its customers many well-known members of the local planter society. The purchases that were made in 1799 by one neighbor, Sarah McCarty Chichester, testify to the complex nature of some of the transactions. Chichester bought 7,000 herrings, 32 gallons of whiskey, and one barrel of flour, with a combined value of $32.78. In exchange, she traded 603 barrels of corn and 243 bushels of wheat, valued at $785.38; the considerable difference was credited to her account. At the other end of the spectrum, the most common transactions were straightforward purchases of one or two barrels of whiskey (valued between $16.50 and $36.42), with most of the payment made in cash and the balance in trade.[16]

Merchants from the nearby town of Alexandria purchased a significant portion of the whiskey and then resold the alcohol through their retail outlets. In 1799, 12 merchants bought 4,300 gallons of whiskey valued at $2,394.59. Most prominent among these customers was George Gilpin, a former army comrade, long-time friend, and business partner of Washington's. Gilpin was a well-known and successful merchant who owned a warehouse and a wharf as well as a store in Alexandria. In 1798 the two men partnered to sell Washington's whiskey on consignment in Gilpin's shop, with Washington reimbursed according to an agreed upon percentage of the value of the whiskey after it had been sold. But in 1799 Gilpin began to purchase the whiskey outright, a change in strategy that probably reflected his success in finding a ready market for Washington's product. Gilpin bought 2,344 gallons of whiskey valued at $1,270 and 58.5 gallons of apple brandy worth $36.56, along with barrels of herring and shad. He paid for the items with a variety of foodstuffs and other goods from his store. The other 11 merchants on average bought just less than 145 gallons of spirits each, with the next largest purchase at 512 gallons.[17]

Another Alexandria merchant, Laurence Hoof, focused his energies on acquiring and butchering livestock fattened on the distillery "slops" to sell the meat in his shop. In 1799 Hoof was the single largest purchaser of livestock, when he bought four calves, four cattle, four cows, and one steer, with a total weight of 3,753 pounds and a sale price of $209.63 (approximately six cents per pound). In addition to the livestock, Hoof purchased 31 gallons (one barrel) of rye whiskey valued at $28.42. He paid for the liquor and the animals with cash and goods: "2 Rams for the Farms"—presumably to support Washington's breeding efforts—and "127 pounds Beef for Mt. Vernon."[18]

A Polish gentleman named Julian Niemcewicz undertook a grand tour of the United States in 1797–99 and he made a special effort in June 1798 to visit Mount Vernon and to meet Washington. Washington appears to have taken considerable pride in showing off the many parts of the plantation to his visitor, including the gristmill property and the distillery. In his journal, Niemcewicz commented quite favorably on the commercial prospects of the new venture: "Just near by [the gristmill] is a *whiski* distillery. Under the supervision of the son of Mr. Anderson, they distill up to 12 thousand gallons a year (they can distill 50 gallons per day if the weather is not too hot); each gallon at 4 Virginia shillings; that alone should bring in up to 16 thousand doll[ars]." While Niemcewicz's calculations may have been a bit off, it is clear that he was duly impressed with the scale and potential success of Washington's distillery.[19]

Raising hogs and fattening them on the spent mash, or slops, leftover from distilling was widely acknowledged to be a significant additional benefit of operating a distillery. In his manual, *The American Distiller*, printed in Philadelphia in 1804, Michael Krafft outlined in great detail the various features of a well-managed livestock raising operation, including the recommendation that the hog pens be positioned so that the discharge from the stills could flow directly into the feeding troughs. Apparently Anderson was similarly solicitous to the needs of the swine at Washington's distillery. In his journal, Niemcewicz concluded: "If this distillery produces poison for men, it offers in return the most delicate and the most succulent feed for pigs. They keep 150 of them of the Guinea type, short feet, hollow backs and so excessively bulky that they can hardly drag their big bellies on the ground."[20]

Like his fellow American distillers, the sales of Washington's whiskey benefited greatly from the fact that it was much cheaper and more readily available than the rum imported from the Caribbean that had been the most popular alcoholic drink in America in the years before the Revolution. Another reason for the popularity of whiskey was that it was relatively easy to produce from ingredients that were readily available. Washington's mash bill was typical of the period in that the main ingredient was ground rye (60 percent), together with 35 percent corn, and 5 percent malted barley meal. The grain was "cooked" in a hogshead—a large barrel usually between 110 and 120 gallons in size, referred to as a mash tub—by adding boiling water, to convert the starches into sugar. At that point, yeast was added to the mix and the concoction was left to ferment. Although the proportions of the grains are slightly different, a recipe for mashing contained in Krafft's *The American Distiller* provides a clear description of the process:

Into each cask or hogshead, throw nine gallons of water heated to ninety degrees of Farenheit's [*sic*] thermometer, to which add forty pounds of Indian corn meal; agitate the mass briskly, and let it stand two hours, that it may open and prepare the grain for dissolution; now twelve gallons of boiling water are added, and briskly worked with the oar, then suffered to stand fifteen minutes—on the top of this, four gallons of luke-warm water are gently poured, and ten pounds of malt gently worked on the top, so as not to intermix with the corn meal, which is in that state suffered to stand thirty minutes, then fourteen gallons more of boiling water are added to the mass, and worked as before: this in that state is suffered to stand sixty minutes, then forty pounds of rye meal are now added, and worked well, and just as before the whole mass is now suffered to stand from two to four hours, in proportion to the state of the weather: the calculation is, when cold water filled to within six inches of the top of the cask, will bring down the whole mass to seventy-five degrees. It is now yeasted...covered as before, and left until fit for the still.[21]

To separate the alcohol from the fermented grain mixture, now referred to as wash or "distiller's beer," it was poured into a copper still that was heated over a wood fire. Since the temperature at which alcohol turns into a gas (approximately 160 degrees) is lower than for water, the alcohol would vaporize and separate from the wash, rising to the upper chamber of the still. An opening at the top allowed the gas to pass into a spiraling copper tube (worm) that wound through another barrel (the worm tub) that was filled with cool running water. As the vapor passed through the worm, the lower temperature of the water helped it condense back into liquid form; the condensed liquid would consist of roughly 20 to 25 percent alcohol. The spirit was reintroduced into the still for at least one more distillation to increase the proof (to 50 percent alcohol or more) and to reduce the level of impurities; the resulting spirit was referred to as "common" whiskey.[22]

All of the steps in making the whiskey were labor intensive: from transporting the meal from the mill to the still house; mashing the grain; transporting the wash by buckets from the tubs to the stills; collecting the first run distillate into large barrels ("low wine coolers"); reintroducing the first-run distillate into the stills; collecting and storing the whiskey in barrels; and, finally, cleaning out the mash tubs in order to begin the process all over again. According to the plantation records, six young enslaved men were assigned to working at the distillery under the direction of young Anderson and his assistant, and it was these workers who provided the muscle power to make the enterprise a success.[23]

According to the Mount Vernon farm ledger for 1799, Washington paid an annual tax of $332.64 on his distillery; his tax bill was based on the rate of 54 cents per gallon capacity (616 gallons total) of his five stills. The three new stills that he purchased in January 1798 were sized at 120, 116, and 110 gallons, and cost him £103 to acquire from George McMunn, a coppersmith who operated a shop in Alexandria. Ironically, when Washington died two years later, it was McMunn, who also worked in lead, who provided the liner for the former president's elaborate three-layered coffin. The documents do not record the exact sizes of the other two stills that had been acquired earlier, but they must have been somewhat larger, as they totaled 270 gallons between them. Distilleries could be found throughout America in the years following the Revolution, and in 1810 there were more than 3,500 grain and fruit distilleries in Virginia alone. However, the typical distillery during this period operated only one still and produced a few hundred gallons of spirit per year.[24]

It is instructive to compare the size of Washington's distillery with the massive enterprises run by the Stein family, one of the distillers in Scotland whose bankruptcy forced Anderson to migrate to America. According to the inventory of the contents found at the Kennetpans distillery at the time it was liquidated in 1788, the size and value of the distilling equipage dwarfs those at Mount Vernon. The capacities of the Scottish stills are particularly impressive, with three copper stills found "in the Still House" ranging from 800 to 1,200 gallons. Thus, the smallest of the Kennetpans stills had a significantly greater capacity than all five of Washington's stills, combined. In addition, another eight stills apparently were not in use at the time, as they were listed as located "In the Yard," but the largest receptacle was 1,656 gallons, and the average capacity was 723 gallons. Similarly, the combined value assigned to the Kennetpans distilling equipment was £1,648; although the total cost to Washington to outfit his distillery is unknown, the fact that he paid only £140 to acquire three of his stills and the boiler suggests that it was a fraction of the value of the Stein's operation. Therefore, while Washington's distillery was exceptionally large in the context of American whiskey makers, the comparison with Kennetpans clearly testifies to the enormous scale that already had been achieved by the most prominent Scottish distillers.[25]

From 1997 to 2005 Mount Vernon's archaeologists excavated at the site of the distillery in hopes of retrieving enough information to be able to justify reconstructing this important and unusual structure. The site of the distillery was extremely well-preserved, and the archaeologists revealed extensive evidence for the building itself, as well as remains of numerous features interpreted as relating to the distilling process. As no 18th-century whiskey distillery survives in this country, and since no full-scale excavation of an American whiskey distillery from this time period had ever been conducted, the project provided a unique opportunity to learn more about the early years of this important industry, as well as to shed light on the commercial activities of George Washington.[26]

The foundation stones of the south and west walls of the building were largely intact, as was a portion of a partition that divided the northern 15 feet of the building from the larger 60-foot-long main section. The foundation was between 2½- and 3½-feet wide, with individual stones brought from the Potomac River measuring up to two feet in diameter. The walls above the ground surface were made of sandstone quarried from Mount Vernon. On the south end one course of the wall survived resting upon the foundation cobbles, with another relatively intact section also surviving in the partition. The character of the masonry illustrates how quickly the distillery was

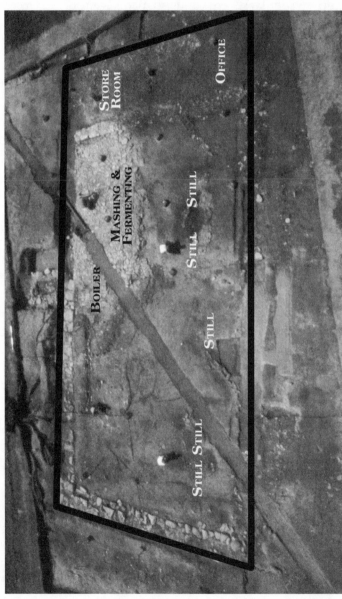

Archaeologists uncovered the footprint of the 75- by 33-foot stone distillery and identified the locations of the stills, drains, mashing floor, cellar, and office.

constructed: the mortar was coarsely prepared, as it contained large inclusions of stones and oyster shell; and the sandstone blocks were irregularly cut and shaped. Neither of these treatments is typically seen in buildings that were carefully constructed, and they also likely reflect the industrial nature of the structure.[27]

Documentary records indicate that wooden floors were installed on both the first and second levels of the building, but the archaeologists discovered two adjoining sections of paving in the western portion of the distilling room, suggesting that roughly half of the floor in this space was masonry and the other half was wood. The masonry paving was further divided between a section comprised of brick and a slightly smaller surface made up mostly of stones, with some brick, which came together at a point just north of the centerline of the distilling room. The presence of the masonry suggests that it was needed to accommodate specialized elements of the distilling operation, and the documentary evidence points to three probable functions: as the base of the stair leading to the upper floor, to support the water boiler for mashing, and to form the mashing floor where the wooden hogsheads were arranged. The masons' weekly reports for the first two weeks of March indicate that they were "building the foundation of the stair" at that time, which provided access to the loft where grain was stored and the distillery manager and his assistant lived. The brick pad seems likely to have been the location for this feature. No evidence was found to indicate the exact location of the stair, but it probably was positioned in the corner of the room in order to maximize efficient use of the space.[28]

Two parallel scars were found in the surface of the brickwork, which suggest that brick piers had been set onto the pad. Together with indications of intensive burning in the area between the piers, they provide strong evidence for the precise location of the water boiler. In January 1798 Washington purchased a 210-gallon copper boiler, essentially a large tub, which was used to provide the hot water needed to "cook" the grain and transform the starches into sugar. Between 12 May and 2 June, 1798, the plantation carpenters, ditchers, and masons all worked together to dig a brick-lined well that the archaeologists revealed located less than 20 feet west of the distillery and conveniently placed in relation to the presumed boiler. To be most efficient, the boiler would have been positioned in proximity to both the well and the mash tubs where the water was used, and this location fits that requirement perfectly.[29]

The stone floor abuts the brick paving, and it is comprised of a surprising mixture of materials, including broken bricks, pieces of sandstone, and mortar interspersed among the cobblestones, which ranged in size from a few inches to more than one foot in diameter. Given the relatively uneven texture of the stone surface, it is hard to imagine that the floor was meant for much foot traffic. Period sources strongly recommended that mashing and fermenting should be carried on indoors, preferably on a solid floor where vibration could be kept to a minimum, so as not to impede fermentation. The makeup of the stone floor would have made it quite stable, and given the proximity to the hypothesized site of the boiler, it therefore seems likely that the mash tubs were located in this area. The size of the space would have allowed up to 12, 120-gallon hogsheads to be arranged there, with ample room for workers to walk between them to carry the grain and water.[30]

A stone foundation, which contained a brick-lined firebox, was revealed just outside and adjoining the west wall of the distillery. Although Washington specified in a letter that he did not make use of malted barley in his whiskey, the distillery accounts clearly indicate that he did. As the barley made up only roughly 5 percent of the mash bill, however, perhaps Washington's remark simply overlooks the small quantities of the grain that were used. The process of malting barley called for the grain to be steeped in water in order for it to sprout, then spread out on a floor to continue to germinate. After several days, the grain was placed in a kiln to dry, before finally taken to the mill to be ground. The first steps would have been carried out in the "malt house," suggesting that the building would have been located within easy access to water. Malt kilns generally were small, freestanding, enclosed structures, primarily consisting of a masonry furnace above which a sheet of iron was placed to hold the grain while it dried. The weekly reports indicate that the malt house was a frame building set on a masonry foundation, but all that is known about the kiln is that the two masons worked on "building the kiln" over a period of six days.[31]

The size and overall character of the masonry feature attached to the exterior wall of the building suggests that it might have been used as the malt kiln, but if so it must have had a somewhat unusual design. One 19th-century distilling manual describes setting up a malt kiln on the upper floor of a distillery, with the flues from the still furnaces providing the hot air to dry the grain. The evidence for the fire having been located within the base of the feature indicates a different arrangement, however, and it is not clear how it could have operated as a malt kiln in this location, as there is no evidence for a covering structure. Furthermore, the masonry feature is roughly adjacent to the boiler on the interior of the building, and situated between the boiler and the well that provided the fresh water used in mashing. Therefore, if both features were in operation at the same time, they would seem to have been in some conflict. Perhaps instead of drying malt the exterior furnace was used in heating water as well, possibly servicing an earlier boiler that was replaced over time.[32]

The archaeologists found three rectangular burned areas arranged in a line along the east side of the building that mark the locations of the furnaces for firing the five stills. The bottom of one of the brick furnaces was relatively intact and the soils surrounding it were reddened from the almost constant fires required to heat the stills. Period sources indicate that it was typical to arrange stills in pairs, so that two furnaces could be served more efficiently by a single centrally located chimney. The size and shape of two of the

Archaeologists revealed evidence for the locations of the five copper pot stills; the remnants of the brick furnace base and fire-reddened clay subsoil indicate the placement of one of the still pairs.

rectangular features indicates this type of arrangement, while the fifth still apparently operated as a separate unit.[33]

This interpretation of the probable locations of the stills was confirmed by the discovery of a series of underground drains that were found in association with them. The historical sources indicate that water was used to help cool the vapor back into a liquid as the alcohol passed from the still through a spiraled copper pipe submerged in special tubs. The water was brought into the building from the millrace by way of an overhead wooden trough, which branched into five smaller channels, each of which distributed water to pour into the top of one of the worm tubs. Once the water passed through the tub, it exited the distillery by way of another complex of underground wood-lined drains. The five sub-floor drains that were discovered each terminated at points directly adjacent to the presumed sites of the furnaces, and thus confirm the locations of the tubs. The drains passed through the foundation to connect with yet another underground drain with a wooden lining that ran parallel with the east façade of the building. In this way the water was channeled away from the building to nearby Dogue Creek.[34]

The north bay of the building (15 by 35 feet) was separated from the larger distilling area by a thick stone wall. This space was also subdivided into two equal parts by a wooden partition; the archaeologists discovered five filled-in holes that held the posts that supported this wall. A four-foot gap occurs between the two post holes at the center of the apparent wall, providing evidence for the placement there of a doorway. Documentary references indicate that a "cellar" was incorporated into the distillery, where the whiskey was stored in barrels while awaiting sale. With two rooms in this space, the inner room most likely served as the "cellar" while the outer room could have been used as an office, where records were kept and where customers came to transact business. With a lock on the door in the partition and on the exterior door leading into the office, the distillery manager could have kept tight control over the valuable whiskey and brandy stored within. At two feet thick, the stone partition was quite substantial, suggesting that its function also was to act as a firewall between the furnaces and the highly inflammable alcohol.[35]

The features and layout of Washington's still house generally correspond with the prescriptions found in a number of distilling manuals of the period. Among the most important features was the size needed to accommodate all of the related steps in the process—storing grain, mashing, and distilling—and the associated equipage. Easy access to grain and an abundant supply of water, together with a means of transporting it through the building and in and out of the worm tubs, were considered equally important. The well presumably supplied the clean water that was the other crucial ingredient of the whiskey. Other recommendations call for the mashing floor to be extremely solid to ensure complete fermentation; that the pens and enclosures for livestock be located nearby; and that the stills be well-supported by sturdy brick furnaces and arranged in a line adjacent to the mashing floor. One major departure that Anderson made from the recommendations found in the manuals was to incorporate the storage room, or cellar, for the finished product within the still house itself, as doing so was considered a fire hazard.[36]

The archaeologists recovered a number of domestic artifacts in the area beneath where the rooms that housed John Anderson and his assistant were located. These included a tea cup made in England, numerous clothing buttons, a drinking glass, and a slate pencil. Pieces of window glass also were found, which probably relate to the glass-paned dormer windows that provided light to their living spaces. The weekly carpenters' accounts indicate that in addition to the windows, the rooms were outfitted with plaster walls, closets, and locks on the doors. All in all, these rooms qualified as relatively well-appointed accommodations for the period.[37]

Five additional artifacts found at the site appear to relate to at least two of the five stills that the building accommodated. These include two small riveted copper fragments that undoubtedly are remnants of the overlapping plates that were used to form the bodies of the stills. A fragment of copper tubing may be from one of the spouts that would have been a feature of every still; these were used to empty the spent wash, or slop, from the receptacle after the distilling process was completed. Two remnants of copper spigots also were found, which recalls the listing of "6 brass cocks" in the inventory of the building that was made after Washington's death in 1799. Although documentary records indicate that the distillery burned, presumably most of the copper distilling equipment was salvaged after the accident, as the archaeologists discovered no other artifacts during their excavation that could be identified as such.[38]

The inventory that was made at the time of George Washington's death provides a snapshot of the distillery operation in 1800. In addition to the five copper stills and the boiler, the distilling furnishings included five worm tubes (also probably copper), five low wine kegs, 50 mash tubs, 15 whiskey barrels, and an assortment of yeast tubs, pails, sieves, funnels, both brass and wooden cocks, and brooms. A cider press also was listed that was likely used in making the small volume of fruit brandies that were produced each year, while a heating stove and an oil lamp, along with a water pump for the well, presumably made life a bit easier for the workers. Livestock consisted of 10 oxen, 14 cows, 2 bull calves, and 2 heifer calves; other sources indicate that upwards of 100 pigs likely were housed there. In terms of product, 693 gallons of common whiskey and 29.5 gallons of rectified whiskey were on hand. Meanwhile, varieties of alcoholic beverages were inventoried in the cellars at the Mansion, and presumably at least some of the spirits found there had been produced at the distillery: peach, apple, and persimmon brandy, rectified apple brandy, and plain and cinnamon whiskey.[39]

In his will, George Washington bequeathed the distillery and the gristmill to Lawrence and Nellie Custis Lewis, Martha Washington's granddaughter and her husband. Lewis took over the business soon after Washington's death in December 1799, with James Anderson continuing to manage the concern until he departed Mount Vernon in 1804. Anderson's departure forced Lewis to find others willing to rent the enterprises. The last mention of the operating distillery occurred in 1808, when an Alexandria merchant named James Douglass advertised in a local newspaper that "liquor made at Maj. Lewis's distillery near Mt. Vernon" was available for sale at his shop. According to an insurance claim filed by Lewis in 1814, the distillery burned in that year, and it was never rebuilt. Although his claim initially was denied, Lewis eventually received full payment in the amount of $960 in return for his annual premium of $35.60.[40]

CHAPTER 4
BIG WHISKEY

America has had a long and sometimes stormy relationship with liquor. Just a few years after the English established their first permanent settlement in the New World at Jamestown Island in 1607, the colonists brewed their first batch of beer. And the ship that brought the Puritans to Massachusetts Bay in 1630 also carried generous supplies of beer and wine to sustain the thirsty settlers. In short order the Americans were brewing, fermenting, and distilling a wide variety of native fruits and grains, and later molasses shipped from the West Indies, to bolster the imported products in satisfying the demands of a growing population. By the early 1800s, alcohol consumption in the United States had reached a peak never before seen, nor equaled since. In the words of historian W.J. Rorabaugh in his classic study, *The Alcoholic Republic:* "Americans drank at home and abroad, alone and together, at work and at play, in fun and in earnest. They drank from the crack of dawn to the crack of dawn. Americans drank before meals, with meals, and after meals. They drank while working in the fields and while traveling across half a continent." But even from the earliest years of settlement there were many who opposed beverage alcohol on social, moral, and religious grounds, and the topic would rise and fall as a bone of contention over the centuries. The schizophrenic nature of America's relationship with liquor is nowhere better captured than by the dramatic success and then the abject failure of the Prohibition movement. After more than half a century of concerted effort on the part of anti-liquor reformers, in 1917 Congress passed legislation prohibiting the consumption of alcohol (which went into effect in 1920), but after an unprecedented period of social turmoil it was repealed only 16 years later.[1]

Imbibing a variety of alcoholic beverages had been common practice in Europe and the British Isles for millennia, and it was this tradition that naturally served as the foundation for colonists' attitudes toward strong drink when they arrived in the New World. The popularity of such liquids was boosted by the general unavailability of trustworthy drinking water, on the one hand, and the widespread perception that alcohol was both a healthful food source and had medicinal properties, on the other. It is possible to produce alcohol from a wide variety of ingredients—any fruit or grain, sugar cane and molasses, even potatoes—in short, anything that can be transformed into sugar and fermented. Europeans learned to distill grain to make whiskey as early as the Middle Ages, and the practice spread rapidly to the British Isles. By definition whiskey is made from grain—usually corn, wheat, rye, and barley—either separately or in combination, and given the traditional focus of British farmers on growing cereal grains, by the 1700s they were the leading producers of whiskey in the world. Distilled spirits like whiskey and brandy, along with other fermented beverages like apple cider, wine, ale, and beer, came to be staples across all classes of English society. It is hardly surprising then that almost as soon as Europeans first settled in the New World they began to produce a variety of alcoholic beverages.[2]

Over time the industry that developed to satisfy the public's demands for liquor took on a distinctively American character. While ale, beer, brandy, and wines were popular drinks in the British Isles, it would be many decades—and in the case of wine, centuries—before American producers of these beverages could begin to satisfy the local market. However, locals soon made a significant contribution to the production of cheap and highly alcoholic distilled spirits, which were particularly well-received by the hard-drinking and cost-conscious populace. Brandy made from apples and peaches was preferred in some parts of the country, while rum distilled from Caribbean molasses achieved widespread popularity during the first half of the 18th century. After the American Revolution, the price of rum—both the spirit imported from the islands and that made in the United States—increased significantly, providing an opportunity for the whiskey industry to expand its share of the market. When George Washington built his distillery at Mount Vernon in 1797, American whiskey producers already were well on their way in supplanting all other distilled beverages and establishing the industry as one of the most prominent in the nation. The influx of large numbers of European immigrants to the United States in the mid-19th century gave a similar boost to the brewing industry, and whiskey and beer together were cemented as Americans' alcoholic beverages of choice.[3]

From a modern perspective, it may be hard to imagine that American colonists in the 17th and 18th centuries had difficulty gaining ready access to clear, unpolluted drinking water. But according to any number of accounts from the period, for much of the population this appears to have been the case. River water was often murky and even muddy; smaller streams were especially prone to fouling from sedimentation due to erosion and from animal waste; and shallow wells were easily contaminated and bred typhoid fever. According to George Percey, writing in 1625, the wells at Jamestown were "at a flood verily salt, at a low tide full of slime and filth, which was the destruction of many of our men." Fresh springs were the most dependable sources of potable water, but they were distributed sporadically across the landscape and thus often not conveniently located. The water problem only worsened as the population grew and hamlets and villages expanded into towns and cities.[4]

Drinking water by itself, even when it was not fouled, was viewed by many as dangerous to the system. One household guide published in 1767 detailed a long list of the ailments that were presumed to derive from "Drinking cold Water, when a Person is hot. It produces Quinseys, Inflammations of the Breast, Cholicks, Inflammations of the Liver, and all Parts of the Belly, with prodigious Swellings, Vomitings, Suppression of Urine, and inexpressible Anguish." Similarly, an English traveler in America in 1793–94 cautioned that "In hot weather it is extremely dangerous to quench great thirst with water alone, without spirit." It was not until the mid-19th century, with the advent of deep wells and municipal water systems fed from reservoirs, that the challenge of providing clean water to broad areas of the country was resolved.[5]

Along with providing a substitute for water, another powerful support for alcohol consumption came from the widely held belief that it had important health benefits. Period sources are filled with recommendations for treating a host of ailments with alcohol, such as the *Virginia Almanack* for 1764: "A Cure for Dropsy. Take a Quantity of dried Huckleberries, and steep them in pure Rum; let the Rum be charged with as many Berries as it can bear, so as to leave a moderate Measure of running Liquid; let the Patient constantly take a Tea Cup full of that Liquid, Night and Morning, until it cures." These publications are bolstered by any number of personal accounts that reported attempts to treat the sick by prescribing alcohol in just about every form imaginable, as on the numerous occasions when George Washington offered or accepted wine as medicine. At about the same time, Nicholas Cresswell of Virginia recorded in his journal that his doctor advised him "to drink a little more rum than I did before I was sicke." Landon Carter, another fellow Virginian, wrote in his diary that he ingested "about 2 teaspoonfuls of brandy and a lump or two sugar" to counter an upset stomach, as well as recorded a recipe "to strengthen the Stomach," consisting of "2 teaspoonfuls of tincture of bark made with a full ounce if not two of a pint of brandy." Given the high alcohol content of these concoctions, it is no wonder that patients felt at least some temporary relief from their ailments, even if the long-term effects were less salutary.[6]

The notion that alcoholic beverages were a source of nutrition stemmed from what passed for conclusive empirical evidence at the time. With such wholesome ingredients as grains like corn, wheat, and rye, and fruits like grapes, pears, apples, and peaches, how could the resulting beverages fail to be healthful? By comparison, water was a thin and tasteless liquid without any obvious benefits as a source of food. Alcoholic beverages also stood up well as a complement to what for most Americans was a bland and monotonous diet featuring fried, salted, and smoked meats, few fresh vegetables, and plenty of corn: either roasted as ears, made into bread, or pounded into hominy. Such heavy, oily, and salty foods called for a strongly flavored beverage to help wash them down, and alcohol and particularly whiskey answered that need much more effectively than tea, coffee, or milk.[7]

Along with a tradition of strong drink, Europeans nevertheless brought with them to the New World a long history of contentious debate over its proper place in society. Given the widespread belief in its nutritional and medicinal benefits, the discussion usually centered on the question of overindulgence and the personal and social costs that plainly could accrue, and whether the perceived benefits outweighed the drawbacks. One of the earliest, and most widely quoted, statements on the topic was made by the Puritan clergyman, Increase Mather, in 1673, which clearly sums up the dichotomy between use and abuse. "Drink is itself a good creature of God, and to be received with thankfulness," wrote Mather, "but the abuse of drink is from Satan, The wine is from God, but the Drunkard is from the Devil." Mather's characterization has echoed through the centuries, with the pendulum of social acceptance swinging wildly back and forth. In fact, decades before the clergyman's pronouncement, it is evident that a backlash against alcohol already had occurred. In 1619, only 12 years after the colony's founding, the Virginia Assembly passed a statute that called for severe penalties for "Drunkenness." The law specified that "if any private person be found culpable thereof, for the first time he is to be reproved privately by the Minister, the second time publiquely, the thirde time to lye in boltes 12 howers in the house of the Provost Marshall." In the case of further breaches of the law, the offender was to "undergo such severe punishment as the Governor and Counsell of Estate shall fitt to be inflicted on him."[8]

While the wording of the 1619 law might seem to imply that the clergy were more or less united in their opposition to alcohol, in fact their attitude varied widely among the different faiths, as well as over time and space. In 1631 the Virginia Assembly even felt obliged to admonish "mynisters" not "to give themselves to excess in drinkinge, or riott," indicating that such behavior was common enough to require regulation. In 1676 the Assembly felt the need to revisit the issue, stipulating that ministers were subject to a fine of "one half of one yeares sallary" as a consequence for becoming "notoriously scandulous by drunkingness." The autobiographical account of Peter Cartwright, a Methodist minister in North Carolina in the 1850s, documents what appears to have been the prevailing attitude toward alcohol among most of the populace, ministers included, that continued to be found in much of the country:

> From my earliest recollection drinking drams, in family and social circles, was considered harmless and allowable sociality. It was almost universally the custom for preachers, in common with all others, to take drams; and if a man would not have it in his family, his harvest, his house-raisings, log-rollings, weddings, and so on, he was considered parsimonious and unsociable; and many, even professors of Christianity, would not help a man if he did not have spirits and treat the company.[9]

Notwithstanding the propensity of many men of the cloth to indulge in strong drink themselves, at various times clergymen were counted among the most vocal critics of drunkenness and the disruptive behaviors that typically resulted. While

Increase Mather pronounced his support for alcohol as a "Good creature of God," four decades later his own son, Cotton Mather, came to the opposite conclusion. One of the intervening developments that led to the younger Mather's stance against strong drink was the increasing availability of cheap, highly intoxicating rum, and a corresponding rise in public drunkenness. What's more, the younger Mather was concerned that this behavior was becoming pronounced even among men of the highest strata of New England society, which was a development that he feared much more than inebriation by their inferiors. Mather therefore admonished these social leaders to renounce abusing alcohol in order to serve as a model for the multitude of men of lesser rank. Similar calls made by the clergy for abstinence, and for the better elements of society to serve as leaders in this cause, would be heard repeatedly over the succeeding centuries.[10]

By 1770 the per capita consumption of distilled spirits alone (excluding beer, wine, and cider) in the American colonies was 3.7 gallons. Since women and children were included in making this calculation, the actual volume of alcohol that the average American male drank would have been far greater. The figure for consumption declined significantly to 2.5 gallons by 1790, primarily due to the decline in rum imports that began during the Revolution and continued afterward. But by the end of the century, cheap whiskey had largely taken the place of rum, and consumption rebounded to the level of the 1770s. And the proportion of alcohol imbibed by males appears to have steadily increased over that time. According to an estimate made by the American Temperance Society, by the late 1820s, nine million women and children drank 12 million gallons of distilled spirits per year, while three million men drank 60 million gallons. Overall consumption reached an all-time high of approximately 5.0 gallons per capita in 1830, before declining under pressure from the temperance movement to 2.0 gallons by 1860. The rate of consumption has remained almost constant at that level ever since, even during the Prohibition years of the 1920s.[11]

A number of first-hand accounts support the finding that by the mid-18th century Americans from all elements of society drank alcoholic beverages in prodigious quantities, and often to the point of intoxication. A doctor writing in 1737 left a graphic description of the range of drinking behavior that he found in his North Carolina community. He contrasted the tendency for many to indulge in "binge" drinking in public with the practice among the upper classes of more restrained consumption in the privacy of their homes:

> For I have frequently seen them come to the Towns, and there remain Drinking Rum, Punch, and other Liquors for Eight or Ten Days successively, and after they have committed this Excess, will not drink any Spirituous Liquor, 'till such time as they take the next Frolick, as they call it, which is generally in two or three Months. But amongst the better Sort, or those of good OEconomy, it is quite otherwise, who seldom frequent the Taverns, having plenty of Wine, Rum, and other Liquors at their own Houses, which they generously make use of amongst their Friends and Acquaintance.[12]

The prominent planter, William Byrd, echoed the doctor's account, recording in his diary that the Virginia populace got drunk regularly at militia musters, on election days, and during the quarterly court sessions. Although the members of the Virginia elite may have practiced more restraint in public, they were also known to drink to excess in private, with Byrd noting that a doctor friend of his frequently "came drunk to dinner."[13]

At the end of the century an English traveler named Thomas Cooper recorded his impressions of Americans' drinking habits, and he weighed in on the age-old debate between use and abuse. First, Cooper maintained that even though he witnessed a great deal of alcohol consumption during his travels, he saw little evidence of detrimental effects: "I do not find however, that the plenty and cheapness of spirituous liquors occasions much intoxication among the common people; nor do I believe the use made of them has any perceptible effect unfavourable to the health of the Americans." Given this finding, it is not surprising that Cooper came down on the side of the pro-liquor camp, arguing that "like other kinds of poisons, [alcohol] deserves that appellation, relatively to the quantity used, rather than the qualities, of the substances so called."[14]

Treating attendees to alcoholic beverages at public events and family gatherings was practiced throughout America during the early years of the country. It is no surprise, therefore, to find that strong drink was commonly pressed into service at funerals to assist the bereaved in their hour of distress. The 22 gallons of cider, five gallons of brandy, and 24 gallons of beer that were consumed at a York County, Virginia, funeral in 1667 seems to have been par for the course. A hundred years later, the expenses for a funeral in Washington County, Virginia, included: "13¼ gallons of Whiskey [at] 10/ per gallon, 6.12.6"— along with a "plank and winding sheet" to accommodate the body of the deceased, at a cost of £1.11.0. The description of a funeral that took place in West Augusta, Virginia, in 1775 included the heart rending observation that "at the Grave the parents [of an infant] and friends Wept and drank Whiskey alternatively." After George Washington died on 14 December 1799, 29 gallons of whiskey were delivered from his distillery to provide some solace for the grieving funeral party. At least some Virginians took issue with this tradition, however, leading one York County citizen to specify that "Having observed in the dais of my pilgrimage the debauches used at burials tending much to the dishonour of God and his true Religion, my will is that noe strong drinke bee p'vided or spirts at my burialls."[15]

The tradition of providing alcohol to voters was well-established in England by the 18th century, even though repeated attempts had been made over the years to discourage the practice. It was one more of the many customs of the Old Country that were transplanted to the New, where it continued as a widespread tactic well into the 19th century, even in the face of various laws that predictably were enacted to prohibit it. Just as George Washington learned first-hand that failing to treat prospective voters to strong drink was a prescription for defeat at the polls, his friend, fellow Virginian and sometime political ally, James Madison, also learned this lesson the hard way. In 1777 Madison was defeated in his bid for election to the newly established House of Delegates, which he attributed to his failure to give away liquor. According to Madison, "the people not only tolerated, but expected and even required to be courted and treated, [and] no candidate, who neglected those attentions, could be elected...forebearance would have been ascribed to a mean parsimony, or to a proud disrespect for the voters." According to one Madison biographer, "there was only one decisive issue. Madison refused to give the voters free whisky." By the 1820s and 1830s treating at the polls made a strong comeback as it took on a more overtly political meaning. Andrew Jackson and others who sought to democratize American society used liquor as a tangible means of demonstrating their ties to the common man, by drinking drams with them, with great success.[16]

Wealthy men, like George Washington and William Byrd, generally purchased their strong drink in bulk from merchant houses in England or via other contacts either at home or abroad. Men of more modest means could satisfy their needs by buying from their wealthier neighbors or from local stores and taverns. In addition to dispensing alcohol, taverns served a variety of important functions in early American society. In an overwhelmingly rural country with a relatively small population spread over an area larger than that of England, taverns were a way station for travelers, venues for public business like elections, militia musters, trials and other court proceedings, and a place to transact business and debate politics. Serving strong drink during these events was viewed as normal practice, and its availability undoubtedly made the sometimes dry proceedings more palatable to the participants.[17]

Given the popularity of beer, ale, and cider among the British rank and file populace, it is no surprise that they were the first alcoholic beverages to be produced by English settlers in the New World. In England, most adults consumed up to one gallon of alcohol per day, and even children drank heartily, as these beverages were standard accompaniments at daily meals, feasts, and religious celebrations. During this period the technical distinction between ale and beer centered on the use of hops as an ingredient. Beer was brewed with hops, which not only imparted a distinctive flavor but also helped it keep much longer than ale, which could spoil in as few as three days. The sweeter, unhopped ale was the traditional brew and was easier and cheaper to make, but hopped beer increasingly gained acceptance over the course of the 17th century.[18]

Brewing, cidering, and even distilling of alcohol, was the province of the women of the household in England well into the 18th century, and that tradition seems to have been brought with the colonists to the New World. This arrangement was alluded to by John Hammond, who wrote an account of the Chesapeake colonies—Maryland and Virginia—in 1656, observing that "Beare is indeed in some place constantly drunken, in other some, nothing but Water or Milk and Water for Beverage; and that is where the goodwives (if I may so call them) are negligent and idle; for it is not for want of Corn to make Malt with (for the Country affords enough) but because they are sloathful and carelesse: but I hope this Item will shame them out of those humours, that they will be adjudged by their drink, what kinde of Housewives they are." But Hammond may have judged Chesapeake housewives too harshly as hops were expensive and difficult to grow in America and the labor that would have been required in their cultivation could not be spared from growing the region's preeminent crop, tobacco.[19]

By the 1640s the Virginians, the Dutch in New York, and even the Puritans of Massachusetts Bay had begun distilling both brandy from fruit and whiskey from grain. Brandy made from pressing, fermenting, and distilling the juice of apples and peaches took the place of ale and beer as the most popular alcoholic beverage in the Chesapeake, as well as in many of the other colonies. Legislation enacted in 1645 indicates that Virginians were distilling fruit brandies well before the middle of the 17th century. The inventory of a store in York County, Virginia, from 1667 included 100 gallons of brandy, along with 20 gallons of wine, and 10 gallons of "aqua vitae" (probably whiskey). By the first quarter of the 18th century, Virginians seem to have had access to the full range of alcoholic beverages that would be the norm for the next 200 years. When Robert Beverley published his History of Virginia in 1722, he recorded that "Their strong drink is Madeira wine, cider, mobby punch, made either of rum from the Caribbee islands, or brandy distilled from their apples and peaches; besides brandy, wine, and strong beer, which they have constantly from England."[20]

Notably absent from Beverley's list is whiskey, but the account of an expedition led by Virginia Governor Alexander Spotswood in 1716 to explore the Blue Ridge frontier indicates that the well-stocked explorers brought that spirit along with them as well: "Virginia red wine, Irish usquebaugh [whisky], brandy, shrub [a mixture of citrus juice, sugar, and rum or other spirit], two sorts of rum, champagne, canary, cherry, punch, water, cider, &c." In his description written almost 80 years later, Cooper indicated that the options for strong drink were little changed, although he pointed out the appearance of marked regional specializations related to the availability of raw ingredients:

> In New England, as the inhabitants of that part of America trade much with the West-Indies, for black cattle and horses; they bring back, among other articles, a great quantity of molasses. Hence the spirit drank in common there, is New England rum. In New York and Pennsylvania states, the chief produce being grain, the spirit used is distilled from some kind of corn, generally rye. In Virginia and Maryland, peaches and apples afford

peach and apple brandy; the latter is an indifferent spirit; the former, when well made, carefully rectified and kept in a cask for some years, is as fine a liquor as I have ever tasted.[21]

The failure of the English American Colonies to develop a native wine industry meant that imported wines continued to enjoy a strong market there, especially among the upper classes. Wines imported from Spain and France were popular, but by the mid-18th century the products of the Portuguese island of Madeira had become the strong drink of choice for many of the wealthiest members of society. Starting in the early 17th century as a substitute for the island's declining sugar industry, Madeira wines were a rather undistinguished product that were sold primarily to ship captains stopping off on their voyages between Europe and the New World. But over the course of the 18th century America became far and away the largest single importer of the island's wines. A crucial factor in this development was the preferred trading privileges that Portugal enjoyed for most of the century, which gave Madeira wines a significant advantage over their European competition. Equally important was that wine produced from the Madeira grapes not only stood up well under the rigors of the Atlantic crossing, but it even benefited as a consequence. The heat and agitation experienced in the holds of ships affected the wine's flavor, which the American consumers found quite to their liking. According to David Hancock, in his exhaustive study of the Madeira wine industry, "By the early nineteenth century, innovation, experimentation, and even happenstance had turned Madeira from the mediocre table wine it had been a century before into a refined manufactured product."[22]

Madeira wine became so closely associated with the North American colonies that its producers adapted their product in accordance with their customers' desires. As Madeira is a blended wine, it was possible for the vintners to alter the ingredients to please specific tastes. In the American South, where there were no concerns about Madeira spoiling from the cold, darker and sweeter blends seem to have been preferred. In the north, consumers requested a paler, drier wine. Other parts of the country made similarly specific requests: in Virginia and South Carolina, extremely pale, dry wine; in New York, a sweet amber, reddish drink, and so on. One innovation that seems to have been the direct result of American input was the practice of fortifying the wine with brandy. Fortification enhanced the body of the wine and made for a potent drink, ranging as high as 22 percent alcohol. This was still well below the level of distilled spirits like whiskey, rum, brandy, and gin, at about 52 percent alcohol, but well above most other wines (13 to 20 percent), ale (7 percent), and small beer (1 percent). American consumers seem to have begun adding brandy to their wine as early as the 1740s, and island growers and exporters are known to have adopted the practice by 1753.[23]

From 1700 to 1775, 76 percent of the wine that was imported into Anglo-America originated in Madeira, and the wine's relatively high price meant that most of this total found its way onto upper class tables. One revealing source is the data provided by examining probate records—listings of the contents and the assigned market values of estates that were made at the time of a property owner's death. Of 325 probate inventories for elite households from the Chesapeake region spanning the period 1740 to 1810, 232 (71 percent) listed wine and 11 (4 percent) specified Madeira. The largest volume of Madeira that any of the men owned was one pipe (approximately 126 gallons), found in four of the inventories, with assigned values from £40 to £90. The others owned bottles of Madeira, ranging from 8 bottles of "Old Madeira," valued at £1, to 380 bottles valued at £50. All of the men whose estates included Madeira owned other alcoholic beverages as well, most often wine and rum.[24]

The 1753 inventory of the estate of Lawrence Washington, George Washington's older half-brother, included a substantial stock of spirits, featuring 1 pipe (two-thirds full) and 16 bottles of Madeira, assessed at a combined value of £21. The other strong drink consisted of rum (7 bottles of "old" rum, 12 jars of rum, 6 of which were specified as coming from Jamaica, and 50 gallons of rum), Port wine (5 bottles), and 1 cask of "Spirits." But the most extensive cellar was kept by Dr. Nicholas Flood, of Richmond County, Virginia, who at the time of his death in 1776 owned 126 bottles of Madeira, along with 47 bottles of "Malmsey," another Madeira wine made from the Malvasia grape. He also owned 33 bottles of white wine, 4 bottles of Fontiniac, 25 bottles of sherry, 27 bottles of "Red Port," 300 bottles of "Wine lately bottled," "5 Large Bottles with Arrack and Chain Spirits," 138 gallons of "spirits" from various sources, 23 gallons of common rum, 30 gallons of peach brandy, 3 gallons of cherry bounce, 20 gallons of "Orange Peel Cordial," and 25 gallons of assorted other cordials.[25]

As wine and spirits increasingly took on the role of prominent props in the rituals of domestic hospitality among upper class Americans, Madeira developed into a potent expression of gentility and a marker of status. Its relatively high price clearly indicated that the owner was well-to-do, and the specialized knowledge required to appreciate the wine conveyed an aura of taste and refinement. Madeira drinking was also soon associated with costly trappings, specialized decanters, bottle tags, and such, which reinforced the inference that the wine and its owner were special. At Monticello archaeologists have recovered the broken fragments of an elaborately decorated decanter, engraved with the name "Madeira," that once belonged to Thomas Jefferson. George Washington's adoption of Madeira as his favorite beverage, his willingness to spend significant sums of money to acquire the wine, and his overriding concern to ensure that it be made available to guests and visitors of sufficient rank, mark him as a devoted follower of the fashion.[26]

While Madeira swiftly rose to claim a prominent position as a marker of status within the highest ranks of American life, rum started out on a much lower rung of the social

ladder. Since rum was highly alcoholic and, for most of the
18th century, both relatively inexpensive and plentiful, it was
particularly attractive to those who were seeking a cheap means
of getting drunk. The price of rum was low in the 1720s, but
over the next two decades steady increases in supply from both
American and Caribbean producers combined to drive the price
lower still, reduced by almost one-half. Thus, the spirit was well
within the means of even common laborers, and it became the
most popular strong drink by far among the working classes.
Increased consumption led to more public drunkenness and
other social problems, which in turn fostered a backlash on
the part of government, clergy, and other leaders of society.
Nevertheless, rum retained its overwhelming popularity, and it
was not until the unnatural restrictions on the supply of rum
that was caused by the disruptions attending the Revolution
that this trend slowed, albeit temporarily.[27]

Rum also came to serve the needs of members of more
polite society, as the liquor was well suited to mixing with other
ingredients to produce a drink that appealed to more refined
palates. Punch was a concoction of five ingredients—spirits,
sugar, citrus, spices, and water—which had appeared in England
by the 1650s, and gained popularity in Colonial America starting
in the late 17th century. Although other spirits like brandy could
be substituted, cheaper rum seems to have been the most popular
choice. The special requirements for preparing the drink were
best suited by mixing the ingredients together in a bowl, and it
became standard practice to serve the drink in the same vessel
in which it was prepared. The size of the bowl naturally related
to the number in the party being served. Punch drinking was
particularly popular in taverns and public places, where it seems
to have been primarily a male activity. On these occasions the
bowl often passed from one person to the next, each drinking
directly from it, and the goal usually seems to have been to get
heartily drunk.[28]

In contrast with the rowdy and bawdy behavior that often
accompanied these public bouts of drinking, punch parties

held in private homes likely were much more restrained, more socially acceptable affairs. Refined women like Martha Washington likely drank punch in these settings, ladled from highly decorated and costly punch bowls into equally fashionable cups or glasses. The probate inventory data reinforces the association of punch and rum with high status households in the 18th century: 151 (46 percent) of the 325 estates in the sample included rum and 121 (37 percent) listed punch implements, such as bowls, ladles, glasses, and strainers. In contrast, only four (1.2 percent) of the inventories contained whiskey, testifying that during this period cheap whiskey remained attractive primarily to those of more modest means.[29]

The first rum distilleries in the Caribbean were probably established in the 1630s and 1640s to make use of the by-products of sugar making, and they became a common adjunct to the operations of large sugar plantations. At first the main ingredient was the "skimmings" of frothy scum that bubbled up when the sugar cane was boiled. Molasses, which is another by-product of making sugar, and which has a higher sucrose content than the skimmings, initially was viewed as too valuable an asset to be used for rum, and it was generally reboiled to produce a lower grade of sugar. Before circa 1700 the vast majority of rum was either consumed locally or sold as provisions to masters of merchant vessels as a more stable substitute for fresh water. As an export market for rum developed, primarily in the North American colonies, the price rose along with it. This made it cost effective to turn to molasses as the primary ingredient and the distilleries expanded their production accordingly. In 1664–1665 the island of Barbados shipped more than 100,000 gallons of rum, making up 4 percent of total exports; by 1699–1701 the volume had increased to just less than 600,000 gallons and 19 percent of the total.[30]

As early as the 1640s a number of distilleries were established in Boston and other Massachusetts communities, although most of these early enterprises likely were using grains for their raw material. Trade between New England merchants and West Indies planters increased steadily over the next decades, with American foodstuffs—principally grain and fish—exchanged for Caribbean sugar, rum, and molasses. By 1648 a rum distillery was operating in Salem, Massachusetts, and in 1661 a still had been set up in New London, Connecticut, "for distilling rum from the molasses procured there in exchange for the exports of the Colony." At the same time most Boston distillers gave up grain in favor of imported molasses, and over the next century the city was the pre-eminent producer of rum in the colonies. In 1716–1717 the 27 Boston distilleries produced over 200,000 gallons of rum, or an average of roughly 5,700 gallons each. Within a decade the number of distilleries increased to at least 40. Low prices and ample supply combined to spur Americans' consumption of rum, which increased dramatically after circa 1720.[31]

American distillers steadily expanded their production, but most of the spirit consumed in the colonies continued to be imported from the West Indies. This is reflected by the records of imports to the port of New York during the decade of 1700–1709. More than 526,000 gallons of rum were received during that period, with 301,000 gallons originating in Barbados and 97,000 gallons provided by the other Caribbean islands. Local imports consisted of 47,000 gallons coming from Boston and another 8,000 gallons from other American cities. Even so, the competition offered by colonial distillers was a point of concern to the British Crown. Rum production was an increasingly important source of revenue for island planters as a complement to sugar exports, and the American colonies were far and away the largest market for their spirit. American rum, therefore, which also was generally cheaper than the Caribbean spirit, was viewed as serious competition by the sugar planters/distillers, who took steps to protect what they viewed as their rightful monopoly. This took the form of refusing to sell their molasses to the Americans, as well as securing passage in 1733 of an act that doubled the duty paid on foreign molasses. Thus, British molasses was largely unavailable, and in response the New Englanders turned to smuggling non-British raw materials to serve their needs. Although some distilleries were driven out of business, most of them were able to survive.[32]

Molasses was shipped in bulk and it was difficult and expensive to transport overland. This led to the concentration of rum distilleries in coastal cities that carried on trade with the West Indies. By the mid-1700s, substantial distilleries were established in every large American city along the Atlantic coast, with Massachusetts and the other northeastern colonies hosting the vast majority of the new still houses. By 1770 the colonies combined to import four million gallons of Caribbean rum, but local production had increased dramatically, to more than five million gallons. Not all of the rum distilled in the northeast found its way to the local market, however, as it became a valuable export commodity sent to Canada, to Africa in exchange for slaves, and to the non-British West Indies. [33]

The first rum distilleries in the North American colonies were generally small family run affairs, but as the market for the spirit grew, and profits improved along with it, producers sought to increase revenues by expanding the scale and complexity of their operations. The distilling apparatus also was refined, with such innovations as adopting larger stills and developing a more advanced system of managing the fermentation and collection processes. According to one observer in 1729, "Our distillers in Boston use large square Cisterns sunk into the floor of the Stilhouse for fermenting their Molasses, and very large Stills of 600 to 1,000 gallons as requiring less firewood in proportion and greater dispatch." The archaeological findings from excavating the site of the Douw-Quackenbush rum distillery, operating in Albany, New York, from circa 1770 to 1810, provide more detail to this picture. The 36- by 60-foot stone foundation contained the bases for two stills and evidence for two generations of fermentation vats (cisterns), linked by wooden distribution pipes to a pump to facilitate transfer of the wash to the stills.

The wooden vats were set deeply into the ground, and each receptacle could have held between 1,250 and 3,000 gallons of liquid. An inventory of the distillery dating to 1784 indicates that three stills were in use at that time, with capacities of 1,500, 500, and 40 gallons. The investigators estimate that the distillery's annual production easily could have approached 50,000 gallons of spirits, testifying to the increasingly industrial nature of rum distilleries in this period.[34]

In contrast, most whiskey distilleries at this time were much smaller affairs, operating only a few months out of the year, distilling a few hundred gallons of whiskey from the farmer-distiller's excess grain. Thomas Cooper, the Englishman from Manchester who toured America in 1793–94, testified to the humble nature of most whiskey distilleries, starting with the observation that "Planters of any consequence frequently have a small distillery as a part of their establishment." He went on to describe one farmer's distillery, "which may serve as a specimen of this kind: he has two stills, the one holding 60, the other 115 gallons." After cooking a mixture of coarsely ground rye, malt, and hops, it was fermented for four to six days. "Of this wash he puts to the amount of a hogshead in the larger still, and draws off about fifteen gallons of weak spirit, which is afterward rectified in the smaller still, seldom more than once."[35]

Freidrich Heinrich Gelwicks was a German immigrant to York County, Pennsylvania, who was a part-time shoemaker and a distiller, in addition to running his 147-acre farm. His account book for the years 1760–83 survives, which provides a record of the types of spirits he produced, the quantities he sold, and the payment that he received from his customers. Gelwicks made and sold rye whiskey, brandy, applejack, and Gassel (a cordial made of a mixture of whiskey, water, sugar, spices, and licorice), along with "punch" by the bowlful. Gelwicks usually sold between one quart and one gallon of spirits per transaction, although he did sell larger amounts on occasion: 111 gallons of rye whiskey in 1766, 117 gallons of brandy in 1767, 112 gallons of brandy in 1768, 66 gallons of applejack in 1773, and 54 gallons of whiskey in 1778. As might be expected, Gelwicks's customers were almost exclusively his neighbors and extended family members living in the surrounding countryside of York County.[36]

Documentary and physical evidence for another distillery that operated in Schaefferstown, Pennsylvania, during the 18th century complements the information provided by the Gelwicks's accounts. The distillery was located in the basement of a stone farmhouse that may have been built as early as 1736. The house was altered and enlarged circa 1771 by a subsequent owner, Alexander Schaeffer, to accommodate the distillery. Schaeffer's son, Henry, inherited his father's property in 1775, which included a tavern in the town and farmland nearby, along with the distillery. According to an 1804 account, the Schaeffer distillery produced "fruit liquors and rye whiskey of superb quality," in addition to "pink grade wine." The account specified that the distillery operated six stills, and that a workshop on the property also made copper stills for retail sale. Surviving physical evidence found in the basement of the house indicates that two stills, which no longer exist, were installed there. According to one source, the Schaeffer farm became one of the largest producers of wine and spirits in Pennsylvania in the early 19th century.[37]

The decline in the popularity of rum was directly related to disruptions in trade with the Caribbean as a consequence of the Revolution, which drastically reduced the imports of both spirit and molasses. Then after the end of hostilities, the price of rum imported from what was now a foreign country increased steeply due to newly imposed tariff fees. On the other hand, one benefit of winning independence was that American farmers were allowed to migrate west of the Appalachians to settle the rich farming lands of the Ohio Valley. Wheat, corn, and rye became the staple products of these farms, which provided the raw ingredients for whiskey. The native industry quickly expanded to meet the demand caused by the decline in

the availability of English rum, and the lower price charged for
the local products cemented the initial advantage that had been
based on scarcity. The decline of rum and the rise of whiskey
occurred over a remarkably short period. Rum accounted for
more than 90 per cent of the distilled spirits consumed in the
American colonies in 1774. By 1790 whiskey had climbed to
one-third of the total, and by 1810 whiskey consumption had
increased to the level claimed by rum 20 years earlier.[38]

Whiskey could so easily replace rum as the most popular
distilled spirit in America because it offered many of the same
benefits—it was highly alcoholic, cheap, and readily available.
Another factor in the rise of whiskey's popularity was the
influx in the mid-1700s of thousands of immigrants from
Scotland and Ireland. These industrious farmers had experience
distilling whiskey in their homelands and they quickly turned to
converting their excess grain into another valuable commodity.
The skill of the Scottish and Irish immigrants in distilling
stimulated the establishment of still houses wherever they
settled. Since many of these immigrants made their way west
of the Appalachians after the war, they were perfectly positioned
to take advantage of the opportunity to help satisfy the demand
for strong drink.[39]

At the same time that the rate of alcohol consumption in
America was entering its phase of most prodigious growth, the
first rumblings of what became one of the strongest arguments
against its use were being heard. By the late 1700s scientific
advances in medicine were leading some doctors to conclude that
drinking alcohol was detrimental to a person's health, rather
than beneficial. Benjamin Rush, a Philadelphia physician who
had trained at the Edinburgh College of Medicine, and who later
achieved prominence as Surgeon General of the Continental
Army, played a particularly important role in advancing this
argument. Rush concluded that alcohol, and particularly
distilled spirits, produced illness and disease by destroying the
body's natural balance. As early as 1772 Rush wrote a pamphlet
in which he urged moderation in its consumption, but he fell

short of recommending total abstinence from strong drink. His experience observing the detrimental effect of spirits on American soldiers during the war strengthened his conviction that alcoholic beverages served no useful purpose. In 1784 Rush published a second essay on the topic entitled, *An Inquiry into the Effects of Spirituous Liquors*, which catalogued a host of drawbacks to liquor and argued for replacing spirits with less alcoholic beverages like light wine and beer.[40]

The argument against distilled spirits put forward by Rush found a receptive audience among a small but influential portion of the American populace, generally the educated and prosperous classes, who already may have observed for themselves the deleterious effects of alcohol abuse. Encouraged by the positive response to his writing, Rush embarked on a campaign to spread his message. His essay was republished in pamphlet form and sold widely, and Rush followed up on that success by preparing "A Moral and Physical Thermometer," which graphically displayed the sliding scale of detrimental effects—vices, diseases, and punishments—associated with different beverages. At the top of the scale was water, which was associated with health, wealth, and serenity of mind. At the other end of the "thermometer" were gin, brandy, rum, and whiskey, which were associated with burglary, murder, suicide, and death. Rush's efforts are credited with leading a significant number of upper class Americans to give up distilled spirits, but the overall impact on drinking habits was minor. Really significant gains in the temperance movement would have to wait until the decade of the 1820s, when the increasing social costs of heavy drinking became too great for most people to ignore.[41]

An unwitting source of support for Rush's successors in the anti-liquor movement came from the legion of drinkers themselves. Between 1800 and 1830 American lovers of spirits outdid themselves, as their rate of consumption increased dramatically, until it exceeded five gallons per person per year, a rate that is more than double that of today's level. A major contributor to the increase was the unprecedented availability of cheap whiskey, which in turn was the result of an overabundance of corn grown on the rapidly expanding western frontier. The early 19th century also was a period of broad social upheaval, and scholars have suggested that heavy drinking was related to a widespread sense of uneasiness. Rapid population growth, the influx of immigrants, urbanization, migration to the interior of the country, war, and hard and boring physical labor, all probably played their part in leading people to drink heartily. For anti-liquor reformers, one of the most troubling aspects of the renewed embrace of hard drinking was the practice of bingeing, or imbibing copious amounts of alcohol in a short period with the expressed goal of getting drunk. In response to what they saw as dire social consequences for this behavior, a number of reform-minded members of the clergy banded together in the 1810s to attempt to persuade their flocks to abstain.[42]

The ministers soon found allies across a broad swath of the American public who were concerned that the liquor menace was sowing social unrest, eroding the authority of church and government, ruining families, and sapping the national spirit. Temperance societies sprang up in response, galvanized by a moral and emotional appeal that ultimately made much more headway with the general public than had Rush's thoughtful and reasoned approach to the problem two decades earlier. By 1831 the American Temperance Society reported that they had enlisted more than 170,000 members who belonged to 2,200 local organizations. The argument for abstinence was distilled into two related assertions: that religious faith could serve as a way for people to ease the anxieties that led to drink, and that hard liquor was the agent of the devil. Another approach was to frame the case for abstinence in a patriotic light, recalling the struggle for independence from Great Britain and equating signing "the pledge" with the same sacrifices that had been born by the founding generation. The rewards for this strenuous effort were impressive, as the all-time high rate of consumption of alcohol per capita that was reached in the 1820s was cut in half within a decade. But this was not the end of the conflict over the place of strong drink in American life, as the renewed debate over prohibition would demonstrate a half-century later.[43]

In Europe the technology of distilling had reached a relatively advanced stage by the mid-1500s, and it remained largely unchanged until the end of the 18th century. A manual published in London in 1651, entitled *The Art of Distillation,* described essentially the same process found in Cooper's *The Complete Distiller,* appearing more than a century later, which was remarkably similar to Krafft's *American Distiller,* from 1804. George Washington's distillery was organized along these traditional lines, divided into the main steps of grinding, mashing and fermenting grain, distilling, gathering the low wines, and distilling for a second time. This was a labor intensive process, which required a force of workers dedicated to carrying out the onerous, repetitive tasks. The procedures were the same no matter the number of stills in use, meaning that few economies of scale applied, and larger operations like Washington's were only slightly more efficient than those of his smaller competitors. Increased production therefore could only be achieved if means could be found to improve efficiency.[44]

The design of the copper pot stills had changed little over the preceding several hundred years. The vessels usually were small, with no more than 150 gallons in capacity and extremely simple in form, consisting of the larger lower chamber in which the wash was placed to be heated over the fire, and the smaller upper chamber (or head) which was fitted tightly onto the body. The vaporized alcohol collected in the head, then traveled through an attached tapering arm and into the spiraling worm tube, submerged in cool water in a tub, where it condensed back into liquid form. While simple in concept, distilling required skill and patience; overheating the still and scorching or burning the contents was a common and disastrous occurrence. Distilling was accomplished in individual batches, and the vessel had to be emptied and thoroughly cleaned between each run. Finally, the first run distillate was gathered and then distilled a second time to increase the proof and reduce impurities. Because of the need for a second distillation, a common method of improving efficiency was to operate two stills. To reduce costs the vessels usually were of different sizes, with the larger still (usually ranging from 100 to 150 gallons) for distilling the fermented wash (beer) and the smaller still (40 to 80 gallons), often referred to as the "doubler," dedicated to the second distillation.[45]

The stills used by early American distillers undoubtedly were imported, with most of the vessels likely coming from England. Coppersmiths in the city of Bristol appear to have been particularly active in the American export trade, and at least two stills marked "Bristol" and dated to the 1780s survive in museum collections. But by the last quarter of the 18th century, numerous American metalsmiths had turned to producing stills from imported copper plates. Pennsylvania appears to have been home to many still makers, and as early as 1788 an advertisement in the Lexington, Kentucky, *Gazette* offered "two Philadelphia-made stills" for sale. On September 5, 1792, a notice ran in the *Pennsylvania Herald and York General Advertiser* advertising for "Journeyman Coppersmiths, Who are compleat Workmen at Stills." Like Alexandria metalsmith George McMunn, who supplied George Washington with three of his stills in 1798, these men usually produced a variety of additional implements. But one craftsman who seems to have specialized in making stills was Daniel Stoehr, who produced 163 stills in his Hanover, Pennsylvania, workshop in the early 1820s.[46]

Another obvious measure to improve efficiency and increase production was to introduce stills with greater capacity, which had lower costs per gallon of output. Fewer batches translated into less time devoted to clean-up, and thus lower labor costs, and less fuel was needed as well. There was both the cost factor and a practical limit to the size of stills one could make, of course. And although the batches were larger in the new stills,

Arranging stills in pairs within a masonry base served by a single chimney was standard practice in large distilleries like Washington's, as with the two brandy stills depicted in Diderot's Encyclopedia.

the vessels still had to be cooled, dismantled, and scoured out after each distilling episode before they could be recharged with the next batch of wash. The solution to this major impediment to production was presented in the form of the so-called "perpetual" still, which could be fed a steady stream of wash while it remained in operation. The traditional worm tube was replaced by a condensing unit that allowed the liquid to be cooled and reintroduced into the still for its second run without any interruption in the process. A second important innovation was to heat the still using steam instead of an open fire, which allowed the temperature to be much more closely regulated, and virtually eliminated the danger of scorching the contents. In 1794 Alexander Anderson of Philadelphia patented a steam still, consisting of "one boiler which worked two stills," followed by a patent in 1801 for a perpetual still condenser. These improvements began to be adopted almost immediately by commercial distillers, and many more innovations were introduced over the succeeding decades. Several sources indicate that by 1815 "patented" steam-heated perpetual stills were in use as far west as Kentucky, and by 1818 the distiller and author Harrison Hall observed that "The old way of distilling is generally pursued only by such as work upon a small scale, or are unwilling to be at the expense of a patent right."[47]

Hall provided a financial analysis to back up his claim that the new patented distilling process was highly profitable. Although the cost of acquiring a still undoubtedly discouraged some, the basic economics of distilling were always attractive to those who possessed surplus grain, no matter on what scale they operated. As one bushel of corn could generate 2.5 gallons of whiskey, the farmer-distiller often could increase the value of his grain by roughly 150 percent. Of course the price of both corn and whiskey varied widely according to time and place, but for most of the period before 1850 the added value from distilling was well worth the effort. Hall updated that analysis by factoring in the costs and benefits of adopting the new technology. Based on a distillery that could process 12 bushels of grain per day and yield 3,000 gallons of spirits in three months, Hall estimated that the total profits for the period would be close to $700—a substantial figure in 1818. The capital required was $1,124 for equipment and livestock, and $1,302 to cover the purchase of grain, firewood, wages, and other essentials. Calculated at a return of 55 cents per gallon on the whiskey sold and a gain of $328 on livestock, total revenues would be $1,978, yielding a profit of $676. At that rate, within six months the owner of the enterprise not only would cover his expenses but also recoup the value of his capital investment. Obviously, this rosy scenario did not take into account the variety of problems that might arise, especially the ones that were most likely—either an increase in the cost of grain or a decrease in the price of whiskey.[48]

In 1830 another major innovation in distilling technology was introduced in Scotland, when a former government official and distiller named Aeneas Coffey invented an even more advanced type of perpetual still. Also known as a "column" still because of its long cylindrical shape, this steam heated device dramatically increased productivity yet again, as it was capable of distilling 3,000 gallons of wash in one hour. The process called for the liquid to pass through a series of chambers in the two parallel columns, where the alcoholic vapor was automatically separated from the less desirable elements of the wash in one continuous flow. Although cheap to operate and simple to control, Coffey's stills came at a high price. Only distilleries operating on a scale that was well beyond the norm found in the United States at the time had either the capital to invest in the machinery or the market potential to make its adoption cost effective. By 1834 Scottish distilleries began to adopt Coffey's equipment, and its widespread use almost immediately caused a striking increase in the output of grain whisky in that country. From about 231,000 gallons in 1835, its production increased to almost 751,000 gallons in 1836. But it would be many decades before column stills following Coffey's general design were adopted in large numbers in the United States.[49]

An early example of an extremely ambitious, and ultimately unsuccessful, commercial-scale distillery was established in 1816 in Louisville, Kentucky. Known as the Hope Distillery, the eastern backers of the concern spared no expense in fitting it out with equipment of the latest design, featuring two English-made copper stills, with a capacity of 1,500 and 750 gallons, operated by a 45 horsepower steam engine. In 1819 daily production was estimated at 1,200 gallons; by 1821 the figure had risen to 1,500 gallons. Almost all well-run distilleries used the nutrient-rich slops (spent wash) left over from distilling grain to fatten livestock for market. In this aspect of the business the Hope Distillery once again was remarkable, as the annual output in pork was estimated at between two and three million pounds. Unfortunately for the investors, however, the business model appears to have been too aggressive, as the product could not be profitably shipped to distant markets, and the enterprise closed within a few years.[50]

The owners of the Hope Distillery are recorded as having used a mixture of rye, corn, and barley as the ingredients to make their whiskey. It isn't possible to determine the proportions of the three grains in the mash bill, but rye traditionally had made up the largest percentage. George Washington's recipe was typical of the era, consisting of 60 percent rye, 35 percent corn, and 5 percent malted barley. The various distilling manuals provided a variety of recipes, with the proportions of the three grains varying according to availability, taste, local conditions, and personal experience. In the West the low price of corn seems to have led to its replacing rye as the principal ingredient, and corn whiskey became particularly associated with Kentucky distilleries. In his manual published in 1818, Hall remarked that "the western whiskey," from Tennessee and Kentucky, was "chiefly" made of corn. Whiskey using rye as the main ingredient continued to be popular in other regions of the country, particularly in Maryland and Pennsylvania, up until Prohibition.[51]

The practice of improving the flavor of alcoholic beverages by setting them aside to age was well-known in the 18th century. When George Washington ordered a barrel of Madeira wine from a supplier in 1759, he specified that it was to be aged, and he understood that he would be obliged to pay a higher price for the premium product. Thomas Cooper's 1795 description of the peach brandy he had sampled in Virginia and Maryland included the observation that when it was "kept in a cask for some years," it was "as fine a liquor as I have ever tasted." Similarly, in 1797 when William Thornton sent Washington a gift of bottles of "old Spirit" that had "obtained the deep colour by standing in Oak Casks" for 28 years, it was clear that both men understood that the rum was a rare and valuable commodity.[52]

The advice found in an influential manual on distilling, written by Ambrose Cooper and published in 1757, provides further evidence for the widespread knowledge that time spent in wooden casks improved the flavor of spirits, as well as gave them a darker color. Cooper provided directions on how to imitate the "dark yellowish brown Colour" of French brandy, presumably because he had reason to believe that consumers preferred the "Softness and Ripeness" of this more refined product. He specified that the changes were a result of the liquid "lying in the Cask," and that "the Ingredient from whence this Colour is extracted, is no other than the Wood of the Cask, and the Brandy in reality is become a dilute of Tincture of Oak." Therefore, Cooper recommended that the best way to imitate "this Colour to Perfection" was by adding oak shavings to the spirit in question, although he added that good results could be attained by using treacle or burnt sugar, as well. Even though the darker cast that liquor achieved as a result of aging in barrels thus appears to have been recognized as a desirable characteristic by the mid-1700s, it would be another century or more before the "red" color so familiar to modern whiskey drinkers became commonplace.[53]

Purposefully aging whiskey in order to improve its taste probably remained an unusual practice before 1830, as it entailed considerable additional expense. In order for distillers to benefit from withholding a percentage of their product for future sales, and thus to bear the costs of storage and deferred revenue in the short-term, the ultimate reward had to be sufficient to warrant the risk. The willingness of consumers to pay a premium for aged spirit and the improved efficiency and increased output that resulted from the perpetual still and other technical innovations eventually combined to make aging whiskey financially viable for some producers. However, since most whiskey distilleries continued to be modest, part-time enterprises, their operators did not command the capital required to engage in aging their spirit.[54]

Aged whiskey was far from unheard of even decades earlier, however. The advertisement in a Kentucky newspaper in 1793 that specified that 500 gallons of "Old Whiskey" were for sale is a particularly early example of the practice. By the 1820s it was fairly common for some merchants to differentiate between "new" and "old" whiskey, with higher prices attached to the aged products. In 1818 Harrison Hall observed that Tennessee and Kentucky distilleries already were earning a reputation for producing superior whiskey, and that aging was at least one factor in their success. "As they depend upon the rise of the rivers to send their whiskey to market," Hall wrote, "it acquires some age: this also, and the motion of travelling, has considerable effect in improving it." The first reference to whiskey of a specific age may date to that same year, when an advertisement appeared in the *Lexington Gazette* offering seven-year-old whiskey for sale.[55]

In the meantime, those distillers who could not afford to age their product continued to find helpful instructions on methods for fabricating a spirit that mimicked the appearance and flavor of genuinely aged liquor. One of the most influential successors to Cooper's *The Complete Distiller*, was *The Practical Distiller: Or an Introduction to Making Whiskey, Gin, Brandy, Spirits, etc.*, by Samuel M'Harry, which was published in Philadelphia in 1809. The book covered a broad range of associated topics, including directions on "how to correct the taste of singed whiskey" and to give it "an aged flavor":

On colouring Liquors. One pound of brown sugar burnt in a skillet almost to a cinder, add a quart of water, which when stirred, will dissolve the sugar—when dissolved, this quantity will color three barrels. A pint of well parched wheat put into a barrel will colour it, and give more the appearance of a naturally acquired colour, and an aged taste or flavor.[56]

To give an aged flavor to Whiskey. Filtered through "a quantity of finely beaten maple charcoal, thro' which let the singlings filter into your usual receiving cask. To each hogshead of whiskey, use a pound of Bohea tea, and set it in the sun for two weeks or more, then remove it to a cool cellar, and when cold it will have the taste and flavor of old whiskey. If this method was pursued by distillers and spirits made 2d and 3d proof, it would not only benefit the seller, but would be an advantage to the buyer and consumer—and was any particular distiller to pursue this mode and brand his casks, it would raise the character of his liquor, and give it such an ascendancy as to preclude the sale of any other, beyond what scarcity or an emergency might impel in a commercial city.[57]

The steady pace of western migration continued unabated for the next eight decades, a process that largely defined the course of the nation's history. Where people led, alcoholic beverages were sure to follow, and the availability of enormous quantities of cheap grain, combined with the growing population, spurred the expansion of the whiskey industry. Migration to the area that in 1792 became the state of Kentucky already had begun before 1783, and the first whiskey distilleries in the region were established soon thereafter. Within 20 years, 5 new states had been added to the original 13, and distilleries were operating in every one of them.[58]

By the year 1810, producing whiskey had grown to be one of the largest industries in America. The industrial census compiled in that year listed more than 14,000 distilleries, making almost 26 million gallons of spirit. Rum production still accounted for almost three million gallons of that total, with the vast majority made in Massachusetts and other New England states. The combined value of rum and whiskey was $15.5 million, or roughly 8 to 9 percent of the total estimated value of the country's manufactured products. Even so, the industry continued to be dominated by small-scale operators, who produced hundreds, not thousands, of gallons of whiskey each year. Virginia was first in the number of distilleries, with 3,662, while Pennsylvania was a close second, and Kentucky was a distant third. By modern standards most of these distilleries were quite small, as the average volume of spirits produced in Virginia and Kentucky was less than 1,000 gallons per year.[59]

In addition to documenting the overall growth of the distilling industry, the results of the 1810 census indicate that the focus of whiskey making already had begun to shift west of the Appalachian Mountains, into upstate New York, western Pennsylvania, Ohio, and Kentucky. Between them the 6,500 distilleries operating in those four states produced more than 10 million gallons of fruit and grain spirits, or roughly 47 percent of the national total, valued at almost $7 million. This trend accelerated over the next several decades, as the mountain barrier fostered two distinct grain markets. Grain continued to be difficult and expensive to ship overland, and when farmers sent their crop down the Mississippi River to New Orleans and beyond, low prices meant modest profits at best. Therefore, the poor market for grain grown west of the mountains spurred its conversion into spirits, while the high prices paid for eastern grain discouraged its use in making whiskey.[60]

Improvements in transportation that began in the 1810s and accelerated in the 1820s had a major effect on the national trade networks, and in turn spurred dramatic changes to the whiskey industry. With the opening of the Ohio Canal and the Erie Canal in New York, and the widespread use of steamboats on the Mississippi and other western rivers, the cost of shipping dropped significantly. In addition, both steamboats and canals allowed for two-way traffic, which had not been possible when the dependence on river currents meant that trade could only travel downstream. Reduced shipping charges allowed producers to transport their goods more widely, taking advantage of varying market conditions. While this development benefited distillers to some degree, it was a particular boon for grain farmers. The enlarged market for their products allowed them to shift their exports accordingly and to choose whether to sell their crop to be made into flour or into whiskey. The effect of nationalizing the market for grain was to concentrate whiskey production in those localities where farmers were at a competitive disadvantage. In areas where farmers could sell their harvest at higher prices, distilling became unprofitable, but where competition for grain was slack, distilleries continued to operate and prosper. For a variety of reasons, farmers in southwestern Ohio, upstate New York, and southeast and southwest Pennsylvania found themselves in the latter situation, and by 1840 more than half of the nation's grain spirits came from those areas.[61]

The number of distilleries nationwide rose from roughly 14,000 in 1810 to 20,000 in 1830, marking both the height of the whiskey glut and the peak of alcohol consumption nationwide. As the supply of whiskey continued to expand, prices inevitably dropped, and by the early 1820s whiskey that had cost 60 cents per gallon in Philadelphia a few years before had declined to less than half that amount. For the western states the cost of overproduction was steep, as whiskey had been one of their few profitable exports, and their economies suffered accordingly. By 1830 the number of distilleries in operation fell to less than half of the total 10 years earlier.[62]

A second development was that small distillers lost business to larger, more efficient competitors who served the national market. This trend is demonstrated by comparing the census figures for distilled spirits between the years 1810 and 1850. In 1810, 14,191 distilleries produced an average of 1,818 gallons of spirit, but in 1850 the number of producers had plummeted to 1,217 while their output had sky rocketed to an average of 39,330 gallons. The totals include all fruit and grain spirits, with 2.8 million gallons of rum (10.1 percent of the total) in 1810 and 6.5 million gallons (13.6 percent) in 1850.[63]

Figures for the distilling industry in the state of New York for the period between 1810 and 1860 provide greater detail for the twinned trends of declining numbers of producers combined with improved output. In 1810, 591 distilleries in the state produced 2.1 million gallons of spirits. Fifteen years later, the spirits industry everywhere was in the midst of its period of unprecedented growth, and in New York almost twice as many operators (1,129) generated more than eight times as much (18 million gallons) product. By 1840, the whiskey glut and changing market conditions combined to reduce the number of distilleries and their level of production, to 212 operators and 12 million gallons of spirits. The number of distilleries continued to dwindle to 77 in 1860, but their output increased to 16.2 million gallons. Thus, the average output per distillery increased from 3,553 gallons in 1810, to 15,943 gallons in 1825, to 56,603 gallons in 1840, and to 210,389 gallons in 1860. The impressive upward trend in the production of spirits in New York was not solely related to beverage alcohol, however, as the state had become a major supplier for industrial uses.[64]

The inclusion of industrial grade distilled spirits in the census data makes it a challenge to compare levels of production of beverage alcohol between the states. In 1810, when industrial alcohol made up a small percentage of the overall volume, the four states that produced far and away the largest quantity of spirits were Pennsylvania, Virginia, New

York, and Massachusetts. Massachusetts remained the primary producer of rum in the country, with 86 percent of the $1.6 million worth of spirits distilled in the state generated from molasses. In the second tier of producers, whose output exceeded $700,000 in value, Kentucky was noteworthy because of the large number (2,000) of distilleries that were listed, ranking the state third overall in that category. By 1850, Pennsylvania was first in the number of distilleries, although Ohio and New York had overtaken Pennsylvania in the volume of spirits produced. It is likely that industrial alcohol made up a significant percentage of the output of all three of those states in 1850. [65]

In the years following the Civil War, Americans turned with relish from the destructive pastimes of war to building a transcontinental commercial colossus. Led by the unprecedented spread of the railroads—and of the steel, oil, and other heavy manufacturing and extractive industries that grew along with them—the American economy expanded at an unprecedented pace. The fortunes of the whiskey industry paralleled those of the nation as a whole. According to the federal manufacturing census, the value of distilled spirits totaled more than $26 million in 1860; 20 years later the figure had grown to $41 million; and in 1900 the value had multiplied to upwards of $96 million. By that year Illinois was far and away the single largest producer of spirits, valued at $38 million, with Indiana, Ohio, and Kentucky, in that order, trailing far behind. The first three states on this list were heavily involved in producing industrial spirits, however, and it is likely that Kentucky had by then taken its place as the largest producer of beverage alcohol in the nation. The scale of the individual distilleries expanded dramatically as well, as their number actually declined by 16 percent between 1860 and 1900, while the average value of output increased four-fold. Once again, much of this increase reflected the impact of producing alcohol for industrial applications rather than for consumption, but the alcoholic beverage industry clearly experienced significant growth.[66]

The burgeoning economy of the post-Civil War decades also provided unprecedented opportunities for unscrupulous men with powerful connections to defraud the public in a variety of ways. The eight years of the administration of President Ulysses Grant (1869–1877) were marked by many scandalous acts of financial and political corruption, and the liquor industry became a ripe target for manipulation. The tax on liquor that had been imposed by the Lincoln administration as a means of raising revenues to help fight the war continued in place after victory in 1865. In 1871 Republican Party operatives seized on the tax revenues as a source of funds to help finance the election campaigns of men in Missouri and in other western states who supported President Grant. Many previous admirers of the president, including former Union general and U.S. Senator Carl Schurz of Missouri, were actively opposing Grant's nomination for reelection in 1872. To combat Schurz and his supporters, Grant dispatched John McDonald, Supervisor of the Internal Revenue, to Missouri to find a way to keep party members in the president's camp. McDonald quickly found the money to finance this effort by establishing a clandestine "whiskey ring" comprised of distillers, storekeepers, and government agents and clerks, who were able to siphon off a portion of the tax revenues that were due the Federal Treasury. The illicit "whiskey money" found its way into the coffers of local Republican Party officials and was used to finance newspapers whose editorial stance was favorable to the Grant administration.[67]

Although Grant was re-elected in 1872, the members of the whiskey ring opted not to dismantle their profitable venture, turning it into a purely criminal enterprise, instead. While St. Louis, Missouri, continued to be the center of the fraudulent activities, the ring spread to Chicago, Milwaukee, New Orleans, and other cities, and by 1873 the conspirators were defrauding the government of an estimated $1.5 million dollars annually. The ring could not succeed without the complicity, or the negligence, of Treasury Department officials, but in 1874 the stance of the department underwent a dramatic change. In June of that year President Grant appointed as the Secretary of the Treasury an aspiring reformer by the name of Benjamin Bristow, who had his own political ambitions. He immediately focused his attention on ending the ring's thievery.[68]

Secretary Bristow launched an in-depth investigation, quickly concluding that Internal Revenue officials were heavily involved in the illegal operation. In an attempt to expose the guilty parties, in January 1875 Bristow ordered that the supervisors be transferred, an action that Grant initially approved. Grant almost immediately changed his mind, however, reasoning that it would be counterproductive to the investigation, as well as politically risky, since it might further weaken support for the president within the local ranks of the Republican Party. Fortunately for Bristow, another opportunity soon arrived in the form of a local journalist, named Myron Colony, who agreed to serve as a secret investigator on behalf of the government. Colony was able to use his contacts within the St. Louis business community to compile detailed records of the volume of whiskey that was distilled, to be compared with the amounts that were reported to the government. The discrepancies clearly indicated the extent of the fraud, and gave Bristow the evidence he needed to arrest more than 300 members of the St. Louis whiskey ring, and to seize the holdings of the implicated distillers and rectifiers. In the end, more than 100 individuals—including John McDonald, the man who launched the conspiracy—were convicted, and more than $3 million in stolen money was recovered.[69]

What may have been an unintended consequence of Bristow's success in exposing the conspirators was heightened political pressure on the already beleaguered Grant administration. The Treasury secretary, who also harbored aspirations to win the Republican presidential nomination in 1876, maintained that Grant's private secretary, Orville Babcock, was implicated as a member of the ring. Bristow also surmised that this connection had led Grant to intervene to hinder the investigation in order to protect his friend. In December 1875, Babcock was indicted by the Grand Jury and brought to trial in St. Louis. The president found himself in the unprecedented position of testifying to the court on behalf of his aide. Babcock ultimately was acquitted, and no direct evidence was produced to link Grant to any illegal activities, but the "whiskey ring scandal" was an additional taint marking the Grant administration as probably the most corrupt in American history.[70]

The distilled spirits industry was beset by a second episode of ethically questionable and sometimes highly illegal behavior that began in 1887 and continued until 1895. A group of midwestern businessmen combined to form a "trust," an elaborate business partnership, with the intention of acquiring a major share of the industry and then manipulating the market to their advantage. Officially named the Distillers and Cattle Feeder's Trust, the group was popularly known as the "whiskey trust." This was a misnomer, as the original combine produced alcohol and neutral spirits exclusively, and later on only one of their distilleries produced a limited quantity of whiskey. The trust was located in Illinois, one of the largest producers of industrial alcohol in the nation, with 24 distilleries initially joining the combine. At first the conspirators were successful in raising prices and profits, but independent producers sprang up to provide strong competition that drove prices back down and reduced revenues. The directors apparently took a variety of extralegal steps in response, and the organization's secretary, George J. Gibson, of Peoria, Illinois, was arrested in 1891 under the charge of plotting to destroy a competing distillery. Two years later the trust directors were indicted on a charge of intent to restrain trade, but the action was not upheld in Federal Court. The State of Illinois sought to cancel the trust's certificate of incorporation (which had been granted in 1890), but further legal actions were forestalled when the trust went into receivership in January 1895, and the corporation was dissolved later that year.[71]

Many of the distilleries operating at this time undoubtedly had incorporated a number of the improvements in distilling technology that had been developed over the preceding century. But the scale and sophistication of the operations continued to vary across a broad spectrum, and comparing two distilleries, one from Kentucky and the other in Ohio, helps to illustrate the range. The Staley distillery was located near the city of New Carlisle, in western Ohio, and produced rye whiskey between 1831 and 1905. The still house was established to complement a substantial gristmill that had been erected in 1818. Andrew Staley took over the property from his father, Elias, in 1866 and ran the distillery in association with the mill until 1877. At that time he discontinued milling for the public and concentrated instead on supplying the needs of his family and of the distillery. Staley continued to operate the distillery until 1905, and a plan that depicts the arrangement of his distilling equipment probably dates to the later years of the enterprise. It shows that Staley had streamlined the process by linking as many as 21 fermenting tubs so that their wash was pumped into the "singling" still, after which the distillate passed through the condenser and finally emerged through the worm tub. The first round distillate then was redistilled in the smaller "doubling" still, positioned nearby, with an attached worm tub, before final barreling. Therefore, even though highly efficient "perpetual" stills had been introduced in the United States almost 100 years before, Staley's operation continued along much more traditional lines.[72]

If the Staley distillery may be taken to represent the mid-scale, rural, traditional enterprises that continued to operate in the latter part of the 19th century, the O.F.C. (Old Fire Copper) distillery located outside of Frankfort, Kentucky, exemplifies the highly capitalized, more overtly commercial distilleries that had grown up to participate in the national whiskey market. O.F.C. was the brainchild of E.H. Taylor, Jr., a legendary character in the history of the Kentucky whiskey industry. Taylor was involved in operating seven distilleries over the course of his career, and he is credited with making significant contributions in transforming whiskey making into a mature industry. This included helping to popularize the notion of brand name marketing, first with his promotion of the Old Crow and Old Pepper brands in the years just before and after the Civil War. Taylor's most ambitious project was the Old Taylor distillery, located just outside Frankfort, which he built in the late 1880s and turned into a showplace, with elaborate architectural and landscaping embellishments. According to one source, "It had pergolas, reflecting pools, stone bridges, gazebos, and a limestone distillery building adorned with turrets, towers and crenellated battlements of a medieval castle." Always attuned to promotional opportunities, Taylor used the site to host elaborate parties to further his own political ends as well as to help market the Old Taylor brand.[73]

In 1869 Taylor was instrumental in establishing the O.F.C. and Carlisle distilleries in Frankfort. Taylor's involvement with the O.F.C. distillery was brief, as he sold his share of its ownership within a year of the company's founding. However, the succeeding owners seem to have followed Taylor's lead, as the building itself was a landmark of self-promotion. The O.F.C. buildings were substantial masonry structures, with handsome arched windows inscribed with the initials "OFC." According to a promotional pamphlet published in 1886, the many up-to-the-minute features of this particular plant were augmented by the authors' claims for the singular merits of the surrounding region for making whiskey: the area's "waters, climate, and special facilities have long since caused it to be known as the almost exclusive locality for the manufacture of pure, old-style, sour-mash whiskey." In their emphasis on the natural advantages of the Kentucky setting for making high-quality whiskey, the breathless language of the pamphlet prefigures the familiar claims to be found in countless advertising pieces that appeared over the succeeding century.[74]

The description of the distilling process at the O.F.C. distillery emphasized the marriage of state-of-the-art equipment with traditional, time-honored methods. The grain was passed through corrugated metal roller mills to produce a "superior" and "more even grind." Mashing was accomplished in traditional hogsheads, however, and was "conducted... by hand," before the liquid was transferred to copper-lined masonry fermentation vats. Distilling was carried out using two pot stills, for singling and doubling, heated over an open fire—a surprisingly retrograde practice almost 100 years after the innovation of perpetual steam-heated stills. But instead of using traditional worm tubs, the alcohol vapor was condensed back into liquid form through the use of cylindrical copper columns, which were connected by copper pipes to receiving tubs.[75]

A distilling manual published in 1889, entitled *Monzert's Practical Distiller*, captures the wide varieties of equipment and processes that had been developed and were available to distillers at that time. These ranged from the "ordinary copper still," which was virtually identical to those that were the norm a century earlier, to elaborate column perpetual stills, and a variety of sophisticated implements to produce various specialized spirits. By the use of highly efficient condensers, it was possible to obtain alcohol of extremely high proof (190 or 95 percent alcohol); the virtually flavorless product would have been used for industrial purposes rather than for beverage alcohol. Monzert also described methods of artificially imparting qualities to new spirits to mimic the characteristics of aging, testifying that a significant number of producers still were taking the cheaper and easier route of doctoring inferior whiskey to approximate the characteristics of more refined spirit.[76]

One of the most important factors that affected the whiskey industry beginning in the years after the Civil War was the practice of branding. As early as the 1820s specific brands of whiskey were being promoted in Kentucky, featured in newspapers and other advertising materials. In 1826 a notice appeared in the Paris, Kentucky, *Western Citizen*, specifying that "Spears's and William's best Old Whiskey" was available by the barrel. The identities of other makers also were prominently displayed, with an auction notice printed in 1849 relating that "a choice lot of copper distilled Whiskey, consisting of about 200 barrels" was included in the items offered for sale, and that "Most of said Whiskey is of Kellar's make, and 35 or 40 barrels of it is 10 years old." A year later, another announcement indicated that more of the distiller's product was available at auction: "Old Bourbon Whiskey at Auction. I will sell, on the public square, on the first Monday in December next, 15 barrels of Old Bourbon Whiskey, made by Solomon Kellar, one of the best Whisky makers in the world, and this lot not to be surpassed by any." In addition to specific brands, these notices indicate that by the mid-19th century, the term "bourbon" had entered the general vocabulary as an accepted descriptor signifying an aged whiskey that probably used corn as its main ingredient. [77]

The question of when the first whiskey was made that generally approximated the characteristics of what is now recognized as "bourbon" has been a subject of considerable debate over the years. A federal law passed in 1964 stipulates that in order for whiskey to be considered bourbon, its ingredients must include at least 51 percent corn and it must be aged for at least two years in newly charred oak barrels. The law essentially codified the developments of the previous century, when for economic reasons corn replaced rye as the dominant ingredient for most of the whiskey that was made in America, and aging the spirit in charred barrels became widespread. The practice of charring barrels has been a particular point of contention, with several fanciful "creation myths" put forward to explain its origin. The most prevalent hypothesis falls into the category of "happy accident," with the charring occurring as a result of using torches to sterilize the inside of reused barrels. After putting their whiskey into these containers, so the story goes, distillers and consumers were pleasantly surprised to find that the taste had improved and the whiskey had taken on a reddish brown color.[78]

That no such convenient chain of events is likely to have occurred is indicated by the various sources that together demonstrate that storing liquor in charred barrels to improve its flavor was generally known long before the term bourbon was ever used to describe Kentucky whiskey. Many 18th-century sources refer to "aged" liquor, and to rum and other spirits whose brown color was attributed to time spent in barrels. A particularly informative source is an English tavern keepers' guide, published in London in 1781, that specifically referred to the practice of "firing" containers used to store rum. In words suggesting that he was reminding his readers rather than providing them with novel information, the author remarked that the range in colors found in Caribbean rum was "owing to the newness of the puncheons [casks], and some being fired more than others." Thus, as with the general practice of aging spirits, using charred containers in which to store the whiskey was neither previously unknown nor the result of accident or the insight of some pioneering frontier distiller. Instead, selecting the ingredients and adopting the processes that combined to produce the defining characteristics of what became the most popular type of American whiskey was a gradual development linked to local conditions, emerging markets, and changing tastes.[79]

The issue of protecting consumers from unscrupulous purveyors of inferior, and sometimes hazardous, spirits took on greater immediacy for the large distillers who sought to protect their industry from the criticisms that such practices evoked. Ambitious producers like E.H. Taylor, who was a major player in the national whiskey market, also embraced the idea of branding as a means of distinguishing their products and building a loyal following of consumers. The lack of government regulations over product purity and the lax enforcement of trademark laws combined to undermine the efforts on the part of industry leaders on both of these fronts. Given that most distillers still were engaged in manipulating their product in a variety of ways to ready it for market, Taylor and his allies were confronted within their own ranks by strong opposition to their effort to solicit government standards to address their concerns. Only after considerable debate and acrimony was the Bottled-in-Bond Act passed in 1897. The law specified that in order to earn the government's designation of approval, whiskey had to be made at one place in one season, aged at least four years in government-supervised warehouses, and bottled at 100 proof (50 percent alcohol). The name of the maker also had to be clearly identified on the label. Although the Act did not guarantee purity, it was a major step forward in regulating the industry, and the bottled-in-bond designation soon became the imprimatur for dependable spirit.[80]

Almost a decade later, the passage of the Pure Food and Drug Act of 1906 gave additional strength to the effort to safeguard consumers. It specifically prohibited "adulterating," or adding non-compatible ingredients to alcoholic beverages, and "misbranding," or misrepresenting the contents of containers. Any grain spirit that was "rectified" (usually passed through charcoal or otherwise subjected to additional methods of purification) or "blended" (a mixture of various spirits and possibly other ingredients) had to be identified as "compound" or "blended" whiskey. Distillers of those spirits objected that the designations unjustly stigmatized their products. This led to continued conflict that was finally resolved when President William Howard Taft ruled that to be considered whiskey the spirit must be made from 100 percent grain. Although far from satisfying all of the concerns of industry members, the resulting regulations gave consumers some guidance as to the nature of the products available to them.[81]

The passage of the Food and Drug Act may have helped to set the record straight in terms of the basic ingredients of whiskey, but it did nothing to dispel the traditional belief that continued to circulate widely about the medicinal qualities of alcohol. The effort that Dr. Benjamin Rush had led to discredit the notion of beverage alcohol as the doctor's friend may have made inroads among many segments of society, but a century later distillers still loudly touted the health benefits of their products. According to an advertisement placed by the makers of Mount Vernon Rye whiskey in a popular outlet, *Munsey's Magazine*, in 1895:

At times we all need a stimulant, either to restore strength after illness, to ward off the effects of chill or cold, and to tone up the system, when by too close attention to business, exposure or other causes, the vitality is below par. The kind and quality of the stimulant to be used is of much importance. Our best physicians prescribe, for our climate, American whiskey, and those who have made an exhaustive study of the subject pronounce whiskey made from rye the best for medicinal use, as not possessing the heating effects of Bourbon or other whiskies made from all or part corn. Naturally the inquiry comes: 'What brand and in what shape can a rye whiskey be obtained that the physician or consumer may feel is strictly pure and reliable?' Upon thorough investigation the

Mount Vernon Pure Rye Whiskey,

bottled at the distillery with an absolutely satisfactory guarantee of purity and original condition, will be found to answer this inquiry. The distillery bottling may be known by its square shaped bottle bearing the guaranteed label of purity. [82]

Within one short paragraph, the advertisers managed to touch on most of the traditional tropes used to promote any number of "quality of life" products. Rather vague but troublesome symptoms—"vitality below par"—were followed by reassurances that the medical community could offer an effective remedy. In this case, the "best" physicians were comfortable prescribing not just any whiskey, but only that which matched the exact qualities of the Mount Vernon brand, as the perfect restorative tonic. And finally, an assurance of purity and quality predicated on the fact that bottling "in the factory" was an effective guarantee of reliability.

The belief that beverage alcohol was beneficial to health continued to have wide currency well into the 20th century, although the views of the medical profession waffled back and forth on the topic. As of 1917 the American Medical Association adopted as their official policy the statement that alcohol had "no scientific value" as a therapeutic treatment. But many physicians continued to prescribe alcohol as a tonic, stimulant, preventive measure, and even as a cure for acute illnesses. The Volstead Act that ushered Prohibition onto the national scene in 1920 nodded in the direction of the interests of these doctors and the public by including the stipulation that "a person may, without a permit, purchase and use liquor for medicinal purposes when prescribed by a physician." Two years later the AMA made a remarkable about-face and countermanded the 1917 ruling. This change of heart may be charitably portrayed as a high-minded protest on their part against the unwarranted encroachment by Congress on their right to treat their patients as they saw fit. It may not be coincidental that doctors were reaping significant profits from the booming prescription trade, however. The act restricted the volume of spirits that could be prescribed to no more than one pint per person over a ten day period, yet that was sufficient to encourage a number of distilleries to participate in the medicinal spirits business. Chief among those entering the market was the American Medicinal Spirits Company, organized in 1920 and headquartered in Louisville, Kentucky, which incorporated a number of well-known brands, including Old Forester bourbon and Mount Vernon Rye whiskey.[83]

In 1870 Old Forester brand bourbon was the first whiskey to be offered for sale solely in bottles; the brand was kept alive during Prohibition as a "medicinal" whiskey, and resumed wide distribution after repeal.

The public relations benefits to be gained from bottling helped to spur the growing popularity of branding during the last decades of the 19th century. As long as most whiskey was sold and distributed in barrels, the security of the product could not be guaranteed. Standard practice had called for whiskey to be transported in barrels and sold by the glass in drinking establishments, and it was a simple matter for unscrupulous retailers to add foreign liquid to adulterate the original spirit. The Bottled-in-Bond Act of 1897 encouraged distillers to bottle their whiskey as a way to guarantee the purity of their product. George Garvin Brown, the founder of the Brown-Forman company, is credited as the first to ship and sell whiskey in bottles in 1870. The brand was Old Forester bourbon, and Brown hoped that making it available solely in bottles would elevate its stature as a dependable product of high quality. Brown's example seems to have had little impact on other distillers, however, and it was not until the early 1900s that whiskey was commonly sold in bottles. Cost remained the major impediment, as bottling was only made affordable with the invention of an automated bottle making machine in 1903. Once the cost of bottling was reduced to an economical level, distillers had an additional incentive to develop distinctive brand labels to identify their products.[84]

The four years of the Civil War slowed the momentum that the temperance movement had enjoyed in the antebellum decades, but with the end of the war it was reinvigorated by a variety of factors. As was the case when temperance first burst onto the American scene in the 1820s and 1830s, its growth was fed in part by fears engendered by widespread social change. Among these developments were the perceived detrimental effects on American society resulting from industrialization, the growth of cities, westward migration, and stepped-up immigration from Eastern Europe. In addition to other social concerns linked to the increased flow of immigrants, they were widely but erroneously believed to have a tradition of particularly heavy drinking that anti-liquor reformers viewed with special alarm. As had been the case during antebellum days, the renewed temperance movement was spearheaded by a powerful combination of concerned women, emboldened clergy, and sympathetic reformers of various stripes. In short order several temperance organizations were formed, led by the most influential of all, the Women's Christian Temperance Union in 1874.[85]

Saloons became the principal target of the WCTU, as they were both the most conspicuous public manifestation of intemperance, and the locus for the many other vices associated with drinking: drunkenness, gambling, profanity, prostitution, political corruption, and crime of all sorts. Thus, saloons were viewed as a danger to family life, republican values, community standards, and even to the cause of women's suffrage. Attempts to form prohibition political parties had only modest success throughout the 1880s, but by the 1890s there was growing sentiment among a broader spectrum of society that temperance was desirable as a national policy goal. Prohibition melded with the broader progressive reform agenda, which viewed temperance as crucial to alleviating poverty, lessening political corruption, and spurring the general improvement of society. From 1899 until 1911, the specific campaign against the evil of saloons was identified with the efforts of Carry A. Nation, a religious zealot and some-time vigilante from Kansas, who literally took matters (and a hatchet) into her own hands to terrorize saloon keepers from coast-to-coast.[86]

The Anti-Saloon League was formed in the early 1890s (the national organization in 1895) to establish a platform that could work effectively with both major political parties to further the anti-liquor goal. The league worked to garner support for any candidate, Republican or Democrat, as long as he was willing to vote for dry legislation. The league exercised its political muscle across a broad spectrum of government, advocating simultaneously at the county, state, and national levels, with considerable success. By 1903 as much as one-third of the country lived under some form of prohibition, a figure that grew to 50 percent 10 years later. By 1914 there was mounting support for a Constitutional Amendment prohibiting liquor, which continued to gain strength during World War I. Entry into the conflict fostered a commitment for national unity and sacrifice to further the war effort that increased popular support for prohibition. The league also exploited Americans' anti-German hysteria by deliberately associating beer with German-American brewers. "Kaiserism abroad and booze at home must go," declared Wayne Wheeler, the league's general counsel and wily Washington lobbyist.[87]

The proponents of prohibition faced, and then found their way around, a significant financial obstruction to achieving their goal. The attempt on the part of the Washington administration to generate much needed revenue for the federal government by taxing beverage alcohol had largely failed in the 1790s. The tax was struck down by President Jefferson in 1802, although it returned briefly to help finance the War of 1812. With the outbreak of the Civil War, the federal government once again looked to the liquor industry as a source of funds, and the tax was reestablished by the Lincoln administration in 1862. This time, the tax was not discontinued at the end of the war, however, and by the last decades of the century the tax on liquor was responsible for contributing more than one-half of federal revenues. Thus, prohibition would mean a major decline in funds, and it is no coincidence that the first federal income tax was passed into law in 1913 as a means of making up the anticipated shortfall.[88]

In 1918 the Volstead Act calling for the prohibition of beverage alcohol throughout the land was passed by Congress. In January 1919 the Act was ratified by the necessary 36 states and duly added to the Constitution as the Eighteenth Amendment, and nationwide Prohibition took effect one year later. The federal authorities embarked on a sincere but flawed campaign to enforce the law, with federal agents confiscating distilling equipment, intercepting shipments of liquor imported from overseas, and destroying vast quantities of illicit alcohol. From the beginning, millions of citizens disregarded the law and continued to drink "bootleg" alcohol, however. Rampant lawlessness and violence attending the bootlegging industry skyrocketed, along with the financial and social costs from attempting to enforce the law, and pressure from the public mounted to call an end to the "noble experiment." By the early 1930s the majority of the American people believed that Prohibition had failed, and the Twenty-First Amendment to the Constitution repealing national Prohibition was ratified in December 1933. While lively debate continues among scholars over the long-term impact of Prohibition, the immediate result of its repeal on the liquor industry was naturally profound. Many of the closed distilleries and breweries never reopened, but a number of firms had found a way to survive the dry years and soon resumed production.[89]

The long-term trend of consolidation within the liquor industry that had begun even before Prohibition continued and accelerated in the decades following repeal. From more than 400 establishments in 1914, only 27 to 33 distilleries continued to operate during Prohibition. Notable among the survivors in the whiskey industry was the American Medicinal Alcohol Company, which had been able to keep a number of distilleries online and in good operating condition. In 1933 the company was renamed the National Distillers Products Corporation, and with control over seven distilleries it was the largest single unit of the American liquor industry. By 1936 the group operated nine distilleries producing as much as 40,000,000 gallons of spirit. According to one source, in 1935 the total production of whiskey in the United States was 184,839,630 gallons, a remarkable increase over pre-Prohibition levels, with the National Distillers share at more than 26 million gallons, or 14 percent of the total. [90]

The landscape of alcohol consumption had changed in other dramatic ways over the period of the enforced 13-year hiatus. Whether because of the influx and popularity of more bland Canadian whiskey, or exposure to a wider range of liquors, changing tastes favored spirits with less pronounced flavor. The sweeter, smoother, corn-based bourbon that was the most popular type of American whiskey before Prohibition rebounded to capture much of its share of the market. But the more pronounced flavor characteristic of rye whiskeys was less amenable to the new taste. Distillers naturally turned to aggressive advertising in the reinvigorated national print media to bolster their brands. Sophisticated campaigns were developed, like that launched by the makers of Mount Vernon Rye whiskey in 1935, which often referred to the historic roots of the industry and the imagined association of the brand with George Washington. Already before Prohibition, rye whiskey was produced almost exclusively in the states of Pennsylvania and Maryland, the historic heartland of the traditional spirit. Over the next several decades production of first one, then another, and finally almost all of the rye whiskeys on the market was discontinued. The venerable Mount Vernon Rye brand, which had been in business almost continuously since the 1850s, was a particularly notable casualty, ceasing operation in 1957.[91]

Steadily increasing competition from other types of alcohol was the rule of the day throughout the last half of the 20th century, with whiskey of all types losing market share to wine, beer, and white liquors at an alarming rate in the 1970s and 1980s. Many more brands have failed in the interim, although in recent years a "whiskey revival" has encouraged distillers to expand both the number and variety of their offerings. Even so, in 2005 only 19 brands accounted for 95 percent of the whiskey made in America, and they were operated by eight companies, almost all of which were international conglomerates operating on a massive scale.[92]

CHAPTER 5

MAKING GEORGE WASHINGTON'S WHISKEY

In 1933, staff with the Commonwealth of Virginia's division of parks proposed constructing a replica of George Washington's whiskey distillery. They hoped that its novelty and strong association with George Washington would transform the property into a major attraction for the burgeoning ranks of tourists drawn to the Old Dominion to learn more of its rich history and to experience the sites where those events occurred. A lack of funding and public support thwarted their plans, but more than 70 years later another group of visionaries banded together and succeeded where the earlier effort had failed. After a decade of planning, research, fundraising, and construction, the meticulously recreated distillery joined the nearby previously restored gristmill to provide a unique picture of these once ubiquitous fixtures of 18th-century American industry. The story of the effort to recreate Washington's distillery features important roles played by historians, archaeologists, museum administrators, and educators, in partnership with some of the most prominent master distillers in the country. None of their efforts would have come to any consequence, however, without the vision and financial support of leaders of the liquor industry itself, which not only supplied the funds to carry out the project, but also shared the commitment to tell the story of a little-known aspect of Washington's career as a canny businessman, entrepreneur, and whiskey distiller.[1]

The first phase of the project began in 1995, when a later generation of officials with the Commonwealth of Virginia approached Mount Vernon to propose that the foundation take over the site of Washington's Gristmill State Park. The state had operated the property as a public park since 1933, but the officials convinced the Mount Vernon board that it could only reach its full potential as an educational resource under their management. While priority was given to restoring the gristmill, which the state already had reconstructed on the footprint of the original building, Mount Vernon's archaeologists surveyed the seven-acre tract in 1997 with hopes of relocating the remains of the still house. The archaeologists succeeded in finding the evidence for the building, and then returned two years later to begin to excavate the site. After the first year of fieldwork, it was clear that the remains were remarkably well preserved, and they promised to provide the physical evidence needed to complement the documentary records in drawing a detailed portrait of the still house and the layout of the distilling apparatus. At this point, the Mount Vernon staff and members of the board were united in their belief that sufficient information was likely to be available to justify reconstructing Washington's distillery. But the cost of conducting years of additional archaeological and documentary research, and then of designing and constructing an authentic replica of the distillery, was well beyond the normal operating resources of the Ladies' Association. To be able to carry out this ambitious and costly project, willing partners would need to be found.[2]

One likely ally was identified almost immediately. The Brown-Forman Company of Louisville, Kentucky, was the largest family-run distilling enterprise in America, and had compiled a distinguished record of support both for historic preservation in general and for the heritage of the distilling industry in particular. Included in their portfolio of brands was Old Forester, the first whiskey to be offered solely in bottles beginning in 1870; Jack Daniels, the most popular whiskey made in the United States; and Woodford Reserve, the only major brand of bourbon in the country that was produced using traditional pot still technology. The site of the Woodford

Reserve distillery (then known as Labrot and Graham) was the historic Old Oscar Pepper distillery, which had been established in the early 19th century. Many of the original structures had been lovingly refurbished, and in 2000 the property was designated as a National Historic Landmark. Coincidentally, a long-time member of the Mount Vernon board, Eleanor Newman, of Louisville, was well acquainted with members of the Brown family, owners of Brown-Forman.[3]

At the behest of Carew Lee, who at the time was the Regent (chairman of the board) of the Mount Vernon Ladies' Association, Mrs. Newman approached Owsley Brown II, Chief Executive Officer of Brown-Forman. Brown immediately expressed the company's willingness to support the distillery project. Mark Smith, Brown-Forman's Director of Government Relations, had worked closely with staff at the National Park Service in developing the National Historic Landmark nomination for the Old Oscar Pepper Distillery. Smith was tasked with meeting with members of the Mount Vernon staff to learn more details of where the project stood at that time and to make plans for the future. In the meantime, Smith contacted Peter Cressy, President of the Distilled Spirits Council of the United States, the liquor industry trade association, which was headquartered in Washington, DC. This was both to inform Cressy of the Mount Vernon proposal, and to discuss the possibility of whether DISCUS might have some interest in joining Brown-Forman in supporting the effort to reestablish the first president's distillery.[4]

In May 2000, Cressy and Smith traveled to Mount Vernon to meet with Richard Dressner and Dennis Pogue, Mount Vernon's Director of Development and Director of Preservation, respectively. The Mount Vernon staffers outlined their ideas for reconstructing and opening the distillery to the public as a major educational facility, but they also made it clear that the organization lacked the resources to carry out the project without outside support. After visiting the site to observe the archaeological team in action, and to see first-hand the remains of the building's stone foundations, the masonry floor of the mashing area, and other features that were emerging from the red Virginia clay, Cressy immediately recognized the potential of the project for its educational and public relations value. As a group that had always embraced its long history and was proud of its important role in the development of American society, Cressy believed that the project represented an opportunity for the spirits industry to help spread its story of the traditional role of beverage alcohol as a normal part of American life. Furthermore, Washington's own habits of modest liquor consumption and his many statements on both the benefits and the drawbacks of strong drink made him a particularly appropriate example for promoting the cause of drinking in moderation.[5]

Cressy agreed to take the idea to his board of directors, and within a few hours and after a half-dozen phone calls, he had secured a commitment of $1.2 million to be provided by a consortium of DISCUS member distillers and the Wine and Spirits Wholesalers Association of America. The plans that the partner organizations ultimately agreed upon called for building an exhaustively researched and rigorously authentic recreation of Washington's distillery. The distilling room was to house replicas of the five furnaces and pot stills, along with a boiler for heating water used in cooking the mash, up to a dozen mash tubs, and a system of troughs and drains used to circulate water to cool and condense the spirits. Costumed interpreters would be on hand to demonstrate the art of distilling as it was practiced in Washington's day. As such, this would be the only site in the country where visitors could come to witness an authentic 18th-century distillery in action. The second floor of the structure was to feature two period rooms representing the domestic spaces set aside for the distillery manager and his assistant, as well as a theater displaying a 10-minute video on the story of Washington's distillery, and a small gallery with exhibits focused on the history of the whiskey industry in America.[6]

MAKING GEORGE WASHINGTON'S WHISKEY   195

It was anticipated that the archaeological excavations could take as long as three more years to complete followed by at least two years devoted to its design and construction. All parties were committed to using that time to generate interest in the project on the part of the public and to begin to tell the largely unknown story of George Washington's foray into whiskey making. Frank Coleman, DISCUS Vice President for Media Relations, was enlisted to work with Mount Vernon staff to develop a plan to ensure maximum public exposure for the ongoing research efforts. Over the next decade the resulting campaign succeeded well beyond anyone's wildest expectations, with hundreds of "hits" in the national and international print, broadcast, and digital media, including feature stories that appeared in dozens of countries around the globe.

The kick-off to the media campaign occurred on May 21, 2001. On that day, empty barrels standing in for 12 of the DISCUS members' finest products—bourbon, Tennessee whiskey, rye whiskey, and rum—were transported to Mount Vernon on a vintage sailing vessel, while barrels containing the real spirits were stowed in a warehouse elsewhere on the estate. The brands represented were Jim Beam, Wild Turkey, Virginia Gentleman, Very Old Barton, Maker's Mark, Woodford Reserve, I.W. Harper, Jack Daniel's, George A. Dickel, Platte Valley, Casa Bacardi, and Cruzan. The plan was to store the barrels at Mount Vernon for at least one year, then to bottle the contents using special "Presidential" labels, under the auspices of the newly licensed George Washington Distillery. Later that day a groundbreaking ceremony was held at the site of the still house, where Peter Cressy of DISCUS proclaimed, "This is a marvelous opportunity for us to demonstrate the role of spirits in our nation's history and the part which our founding father played in that great tradition."[7]

The response on the part of the press to the groundbreaking events was entirely positive, with the story carried in several major newspapers around the country. At the outset, both Mount Vernon staff and the board shared some concern about the possible mixed reaction by some members of the public to publicizing and interpreting Washington's career as a whiskey maker. With the notoriety that the plan received after the ceremony, staff braced in anticipation of receiving angry telephone calls from those with an anti-liquor perspective. To their relief, the reaction was overwhelmingly favorable, with only two or three individuals calling to declare, "the father of our country surely would never have engaged in such immoral behavior" as operating a distillery. No matter how much documentary evidence was cited to demonstrate Washington's role as both a consumer and a producer of alcoholic beverages, these callers were not convinced. Although a few individuals were quite unwilling to let the facts get in the way of their image of Washington as a symbol of temperance, the vast majority of the public were more open-minded, and they demonstrated keen interest in learning about an aspect of his career that they had never imagined.

As the Mount Vernon staff conducting the research on Washington's distillery began their work in earnest in 2000, their attention was naturally drawn to any objects, images, or records thought to be associated with his whiskey making. One particularly intriguing object is a small copper pot still, stamped with the maker's name and the location and date of its manufacture ("R. Bush & Co. / Bristol / 1787"), that is housed in the collection of the Smithsonian Institution National Museum of American History. Federal agents confiscated the vessel circa 1940 from a house in rural Fairfax County, located only a few miles from Washington's former home. Since it was known that Washington had operated a distillery, the still's age and its proximity to Mount Vernon at the time of its seizure suggested to the agents that the vessel may have been owned by the former president. The object was transferred from the Internal Revenue Service to the safekeeping of the Smithsonian in 1965, where it was catalogued as "alleged to have belonged to George Washington." Over the next decade, the still was intermittently put on display at the museum and loaned to

This copper pot still was made in 1787, probably in Bristol, England, and was confiscated from moonshiners by federal authorities circa 1940; the piece was erroneously identified as having been owned by Washington.

other institutions. According to the Mount Vernon plantation financial records, Washington acquired five stills in 1797–98 to outfit the distillery, at least three of which were provided by a local metalsmith. The vessels varied in capacity from 110 to 135 gallons, placing them comfortably within the normal range for stills in use at that time. In addition to the earlier date and apparent English place of manufacture, the Smithsonian still is only between 25 and 30 gallons in capacity, suggesting that it was not used in a commercial setting. Thus, while a rare and important example of an 18th-century pot still, it appears highly unlikely that the artifact had been owned by Washington.[8]

The bottom half of a second still, almost identical in size, shape, and overall appearance to the one at the Smithsonian, and also bearing an 18th-century date and the name of the same city of manufacture ("R & T Hale / Bristol / 1784"), recently came to light. According to information provided by the owners, the still body was confiscated in 1932 from a moonshiner in Banner Township, North Carolina. But instead of destroying the illicit vessel, the constable sold it for four dollars to a local man, Herschel Vaughn Rose. Rose used the object as a handy receptacle to store grain until it was stolen in 1957; the thief at least left the grain behind, deposited in a pile on the floor of the barn. A few years later, Rose's son-in-law, Melvin L. Wilkins, received a tip as to the still's whereabouts, submerged in a local pond. Wilkins used a tractor to retrieve the still, which then remained in the possession of his family until it was finally donated to Mount Vernon to be put on display at the reconstructed distillery in spring 2011.[9]

A second group of objects with an even more puzzling and less likely association with Washington's distillery had surfaced a few years earlier. These consist of several bottles of whiskey that, according to the writing on the labels, had been filled in 1918 from a cask that had been found at the site of the "Mount Vernon distillery." As Washington's distillery is known to have been destroyed by fire in 1814, it seems virtually impossible that it was the place where the whiskey was made.

What seems more likely is that the bottles contain the product of the Mount Vernon Rye whiskey brand, which was produced in Baltimore beginning in the mid-19th century and continued to be distilled as beverage alcohol up until Prohibition. In hopes of determining whether the liquid could possibly be 200 years old, a sample was taken to Louisville to be analyzed by chemists at the Brown-Forman product-testing laboratory in the fall of 2000. The tests confirmed that the liquid was whiskey that had been made from a mixture of grains, probably including rye, but it was not possible to determine its age.

According to plan, distillers and other staff from the companies that had sent their spirits to Mount Vernon the year before returned to the estate in October 2002 to bottle the product. The list of master distillers in attendance was a who's who of America's best-known spirits makers. The companies designed and produced special commemorative labels for the event, with each evoking an association with George Washington and his distillery. Each barrel of spirit had been specially selected as the best of its kind, and ranged in age from 6 to 10 years at the time they were shipped. After aging at Mount Vernon for an additional 17 months, the distillers and the other participants had high expectations that they were about to taste some remarkably fine liquor. The consensus of the assembled media and spirits experts was that the unique products lived up to their billing, with the special Jack Daniel's expression possibly taking the top prize. Later that day a selection of the bottles were auctioned at a dinner and industry event organized by DISCUS, with more than $170,000 in donations raised for Mount Vernon.[10]

The attention given to the special bottling fueled even more interest in the type of whiskey that Washington had made 200 years before. Almost the first questions any writers or visitors asked was about the character of that whiskey, followed by whether there were plans to make it, and if it would be offered to the public for sale? Although the Mount Vernon board had not envisioned reconstructing the distillery to become a commercial enterprise, making a limited batch of the antique whiskey seemed to offer an outstanding educational and promotional opportunity. Furthermore, as the plan called for replicating the distillery experience for visitors as authentically as possible, experimenting with making whiskey as it was done 200 years ago would be of enormous practical benefit in planning for the reconstruction. Therefore, the project staff focused on the research needed to guide the experiment, to include determining the ingredients in Washington's mash bill, fabricating a replica of an 18th-century still, and learning the detailed steps in making whiskey that were followed at the time.

In relatively short order the planners were able to find all of the necessary information and get the outside cooperation to secure the various distilling apparatus that would be needed. Several distilling manuals dating to the late 18th and early 19th centuries were consulted, which provided the step-by-step instructions on mashing, fermenting, and operating the pot still. The manuals also included several different recipes for rye whiskey, and since Washington's own recipe had not been found, selecting one of them was an option. However, Esther White, Mount Vernon's Director of Archaeology, came up with the idea of tabulating all of the grain that was recorded in the plantation accounts as having been ground and sent to the distillery as a way of determining Washington's mash bill. The records of the grain transactions survived for a 15-month period in 1798–99, which yielded the proportions of 60 percent rye, 35 percent corn, and 5 percent barley—a typical mash bill for rye whiskey at that time. While it was highly unlikely that the Smithsonian still actually had been owned by Washington, it was an authentic 18th-century vessel, and therefore was deemed to be an appropriate model upon which to base the replica. Tom and Mike Sherman, President and Vice President of Vendome Copper and Brass Works, of Louisville, Kentucky, and the industry leaders in fabricating distilling equipment, agreed to produce a replica still for the purpose. The curators of the Smithsonian kindly agreed to allow the team to examine and measure their artifact, and the Vendome craftsmen used that information to produce an exact copy, down to the hammer marks around the rivets and the name of the maker stamped on the shoulder of the body. Two oversized, 120-gallon barrels were supplied by Kentucky's Independent Stave Company to be used as mash tubs.

The efforts of the historians could take the experiment only so far, of course, so Frank Coleman at DISCUS once again put out the word that Mount Vernon was soliciting volunteers to participate in a once-in-a-lifetime enterprise. Many of the same master distillers who had attended the barrel tapping and bottling event the previous year expressed interest in participating, and a task force was formed to plan the project. Given the groundbreaking nature of the proposed experiment, the team determined that it would be prudent to conduct a trial run before inviting the public to observe the event at Mount Vernon in October. At their Woodford Reserve distillery, Chris Morris and Lincoln Henderson, of Brown-Forman, oversaw producing several barrels of wash according to Washington's recipe. One of the barrels was trucked to the Jim Beam distillery where Jerry Dalton and Mike Sherman used it to put the replica still through its paces. Predictably, there were bugs to be worked out, as the temporary base in which the still was seated did not enclose the vessel sufficiently to properly convey the heat. Several hours later, the hot and tired distillers finally were rewarded with the appearance of a tiny stream of distillate, just enough to encourage them that a better designed furnace should solve the problem.[11]

With the return of the replica still to Mount Vernon, the estate's masons erected a small brick structure to house it, located just a few hundred feet from the site of the original still house. The new furnace was designed to enclose the entire bottom portion of the vessel, allowing the heat from the fire to come into contact with more of its surface area. Described by one journalist as looking like a backyard barbecue "with a still sunk into the top," the primitive installation nevertheless worked remarkably well. As part of the demonstration, rye, corn, and barley were mixed and then fermented nearby in two wooden hogsheads. But since the fermentation process could take up to five days to complete, the distillers filled the still with more of the wash that had been made earlier in Kentucky. Once again, some lessons were learned the hard way. At the mashing operation, a handle on one of the buckets used to transfer water to the tubs broke, dumping scalding water and causing Jimmy Russell, of Wild Turkey, and James Graf, from McCormick Distilling, to scamper to safety. Regulating the heat from the fire under the still continued to be a challenge, and led to one batch that, according to Virginia Gentleman's Joe Dangler, "tasted like burnt rye bread toast." But the crew took most of the setbacks in stride, and as Lincoln Henderson observed, "Essentially we're looking back at history and using techniques that are now obsolete. But we're doing a pretty good job of making it work."[12]

After several days of hard work and with only a few burned and blistered fingers, the experiment ended with almost 10 gallons of rye whiskey safely in the barrel. With a generally spicy flavor profile and just a hint of corn sweetness that is characteristic of the ingredients, some of the twice-distilled spirit reached 140 proof, or 70 percent alcohol. Although unceremoniously referred to as "white dog" at modern distilleries where the next step would be to stow the whiskey away for several years to mellow and darken in oak barrels, this raw, unaged spirit would have been considered a high-quality product in 1797. While not to everyone's taste, David Pickerell, of Maker's Mark, summed up the assessment of the more adventurous imbibers in the crowd, putting down a tiny glass after tasting and pronouncing, "Oh, that's really nice."[13]

With the success of the initial attempt in 2003 to replicate Washington's whiskey, making one variety of vintage product or another was adopted as almost an annual activity over the next several years. Rum was the focus in 2005, using fermented

In 2003 a team of master distillers gathered at Mount Vernon to produce a batch of rye whiskey according to Washington's recipe and using a replica 18th-century pot still.

IMAGE: COURTESY OF THE MOUNT VERNON LADIES' ASSOCIATION

blackstrap molasses brought in from St. Croix, and distilled under the direction of the rum experts, Gary Nelthropp and Ron Call from Cruzan and Willie Ramos from Bacardi. Frank Coleman also had the bright idea to blend together the whiskeys in the barrels that had been brought to Mount Vernon in 2001, which were left over from the special bottling that had occurred the next year. Remarkably, all of the distilleries agreed to allow their whiskey to be melded into one unique product. It took a special act of the Virginia General Assembly to allow Mount Vernon to be able to sell this and other spirits on site, and the blended whiskey finally was offered for sale to the public beginning in 2008. The distillers returned to produce small batches of rye whiskey in 2006, when HRH Andrew, the Prince of Wales, dedicated the distillery building, and again in 2007, when the structure was completed and the site was opened to the public. All of these products were auctioned at different times, with the proceeds devoted to supporting Mount Vernon's educational programs.[14]

Although a number of relatively minor compromises had to be made in the name of visitor safety, the building that opened in the spring of 2007 was an authentic recreation of the 18th-century still house, where whiskey could be made as faithfully as possible according to the procedures of Washington's day. Most of the modifications that were made to the building's design were required to meet modern building codes. The most significant was adding a 15-foot-long section to the north end to accommodate an elevator and a staircase to the floor above, to provide handicapped access and a second exit in case of a fire. But the addition was constructed to blend visually with the replica, and the distilling room remained largely unchanged from what the archaeological and documentary evidence indicated. The five stills are arranged in a line on the east side of the room, with the interior walls of their furnaces lined with modern fire-resistant materials. The fires under the stills are vented by three brick chimneys outfitted with modern flue liners. The water in the copper boiler, located along the west side of the building opposite the stills, is heated by electric heating coils, as its wooden fume hood simply could not be made to pass the fire code without dramatically changing its appearance. Thus, while the structure remained true to the evidence found for its 18th-century predecessor, it also could accommodate the needs of the modern public as an educational facility as well as occasionally become an honest-to-goodness operating distillery.

Given the continuing strong interest on the part of the public in tasting Washington's whiskey, Mount Vernon hired David Pickerell, formerly the master distiller with Maker's Mark and one of the volunteers who had banded together to produce the earlier limited runs, to oversee the production. Pickerell agreed to spend two weeks at the site working with Mount Vernon staff from the estate's historic trades program. The goal was to make up to 100 gallons of rye whiskey, not only using Washington's mash bill and distilling on site, but also for the first time grinding all of the needed grain in the nearby gristmill and mashing and fermenting in the reconstructed still house. Since this was the first distilling that had been carried out at the site since the building was opened in 2007, and because of the much larger scale of the effort, the preparations leading up to distilling were time consuming. The 12 barrels used for mashing the grain, which had been on display in the building for almost two years, had to be thoroughly cleaned and filled with water so that they would swell and become sufficiently tight, and the stills and the copper boiler were cleaned as well. At the same time, the resident miller, Steve Bashore, acquired about 2,000 pounds of rye, corn, and barley from local suppliers, and then spent almost 20 hours next door in the mill grinding the ingredients.

With the mash tubs finally at the ready, it took three days of backbreaking labor to mix and cook the grain in the 120-gallon barrels. In addition to the physical demands, the work required lots of attention to detail, as it is a process with multiple, time-sensitive steps. First the corn was mixed with water that had been heated to about 140 degrees, while stirring the mixture rapidly with a wooden mash "rake" to help the grain dissolve and to retard clumping into balls of dough. Next the tub was filled two-thirds full with boiling water, and left to sit for 20 minutes while the corn starch turned to gelatin. Then the rye was added and the mixture stirred continuously as the solution turned into the consistency of a thick soup. When the temperature dropped to about 148 degrees, the malted barley was stirred in—the barley helps to break down the starches even further, making the mixture much thinner and easier to stir. Finally, when the temperature dropped to about 90 degrees, yeast was added to begin the fermentation. Then it was time to take a break, rest arms, and get ready for the next barrel.

Four days later, the first barrels of mash had finished fermenting and the liquid was ready to be distilled. The crew hauled the wash in buckets to the waiting still, with the head removed to allow the liquid to be poured into the body. After the vessel was filled to about 60 percent capacity, they replaced the head and attached the arm to the copper coil (worm) in the nearby worm tub (condenser), and the spigots were opened so that water could flow in and out of the tub. After building the fire and heating the wash to about 160 degrees, the alcohol vaporized and collected in the head of the still, where it began to condense back into liquid form. From there it traveled across the arm and down through the worm, with the cool water in the tub aiding the condensation, and finally appearing, first as a few drops and then as a steady stream, from the end of the worm at the bottom of the tub. The first part of the flow, known as the "heads," is of poor quality, so it was dumped back into one of the fermenters to be redistilled later. Once the spirit reached at least 40 proof (20 percent alcohol) it was collected and set aside to be distilled a second time. When the proof dropped below 40 again, the batch was cut off and either the still was emptied and cleaned out, or new wash was added to continue the run. Pickerell calls the latter procedure "turn and burn," which allows him to continue distilling with less down time.

The folks at Vendome Copper and Brass Works, who made the stills, suggested that it would be a good idea to install a small vent hole in the shoulder of the vessels as a pressure release device. But the hole also acts as a handy inlet for adding the fresh wash to the previous batch.

After several days of working with the stills, Pickerell had pretty well identified their different idiosyncrasies, determining which ones worked best for distilling the wash and which were better suited for redistilling the first run spirit. According to Pickerell, "Each still has a happy place that it likes to run. The trick is not to make it run how you want, but rather to figure out how to make it happy where it wants to run, and then encourage it." After exhausting all of the wash, the distillate that had been collected and set aside was reintroduced to the "spirit" still for the second and final run, after which the alcohol content reached between 140 and just below 100 proof. At the end of the two weeks, Pickerell and his team had hit their target almost exactly, with 96 gallons of approximately 90 proof rye whiskey safely stored in the warehouse at Mount Vernon.[15]

One of the most valuable outcomes of this first experiment in making a significant quantity of whiskey according to the vintage techniques, was to instill an even greater appreciation of just how successful Washington's distillery had been. According to period sources, Washington's distillers had been able to produce approximately 10,500 gallons of spirits in the year 1799 alone. If the distillery operated 365 days that year, which is unlikely, that would translate into roughly 30 gallons per day. A visitor to the plantation in 1798 remarked that the distillery had the capacity to produce 50 gallons per day. With the benefit of the experience from the 2009 trial, when it took two full weeks to distill 96 gallons of spirit, both of those numbers seem impressive, indeed. Washington's distillery manager, John Anderson, and his assistant and crew of six enslaved workers, had a considerable advantage over their 21st-century counterparts in terms of experience working with the equipment available at the time. But Pickerell and his crew were fast learners, and their performance improved significantly during two subsequent distilling episodes, as they increased their efficiency considerably. Over a three-week period in March 2011, the team produced 145 gallons of whiskey, using only 2,700 pounds of grain and 15 fermentations, or an increase of 34 percent in production with only a 26 percent increase in raw ingredients. Even so, it seems highly unlikely that the Mount Vernon crew will be able to approach the level of performance of the 18th-century distillers any time soon.[16]

As predicted, when the first bottles of the rye whiskey that had been made in 2009 were finally offered for sale on July 1, 2010, the public was eager to taste the product. At a ceremony held at the distillery to mark the occasion, free tastings of the spirit were offered, and within a few hours all 470 bottles were sold, for the not inconsiderable price of $85 each. At the ceremony, a professional actor playing the role of George Washington offered the final words of the day, proclaiming the whiskey to be "fine," and offering a toast, "To all our friends." His words were followed by enthusiastic "huzzahs" of approval from the gathering.[17]

On 1 July, 2010, 470 bottles of unaged rye whiskey made according to *Washington's recipe at the reconstructed Washington distillery were offered for sale to the public; George Washington, as portrayed by actor Dean Malissa, offered a toast, "To all our friends."*

Appendix A
George Washington on Alcohol

Regarding the need to supply the troops with alcohol:

"And as an encouragement to them to behave well, and to attend diligently to their Duty, the Colonel [Washington] promises to give them, so long as they deserve it, four gallons of rum, made into punch, every day."

—General Orders, 7 August 1756

"Since our Imports of Spirit have become so precarious, nay impracticable, on Account of the Enemy's Fleet which infests our Whole Coast, I would beg leave to suggest the propriety of erecting Public Distilleries in different States. The benefits arising from moderate use of strong Liquor, have been experienced in All Armies, and are not to be disputed."

—GW to John Hancock, 16 August 1777

"It is necessary, there should always be a Sufficient Quantity of Spirits with the Army, to furnish moderate supplies to the Troops. In many instances, such as when they are marching in hot or Cold weather, in Camp in Wet, on fatigue or in Working Parties, it is so essential, that it is not to be dispensed with. I should be happy if the exorbitant price, to which it has risen, could be reduced."

—GW to William Buchanan, 20 August 1777

"...the Serjeants [should] see it [liquor] duly distributed daily
and mixed with Water at stated times; in which case...it will
become refreshing and salutary."

—General Orders, 16 May 1782

On the debilitating effects of over indulging in alcohol:

"It gave me infinite satisfaction to hear Colonel Stephen
express his approbation of your conduct. Assure yourself,
dear Charles, that activity and Bravery in Officers are the
means to recommend them to their Country's applause—and
will ever endear them to me! Your Courage and abilities were
always equal to my wishes: But I dreaded the pernicious
effects of liquor; especially as I knew it bereft you of that
prudent way of reasoning, which at other times you are
master of. Such inconsistent behavior as liquor sometimes
prompts you to, may be borne by your Friends; but can not
by Officers; and in a camp, where each individual should
regulate his conduct for the good of the whole; and strive to
excel in all laudable Emulations. This comes from me as your
Friend, not as a Superior Officer; who must, when occasion
requires, condemn as well as applaud.

—GW to Charles Lewis, 27 January 1756

"The General is extremely concerned that an Article
so salutary as that of distilled Liquors was expected
to be when properly used, and which was designed
for the comfort and refreshment of the troops has been in
many instances productive of very ill consequences. He
calls attention to the officers of every grade to remede these
abuses and to watch over the health of their men.

—General Orders, 16 March 1782

"I could wish to see the direct commerce with France
encouraged to the greatest degree; and that almost all the

foreign Spirits which we consumed should consist of the Wines and Brandies made in that Country. The use of those liquours would at least be more innocent to the health and morals of the people, than the thousands of Hogsheads of poisonous Rum which are annually consumed in the United States."

—GW to Comte de Moustier, 15 December 1788

"An aching head and trimbling limbs are the inevitable effects of drinking [and] disincline the hands from work hence begins sloth and that Lestlessness which end in idleness."

—GW to Thomas Green, 31 March 1789

"Before any nomination, or appointment of a Keeper of the Lighthouse on Cape Henry takes place, it would be proper to examine the List of Applicants...If the person recommended by Colo. Parker is intemperate in drinking, it is immaterial whether you can recollect his name or not; for me, this would be an insuperable objection."

—GW to Alexander Hamilton, 1 October 1792

"So long as the vice of drunkenness exists in the Army so long I hope, Ejections of those officers who are found guilty of it will continue; for that and gaming will debilitate and render unfit for active service any Army whatsoever."

—GW to Henry Knox, 1 August 1792

"I shall not close this letter with out exhorting you to refrain from Spirituous liquors, they will prove your ruin if you do not. Consider how little a drunken Man differs from a beast; the latter is not endowed with reason, the former deprives himself of it; and when that is the case acts like a brute; annoying, and disturbing everyone around him. But this is not all, nor as it respects himself the worst of it; By degrees it renders a person feeble and not only unable to serve others but to help himself, and being an act of his own he fall[s] from a state of usefulness into contempt and at length suffers, if not perishes in penury and want."

—GW to John Christian Ehler, 23 December 1793

"I am very willing to allow them [John Christian Ehler and his wife] enough, and of such provisions, day by day, as is wholesome and good, but no more—they have, each of them been allowed a bottle of Beer a day—and this must be continued to them. The Gardener has too great a propensity to drink, and behaves improperly when in liquor; admonish him against it as much as you can, as he behaves well when sober—understands his business—and I believe is not naturally idle—but only so when occasioned by drink."

—GW to William Pearce, 23 December 1793

Reference to George Washington's imbibing whiskey:

"As the President will be going, if he proceeds, into the Country of Whiskey he proposes to make use of that liquor for his drink."

—Bartholomew Dandridge to Henry Knox, 9 October 1794

Giving permission to James Anderson to erect a distillery at Mount Vernon:

"I consent to your commencing a distillery, and approve of your purchasing the Still, and entering of it. And I shall not object to your converting part of the Coopers shop at the Mill to this operation...If the advantages were certain, of wch. From want of experience in the business I have no adequate idea; I should have no objection to the building of a house for the purpose of distillation; and in that case (unless the house ought to be so situated as that water can be carried through it) I should prefer for this purpose the point below your house at what used to be the ferry landing."

—GW to Anderson, 8 January 1797

"Distillery. Is a business I am entirely unacquainted with; but from your knowledge of it and from the confidence you have in the profit to be derived from the establishment, I am disposed to enter upon one."

—GW to Anderson, 18 June 1797

Asking for and receiving advice from John Fitzgerald regarding the potential for the distillery to be a financial success:

"Mr Anderson *has* engaged me in a distillery, on a small scale, and is very desirous of encreasing it: assuring me from his *own* experience in *this* country, and in *Europe*, that I shall find my acct in it, particularly in the benefits my stock would derive from it. The thing is new to me, in toto; but in a distillery of another kind (Molasses) you must have a good general knowledge of its profits, and whether a ready sale of the Spirit is to be calculated on from grain (principally to be raised on my own Farms) and the offal of my Mill. I, therefore, have taken the liberty of asking your opinion on the proposition of Mr Anderson."

—GW to Fitzgerald, 12 June 1797

"As I have no doubt Mr. Anderson understands the Distillation of Spirit from Grain I cannot hesitate in my opinion that it might be carried on to great advantage on your Estate...as to a Sale of the Whiskey there can be no doubt if the Quantity was ten times as much as he can make provided it is of good Quality."

—Fitzgerald to GW, 18 June 1797

Appendix B

The American Whiskey Trail

The American Whiskey Trail is a vehicle for enthusiasts to embark on an educational journey into the cultural heritage and history of spirits in America. From the Colonial Era, when whiskey and rum served a particularly important social and economic function within the fabric of the community, through the Whiskey Rebellion, to Prohibition, and into modern times, spirits have occupied a sometimes controversial but always fascinating place in the nation's history. All of the sites included on the American Whiskey Trail are united by their association with important events and activities relating to the history of American spirits, and they each have their unique story to tell.

Historic Sites:

George Washington's Distillery, Mount Vernon, Virginia

Open from April through October each year, George Washington's Distillery is the only place in the country where visitors may observe how whiskey was made in 18th-century America. The distilling room is outfitted with five copper pot stills, the boiler, and mash tubs for cooking and fermenting grain. Costumed interpreters provide guided tours of the building and demonstrate the various steps in the whiskey making process. The theater, showing a 10-minute video that relates the story of Washington's distillery, and the gallery, with exhibits on the history of the spirits industry in America, are located on the second floor. The distillery has been designated as the "gateway" to the American Whiskey Trail, and provides an overview of all of the sites that are included.[1]

West Overton Museum, Scottdale, Pennsylvania

West Overton Village was the site of the Overholt family distillery, established by Abraham Overholt in 1838. In 1800 a group of German Mennonites led by Henry Overholt crossed the Allegheny Mountains and established a farming settlement on the fertile plains just west of the Chestnut Ridge. Overholt's son, Abraham, established a large grist mill and distillery, which later were housed in the surviving six-story brick structure (built in 1859), located adjacent to his three-story brick home. Prior to 1870, the rye whiskey that he made was known by the Monongahela and A. Overholt and Co. Pure Rye Whiskey brands. After Abraham Overholt's death in 1870, the name of the brand was changed to Old Overholt. West Overton was named to the National Register of Historic Places as a district in 1985, cited as an outstanding example of a 19th-century rural industrial village. From May through October visitors may tour the farmstead and two floors of the former Overholt mill and distillery, where artifacts and artwork relating to the distillery are on display.[2]

Gadsby's Tavern Museum, Alexandria, Virginia

The tavern operated by the proprietor John Gadsby was a center of political, business, and social life in 18th-century Alexandria. The tavern hosted many social events, dancing assemblies, theatrical and musical performances, and meetings of local organizations. George Washington frequently visited the tavern, and he and his wife Martha twice attended the annual Birthnight Ball held in his honor. Other prominent individuals who were entertained there included John Adams, Thomas Jefferson, James Madison, and the Marquis de Lafayette. The museum consists of two historic buildings, both listed in the

National Register of Historic Places: the Tavern built circa 1770, and the adjoining City Tavern and Hotel, built in 1792. Meticulously restored in 1976 to their 18th-century appearance, the buildings are open year-round, Tuesday through Sunday, when visitors are given a guided tour of the historic rooms in both buildings.[3]

Fraunces Tavern Museum, New York, New York

Best known as the site where George Washington made his farewell to the officers of the Continental Army in 1783, Fraunces Tavern was built in 1719 as an elegant residence for merchant Stephan Delancey. The building was purchased in 1762 by Samuel Fraunces, who turned it into one of the most popular taverns in the city. After the Revolution, when New York was the nation's first capital, the tavern was rented to the new government to house the offices of the Departments of War, Treasury, and Foreign Affairs. In addition to operating the tavern, Samuel Fraunces gained notoriety by serving as the steward for George Washington and his household during his two terms as president. In 1904 the Sons of the Revolution in the State of New York purchased the building and set about restoring it to its 18th-century appearance. In 1907 the Fraunces Tavern Museum opened to the public and it has been listed in the National Register of Historic Places. Open to visitors year-round, the tavern displays two period rooms and numerous temporary and permanent exhibitions, and includes four adjoining 19th-century buildings.[4]

Woodville Plantation, The John and Presley Neville House, Bridgeville, Pennsylvania

A National Historic Landmark and one of the oldest houses in western Pennsylvania, Woodville Plantation was the home of John Neville, a noted soldier who was the commandant of Fort Pitt and who served as a general officer with the Continental Army during the Revolution. Neville was appointed as the collector of the federal excise tax on whiskey for the four-county western Pennsylvania area, and he was one of the first to bear the brunt of widespread resistance to the measure. In 1794 local farmers besieged Neville in his home at the time, Bower Hill; Neville and his supporters successfully resisted the attack, but the house was destroyed by fire during the event. His earlier house was Woodville, which was built in several stages, beginning with a portion constructed by John Neville circa 1785; later additions were made by his son, Presley, and subsequent owners in the 19th century. Today Woodville is a museum owned and operated by the Pittsburgh History and Landmarks Foundation, and has been restored to its late 18th- and early19th-century appearance. The building is open year-round, Wednesday through Saturday, for guided tours.[5]

The Oliver Miller Homestead, Allegheny County, Pennsylvania

Some of the first gunshots signaling the outbreak of the Whiskey Rebellion were fired at this site, the original homestead of Oliver Miller. One of the first settlers to cross the Allegheny Mountains, Miller claimed the property and erected a log house in 1772. After his death in 1782, the property passed to his sons, three of whom were directly involved in the Rebellion as leaders of the rebel cause. In 1794, the local citizens took up arms in opposition to the federal excise tax on whiskey, with one of the first conflicts occurring at the Miller property when William Miller resisted an attempt by federal officers to register his still. Miller later led a group of irate farmers to the home of General John Neville, who was appointed as collector of the "whiskey tax," where they succeeded in burning his house. The original Miller log house was replaced with a two-story stone structure in 1830. In total, five generations of the Miller family lived on the property until it was purchased by the Allegheny County government in 1927. Visitors may tour the restored James Miller house, which has been listed in the National Register of Historic Places, every Sunday from May through December.[6]

The Oscar Getz Museum of Whiskey History, Bardstown, Kentucky

The Oscar Getz Museum of Whiskey History houses the country's largest collection of rare whiskey artifacts and documents, dating from the Colonial Era to post-Prohibition days. The core of the museum's holdings was collected over a 50-year period by Oscar Getz, a local entrepreneur who established and operated the Barton Distillery in Bardstown. Among the artifacts on display are rare antique bottles, a moonshine still, advertising art, novelty whiskey containers, and Abraham Lincoln's liquor license. The museum is housed in historic Spalding Hall, which was built circa 1826 to serve as a college and seminary, and is listed in the National Register of Historic Places. Together with the Bardstown Historical Museum, the Getz Museum occupies the first floor of the Hall, and it is open to visitors from May through October.[7]

Distilleries:

Woodford Reserve Distillery, Versailles, Kentucky

Located in the heart of Kentucky's famous horse country, the Woodford Reserve Distillery was designated as a National Historic Landmark in 2000. The first distillery on the site was established in 1812 by Elijah Pepper, and the current distillery incorporates the walls of the stone still house that was erected in 1838. The other historic structures include the Pepper family's log farm house, built circa 1812; the scale house and office, both built in 1883; the watchman's guard house built in 1911; and stone and brick warehouses dating to the 1890s and 1930s. A feature that is unique to the site is the metal rail track, built in 1934, that operates by gravity to transport barrels of whiskey to the warehouses. A highlight of the tour of the still house is the chance to view three traditional copper pot stills, which are used in the time-honored production of Woodford Reserve bourbon. The visitors' center built in 1996 houses a retail shop, orientation film, and exhibits; the site is open to the public year-round.[8]

Jim Beam Distillery, Clermont, Kentucky

A visit to the Beam distillery offers a unique opportunity to learn about America's first family of bourbon and the bourbon-making process. While tours of the plant itself are not offered, visitors may walk the grounds and tour a rack house and the cooperage. T. Jeremiah Beam, the son of the distillery's founder, Jim Beam, was the master distiller from 1938 to 1960. His home, built in 1911 and fully restored, is listed in the National Register of Historic Places and is open to visitors. The American Outpost visitor center displays exhibits and artifacts spanning a 200-year period of Kentucky whiskey making. The site is open to the public year-round.[9]

Maker's Mark Distillery, Loretto, Kentucky

Established in 1805 as a combined gristmill and distillery, Maker's Mark is the oldest working distillery on its original site in America, and is listed in the National Register of Historic Places. Originally established by Charles Burks, the distillery operated until the 1830s; after sitting idle for a number of years, it was reopened by George R. Burks in the 1880s. At that time the plant was considerably expanded, and the complex as it appears today dates largely from the late 19th century. The distillery reopened and operated under different ownership shortly after the repeal of Prohibition, and in 1953, T. William Samuels took over the property and introduced the Maker's Mark brand of premium whiskey. In addition to the still house, which rests on the foundations of the 1805 structure, there are warehouses, the boiler house, and the master distiller's house, all probably built in the 1880s. The distiller's house has been renovated to serve as the visitors' center, and site tours are offered year-round, seven days a week.[10]

Wild Turkey Distillery, Lawrenceburg, Kentucky

The original distillery on the site was established by the Ripy family in 1869, and, except for the era of Prohibition, it has been in operation ever since. In 1939 Austin Nichols, who had operated a wholesale grocery business in New York City, focused his business exclusively on producing and marketing fine wines and spirits. The Nichols Company contracted with the Ripy distillery to supply them with whiskey, and in 1971 Nichols purchased the distillery itself. The Wild Turkey brand was established in 1940, and it has been the distillery's primary product ever since. Tours of the plant are offered from Monday through Saturday, year-round, when visitors can follow the entire production process from grain delivery to bottling.[11]

Barton 1792 Distillery, Bardstown, Kentucky

Tom Moore, a Kentuckian whose product earned him a reputation as one of the finest bourbon distillers in the country, established his distillery at this location in 1879. The plant operated more or less continuously until Prohibition, after which the buildings were renovated and enlarged. Barton Brands acquired the Tom Moore distillery in 1944 and continues to operate it on the same site. Today the plant is dedicated to producing the 1792 Ridgemont Reserve brand, but among the vintage whiskies that were previously made here were Tom Moore, Kentucky Gentleman, and Very Old Barton. A state-of-the-art visitors' center opened to the public in 2011, and is the beginning point for guided tours of the inner workings of the bourbon making process, from corn delivery to the bottling line. Open year-round, guided tours are by reservation only, from Monday through Friday.[12]

Buffalo Trace Distillery, Franklin County, Kentucky

The current Buffalo Trace Distillery incorporates part of the old O.F.C. still house, which was built in 1869 by E. H. Taylor Jr., an early leader in the Kentucky bourbon whiskey industry. Although Taylor sold his interest in the company soon thereafter, the plant has operated under various owners, with the exception of the Prohibition years, almost continuously ever since. Taylor's original partner in the venture was George T. Stagg, after whom the distillery was named up until 1999. Buffalo Trace has earned the reputation as one of the most innovative whiskey producers in America, annually offering several well-received bourbon expressions. A number of the buildings survive from the late 19th century, and the property is listed in the National Register of Historic Places. Visitors may tour the site, including a rack house and the bottling plant, Monday through Saturday, year-round.[13]

Jack Daniel's Distillery, Lynchburg, Tennessee

The Jack Daniel's Distillery is the oldest registered distillery in the country and is listed in the National Register of Historic Places. The distillery was established in 1866, and remained in the Daniel family until it was sold to the Brown-Forman Company in 1956. The making of Jack Daniel's whiskey was set down by its founder and the recipe and special production process have been maintained and preserved for over 140 years. Jack Daniel's is a Tennessee whiskey, which means that the spirit is subjected to an additional step of filtering through a 10-foot column of maple-wood charcoal. Tours of the distillery are offered year-round, which include the visitor center, where historical exhibits and artifacts are on display, Jack Daniel's office, as well as the opportunity to observe the process of producing the maple-wood charcoal through which the whiskey is finally filtered.[14]

George Dickel Distillery, Tullahoma, Tennessee

George A. Dickel was a successful merchant who dreamed of creating the "finest, smoothest sippin' whisky" in the United States. Dickel migrated from Germany to Tennessee in 1853 and established a wholesale whiskey business and a liquor store in Nashville. In 1888, Dickel and his associates bought the rights to bottle and distribute the product of the Cascade Distillery, which had been established in 1877. After Dickel's death in 1894, the enterprise passed through several owners until it was forced to close in 1911 when the State of Tennessee implemented its own prohibition legislation. It was not until 1958 that the distillery reopened under new management, using the original whiskey recipe found in George Dickel's papers. Like Jack Daniel's, the George Dickel brand is a Tennessee whiskey, which means that it is finished by filtering through a stack of maple-wood charcoal. In addition to the distillery tour, which is open year-round, the visitors' center offers an array of antiques and whiskey making memorabilia.[15]

Bacardi Visitor Center, Catano, Puerto Rico

Originally founded in Cuba by Don Facundo Bacardi in 1862, the Bacardi rum distillery in Puerto Rico was established in 1936 to more effectively supply its product to the United States market. After the Cuban Revolution in 1959, the Bacardi Company transferred its operations to other countries, and the Puerto Rican distillery took on a greater role in its corporate fortunes. Tours of the site are available year-round, from Monday through Saturday, when visitors can enjoy an interactive trip through history, observe the production process, and experience the party spirit of the Bacardi brand.[16]

Cruzan Rum Distillery, St. Croix, U.S. Virgin Islands

Founded in 1760, the Cruzan Distillery has supplied rum to America for more than two centuries. Throughout the 18th century, rum was the most popular distilled spirit in America, and

tradition holds that rum from St. Croix was supplied to General
George Washington's troops during the Revolutionary War.
For eight generations, through various changes in corporate
ownership, the distillery has been managed by members of
the Nelthropp family. Today the Cruzan Distillery is the only
remaining rum distiller operating in the Virgin Islands; tours
of the distillery are given year-round during week days.[17]

APPENDIX C
PORTFOLIO OF
DISTILLERY IMAGES

A remnant of the three-foot-wide stone distillery foundation.

Brass and copper fragments of the 18th-century stills: upper right, three body fragments; lower right, drain spout; left, spigot fragments (the largest of the artifacts is approximately four inches long).

IMAGE: COURTESY OF THE MOUNT VERNON LADIES' ASSOCIATION

Building the brick furnaces for the stills in the replica distillery.

IMAGE: COURTESY OF THE MOUNT VERNON LADIES' ASSOCIATION

In 2007 the replica of George Washington's distillery was completed and the building was opened to the public.

IMAGE: COURTESY MOUNT VERNON LADIES' ASSOCIATION

Inside the replica distillery, showing two stills and mash tubs.

IMAGE: COURTESY RUSS FLINT

Workers tending three of the stills in the replica distillery.

IMAGE: COURTESY RUSS FLINT

NOTES

Frequently Used Abbreviations

GWD: *The Diaries of George Washington*

LGWMV: Library, George Washington's Mount Vernon

PGW: *The Papers of George Washington*

WGW: *The Writings of George Washington*

INTRODUCTION

NOTES

1   GW to William Buchanan, 20 August 1777, *The Papers of George Washington Digital Edition*, ed. Theodore J. Crackel (Charlottesville: University of Virginia Press, 2008).

2   The standard work on the Whiskey Rebellion is Thomas P. Slaughter, *The Whiskey Rebellion: Frontier Epilogue to the American Revolution* (New York: Oxford University Press, 1986). For a recent appraisal of Washington's attitudes toward the whiskey rebels, see Ron Chernow, *George Washington: A Life* (New York: Penguin Press, 2010), 718.

3   For details on the development and the operations of the distillery, see Chapter 3: "A Considerable Distillery." The financial records of the distillery are provided in, Anna C. Borden, "A Study of Transition in Plantation Economy: George Washington's Whiskey Distillery, 1799" (master's thesis, College of William and Mary, 2002). The documentary evidence for the demise of the distillery is contained in the records of the Mutual Assurance Society of Virginia (1815), Declaration of Assurance No. 1750 (Virginia State Library and Archives, Richmond).

4   Christopher R. Eck, "The Spirits of Massachusetts: Distillers and Distilling in Seventeenth- and Eighteenth-Century Boston," (master's thesis, University of Massachusetts at Boston, 1993), 27–34. William J. Rorabaugh, *The Alcoholic Republic: An American Tradition* (Oxford: Oxford University Press, 1979), 29–31, 66–69.

5   Tench Coxe, comp., *A Statement of the Arts and Manufactures of the United States of America, for the Year 1810* (Philadelphia: A. Cornman, 1814), 22. William F. Micarelli, "Evolution of the United States Economic

Censuses: The Nineteenth and Twentieth Centuries," *Government Information Quarterly* 15, no. 3 (1998): 336; Rorabaugh, *Alcoholic Republic*, 69–73.

6   Mark E. Lender and James K. Martin, *Drinking in America: A History* (New York: Free Press, 1987), 64–131.

7   Ibid., 74–77.

8   James H. Bready, "Maryland Rye: A Whiskey the Nation Long Fancied—But Now Has Let Vanish," *Maryland Historical Magazine* 85, no. 4 (1990): 354, 369.

9   GW to Fitzgerald, 12 June 1797, *The Papers of George Washington: Retirement Series*, ed. W.W. Abbot (Charlottesville: University Press of Virginia, 1998) 1: 180. Fitzgerald to GW, 12 June 1797, Ibid., 181.

10   *Time*, September 30, 1935.

11   Esther C. White and Christy E. Leeson, *Results of Phase I and Phase II Archaeological Investigations at Washington's Mill Historical State Park (44FX2262)* (Mount Vernon Ladies' Association, Mount Vernon Archaeology File Report No. 6, 1999).

12   R.E. Burson, *A Report of the Findings of Mr. R.E. Burson on the George Washington Grist Mill, Situated on Dogue Run Creek, Mt. Vernon, VA* (Conservation and Development Commission of Virginia, 1932, photocopy). White and Leeson, *Washington's Mill*, 35–46.

13   For Carson's public career and his leadership of the Commission, see John F. Horn, Jr., "Will Carson and the Virginia Conservation Commission, 1926–1934," *Virginia Magazine of History and Biography* 92, no. 4 (1984): 391–415. *Public Opinion*, December 1936, 20–22.

14   Dennis J. Pogue and John P. Riley, *An Assessment of the Condition of George Washington's Gristmill and a Proposal for its Restoration* (Mount Vernon, Virginia: Mount Vernon Ladies' Association, 1995).

15   White and Leeson, *Washington's Mill*, 51–94.

16   Dennis J. Pogue and Esther C. White, *George Washington's Gristmill at Mount Vernon* (Mount Vernon, Virginia: Mount Vernon Ladies' Association, 2005), 55–63.

CHAPTER 1

NOTES

1   GW to Thomas Green, 31 March 1789, *The Papers of George Washington: Presidential Series*, ed. Dorothy Twohig (Charlottesville: University of Virginia Press, 1987) 1: 468–469.

2   Rorabaugh, *Alcoholic Republic*, 25–57, 95–122.

3   Adam Stephen to GW, 23 December 1755, *The Papers of George Washington: Colonial Series*, ed. W.W. Abbot (Charlottesville: University of Virginia Press, 1983) 2: 226–229. GW to James Wood, 28 July 1758, *The Papers of George Washington: Colonial Series*, ed. W.W. Abbot (Charlottesville: University of Virginia Press, 1988) 5: 349. Charles Smith to GW, 26 July 1758, Ibid., 331–334. Charles Smith to GW, 5 August 1758, Ibid., 373–374.

4   Invoice from Richard Washington, 20 August 1757, *The Papers of George Washington: Colonial Series*, ed. W.W. Abbot (Charlottesville: University of Virginia Press, 1984) 4: 380. Invoice from Thomas Knox, 18 August 1758, *PGW: Colonial* 5: 400. Invoice to Robert Cary and Company, 28 September 1760, *The Papers of George Washington: Colonial Series*, ed. W.W. Abbot (Charlottesville: University of Virginia Press, 1988) 6: 463. Invoice from Robert Cary and Company, 31 March 1761, *The Papers of George Washington: Colonial Series*, ed. W.W. Abbot and Dorothy Twohig (Charlottesville: University of Virginia Press, 1990) 7: 24. Invoice to Robert Cary and Company, 12 October 1761, Ibid., 77. GW to Robert Cary and Company, 10 August 1760, *PGW: Colonial* 6: 449. Invoices to Robert Cary and Company, 15 November 1762, *PGW: Colonial* 7: 165. Invoice to Robert Cary and Company, 28 September 1760, *PGW: Colonial* 6: 462. In this period the liquid capacities for barrels and casks were generally standardized: pipe (126 gallons), hogshead (63

gallons), tierce (42 gallons), and barrel (31½ to 34 gallons), see James I. Walsh, "Capacity and Gauge Standards for Barrels and Casks of Early America," *Chronicles of the Early American Industries Association* 52, no. 4 (December 1999), 151–154. However, in several instances GW indicated that the hogsheads of rum that he purchased or sold held between 111 and 125 gallons, see Mount Vernon Accounts Kept by John Kirkpatrick and Lund Washington, 1772–1787 (LGWMV), 51–52, 152, 155.

5   GW to Lafayette, 29 January 1789, *The Papers of George Washington Digital Edition*, ed. Theodore J. Crackel (Charlottesville: University of Virginia Press, 2007), 264. GW to Biddle, 20 July 1788, *PGW: Confederation* 6: 387. Lear to Biddle, 20 June 1790, George Washington Papers at the Library of Congress, 1741–1799: Series 2, Letterbooks, 212 (Washington, DC., Library of Congress). Lear to GW, 31 October 1790, *The Papers of George Washington: Presidential Series*, ed. Mark A. Mastromarino (Charlottesville: University of Virginia Press, 1996) 6: 606. GW to Lear, 7 November 1790, Ibid., 635. George Augustine Washington to GW, 16 July 1790, *PGW: Presidential* 6: 91.

6   Lund Washington to GW, 4 March 1778, *The Papers of George Washington: Revolutionary War Series*, ed. David R. Hoth (Charlottesville: University of Virginia Press, 2004) 14: 60. Memoranda, 17 September— 15 November 1757, *PGW: Colonial* 4: 405.

7   Rorabaugh, *Alcoholic Republic,* 110–112. An entry in the Mount Vernon Store Account, 1787 (LGWMV), 26, stipulated that, "The white people have one bottle per day from this date on acct of the Cyder's being out." GW noted in his diary that he had finished filling "91 dozn." bottles of cider, 1 March 1760, *The Diaries of George Washington*, ed. Donald Jackson (Charlottesville: University of Virginia Press, 1976) 1: 249. On 11 August 1768 GW noted, "Began to beat Cyder at Doeg Run Muddy hole, & in the Neck (three of the farms)," *The Diaries of George Washington*, ed. Donald Jackson (Charlottesville: University of Virginia Press, 1976) 2: 91. Invoice from Richard Washington, 20 August 1757, *PGW, Colonial* 4: 380. Invoice from Thomas Knox, 18 August 1758, *PGW, Colonial* 5: 400.

8   Cash Accounts, 16 June, 1774, *The Papers of George Washington: Colonial Series*, eds. W.W. Abbot and Dorothy Twohig (Charlottesville: University of Virginia Press, 1995) 10: 76. GW to Lafayette, 8 June

1786, *PGW: Confederation* 4: 105. GW to Moustier, 15 December 1788, *PGW: Presidential* 1: 181 Mount Vernon Farm Accounts, 1799–1800 (Photostat, LGWMV), 45.

9   Rorabaugh, *Alcoholic Republic,* 64–69 Frederick H. Smith, *Caribbean Rum: A Social and Economic History* (Gainesville: University Press of Florida, 2005), 80–81. John E. Latta, *Visit to Mount Vernon in 1799* (Photostat, LGWMV), 2. Julian Niemcewicz, *Under Their Vine and Fig Tree: Travels Through America in 1797–1799, 1805,* ed. and trans. Metchie J.E. Budka (Elizabeth, New Jersey: 1965), reprinted in Jean B. Lee, ed., *Experiencing Mount Vernon: Eyewitness Accounts, 1784–1865* (Charlottesville: University of Virginia Press, 2006), 71.

10 Invoice from Thomas Knox, 18 August 1758, *PGW: Colonial* 5: 400. Invoice from Robert Cary and Company, 17 November 1766, *PGW: Colonial* 7: 475. Carol Cadou, *The George Washington Collection: Fine and Decorative Arts at Mount Vernon* (Manchester, Vermont: Hudson Hills Press, 2006), 54–55. Invoice from Richard Washington, 20 August 1757, *PGW: Colonial* 4: 378. Cadou, *George Washington Collection,* 190.

11 Dennis J. Pogue, Esther C. White, and Eleanor E. Breen, "Digging for Trash and Finding Treasure at Mount Vernon," *The Magazine Antiques* 168, no. 3 (December 2005), 88–95. Frederick H. Smith, *The Archaeology of Alcohol and Drinking* (Gainesville: University Press of Florida, 2008), 17–18. For more about Posey, see John Thornton Posey, "The Improvident Ferryman of Mount Vernon: The Trials of Captain John Posey," *Virginia Cavalcade* 39 (Summer 1989), 36–47.

12 To Make Excellent Cherry Bounce (Photostat, LGWMV). For an in-depth portrayal of Washington's expedition to visit his western lands in 1784, see Joel Achenbach, *George Washington's Potomac and the Race to the West* (New York: Simon & Schuster, 2004), 47–64. Entry for 22 September 1784, *The Diaries of George Washington,* eds. Donald Jackson and Dorothy Twohig (Charlottesville: University of Virginia Press, 1978) 4: 32.

13 Pamela Scott, *Temple of Liberty: Building the Capitol for a New Nation* (New York: Oxford University Press, 1995), 50–51, 55. Thornton to GW, 6 October 1797, *PGW: Retirement* 1: 386. GW to Thornton, 10 October 1797, Ibid., 401.

14 Niemcewicz, *Under Their Vine and Fig Tree*, in Lee, *Experiencing Mount Vernon*, 82. Enclosure, Invoice to Robert Cary and Company, *PGW: Colonial* 6: 463. G. Deneale to Colonel Joseph May, 21 July 1802 (Photostat, LGWMV).

15 David Hancock, *Oceans of Wine: Madeira and the Emergence of American Trade and Taste* (New Haven: Yale University Press, 2009), 112, 115–124. GW to Wakelin Welch and Son, 16 August 1789, *The Papers of George Washington: Presidential Series*, ed. Dorothy Twohig (Charlottesville: University of Virginia Press, 1989) 3: 479. GW Household Account Book, 1793–1797 (LGWMV), 33. Louis B. Wright and Marion Tinling, eds., *Quebec to Carolina in 1785–1786: Being the Travel Diary and Observations of Robert Hunter, Jr., a Young Merchant of London* (San Marino, CA, 1943), reprinted in Lee, *Experiencing Mount Vernon*, 28–30. William Spoon Baker, *Washington After the Revolution, 1785–1799* (Philadelphia: J.B. Lippincott Company, 1898), 231–232. Household Expenses, 15–22 March 1790, *The Papers of George Washington: Presidential Series*, ed. Dorothy Twohig (Charlottesville: University of Virginia Press, 1996) 5: 232.

16 Wright and Tinling, *Quebec to Carolina*, in Lee, *Experiencing Mount Vernon*, 30. Earl of Buchan to GW, 28 June 1791, *PGW: Presidential* 8: 305–307. Baker, *Washington After the Revolution*, 231–232.

17 GW to Mazzei, 1 July 1779, *The Writings of George Washington*, ed. John C. Fitzpatrick (Washington, DC: United States Government Printing Office, 1936) 5: 347. Entry for 21 March 1763, *GWD* 1: 315. John Marsden Pintard to GW, 24 January 1786, *PGW: Confederation* 3: 522–523. Entry for 20 November 1774, *The Diaries of George Washington*, ed. Donald Jackson (Charlottesville: University of Virginia Press, 1978) 3: 73. GW to Anthony Whitting, 13 January 1793, *The Papers of George Washington: Presidential Series*, ed. Christine S. Patrick, (Charlottesville: University of Virginia Press, 2002) 11: 630–631. George Ordish, *The Great Wine Blight* (London: Sidgwick & Jackson, 1987).

18 Enclosure, Invoice to Robert Cary and Company, 1 May 1759, *PGW: Colonial* 6: 318. GW to Robert Cary and Company, 10 August 1760, *PGW: Colonial* 6: 449. GW to Scott, Pringle, Cheap, and Company, 23 February 1768, *The Papers of George Washington: Colonial Series*, eds. W.W. Abbot and Dorothy Twohig (Charlottesville: University of

Virginia Press, 1993) 8: 68. See T.H. Breen, "'Baubles of Britain': The American and Consumer Revolutions of the Eighteenth Century," in *Of Consuming Interests: The Style of Life in the Eighteenth Century*, eds. Cary Carson, Ronald Hoffman, and Peter J. Albert (Charlottesville: University Press of Virginia, 1994), 444–482, for a convincing argument that Washington and others' increasingly frustrating experiences in acquiring fashionable consumer goods from England had a role in fanning the flames of independence.

19 Invoice from Robert Cary and Company, 31 March 1761, *PGW: Colonial* 7: 27. GW to Robert Cary and Company, 1 August 1761, Ibid., 62.

20 As early as 1758, GW wrote to an English supplier stipulating that if the table wares that he was ordering were not "neat and fashionable," then he should not bother to send any, to Richard Washington, 8 January 1758, *PGW: Colonial* 5: 80.

21 For a discussion of the different vessels used to transport, store, and serve alcoholic beverages, see Smith, *Alcohol and Drinking*, 7–28. Invoice from Richard Washington, 20 August 1757, *PGW: Colonial* 4: 378. Enclosure, Invoice to Robert Cary and Company, 15 July 1772, *The Papers of George Washington: Colonial Series*, eds. W.W. Abbot and Dorothy Twohig (Charlottesville: University of Virginia Press, 1994) 9: 66. Joshua Brookes, "A Dinner at Mount Vernon—1799: From the Unpublished Journal of Joshua Brookes (1773–1859)," *The Mount Vernon Ladies' Association of the Union Annual Report, 1947* (Mount Vernon Ladies' Association of the Union, 1947), 21. Invoice from Robert Cary and Company, 13 April 1763, *PGW: Colonial* 7: 195, 198.

22 Invoice from Richard Washington, 20 August 1757, *PGW: Colonial* 4: 378. Invoice from Robert Cary and Company, 31 March 1761, *PGW: Colonial* 7: 28. Enclosure, Invoice to Robert Cary and Company, 15 July 1772, *PGW: Colonial* 9: 66. Reminiscences of the Reverend Ashbel Greene, quoted in, George Washington Parke Custis, *Recollections and Private Memoirs of Washington* (New York: Derby & Jackson, 1860; reprinted, Bridgewater, Virginia: American Foundation Publications, 1999), 169. Cadou, *George Washington Collection*, 94–95.

23 GW to Gouveneur Morris, 13 October 1789, *The Papers of George Washington: Presidential Series*, ed. Dorothy Twohig (Charlottesville: University of Virginia Press, 1993) 4: 178.

24 Ibid. Morris to GW, 12 April 1790, *PGW: Presidential* 5: 329. GW to Morris, 17 December 1790, *The Papers of George Washington: Presidential Series*, ed. Jack D. Warren (Charlottesville: University of Virginia Press, 1998) 7: 92–94.

25 GW to Tobias Lear, 7 November 1790, *PGW: Presidential* 6: 633–634.

26 Cadou, *George Washington Collection*, 144. GW to McHenry, 14 August 1797, *PGW: Retirement* 1: 299–300. GW to Hamilton, 21 August 1797, Ibid., 313.

27 GW to Lawrence Sanford, 29 September 1770, *PGW: Colonial* 8: 385. GW to Daniel Jenifer Adams, 20 July 1772, *PGW: Colonial* 9: 70.

28 Accounts, Kirkpatrick and Washington, 15b, 31, 34, 52.

29 For a presentation of Washington's evolving attitudes toward slavery, see Fritz Hirschfeld, *George Washington and Slavery: A Documentary Portrayal* (Columbia: University of Missouri Press, 1997), 11–20. GW to Joseph Thompson, 2 July 1766, *PGW: Colonial* 7: 453–454.

30 Mount Vernon Store Account, 1787 (LGWMV), 25–33.

31 Ibid., 26–27, 29–30, 32.

32 Mount Vernon Ledger B (Photostat, LGWMV), 42. Store Account, 1787, 29–30.

33 Ibid., 31–33.

34 Ibid., 27, 29, 33.

35 GW to Sarah Cary Fairfax, 15 November 1757, *PGW: Colonial* 5: 56. *Travels in North America in the Years 1780, 1781, and 1782 by the Marquis De Chastellux*, Howard C. Rice, Jr., trans. (Chapel Hill: University of North Carolina Press, 1963) 1: 280.

36 For a portrayal of Washington's efforts to acquire the Spanish jacks, see Alan Fusonie and Donna Jean Fusonie, *George Washington: Pioneer Farmer* (Mount Vernon, Virginia: Mount Vernon Ladies' Association, 1998), 33–35. William Hartshorne and Company to GW, 26 November 1785, *PGW: Confederation* 3: 410–411.

37 Farm Accounts, 1799–1800, 46. Articles of Agreement Between Washington and Philip Bater, 23 April 1787 (LGWMV).

38 Farm Accounts, 1799-1800, 33, 45–46.

39 GW to Lear, 23 November 1790, *PGW: Presidential* 6: 689.

40 Robert F. Dalzell and Lee Baldwin Dalzell, *George Washington's Mount Vernon: At Home in Revolutionary America* (New York: Oxford

University Press, 1998), 145–147. Green to GW, 15 May, 1788, *PGW: Confederation* 6: 274. Whitting to GW, 16 January 1793, *The Papers of George Washington: Presidential Series*, eds. Christine S. Patrick and John C. Pinheiro (Charlottesville: University of Virginia Press, 2005) 12: 5. GW to Whitting, 3 March 1793, Ibid., 258.

41 GW to Green, 23 December 1793, *The Papers of George Washington: Presidential Series*, ed. David R. Hoth (Charlottesville: University of Virginia Press, 2008) 14: 598. GW to Williams Pearce, 16 February 1794, *The Papers of George Washington: Presidential Series*, ed. Christine S. Patrick (Charlottesville: University of Virginia Press, 2009) 15: 239. Dalzell and Dalzell, *George Washington's Mount Vernon*, 146–147.

42 Tobias Lear to GW, 24 June 1793, *The Papers of George Washington: Presidential Series*, ed. Christine S. Patrick (Charlottesville: University of Virginia Press, 2007) 13: 135. GW to William Tilghman, 21 July 1793, Ibid., 263. GW to William Pearce, 18 December 1793, *PGW: Presidential* 14: 561.

43 GW to Robert Lewis and Sons, 12 April 1785, *The Papers of George Washington: Confederation Series*, eds. W.W. Abbot and Dorothy Twohig (Charlottesville: University of Virginia Press, 1992) 2: 493. GW to Robert Lewis and Sons, 1 February 1785, Ibid., 317.

44 GW to Patrick O'Flynn, 15 April 1798, *PGW: Digital*, 241–242. William Booker to GW, 15 May 1799, *PGW: Retirement* 4: 73–74.

45 For more on GW's service in the French and Indian War, see John E. Ferling, "School for Command: Young George Washington and the Virginia Regiment," in *George Washington and the Back Country*, ed. Warren R. Hofstra (Madison House: Madison, Wisconsin, 1998), 195–217. Orders, 19 September 1755, *PGW: Colonial* 2: 53. Robert Dinwiddie to GW, 8 April 1756, Ibid., 343. GW to Dinwiddie, 18 April 1756, *The Papers of George Washington: Colonial Series*, ed. W.W. Abbot (Charlottesville: University of Virginia Press, 1984) 3: 13–14. Orders, 1 May 1756, Ibid., 70.

46 GW to William Buchanan, 20 August 1777, *The Papers of George Washington: Revolutionary War Series*, eds. Philander D. Chase and Edward G. Lengel (Charlottesville: University of Virginia Press, 2001) 11: 11. GW to John Hancock, 16 August 1777, *The Papers of George Washington: Revolutionary War Series*, ed. Frank E. Grizzard (Charlottesville: University of Virginia Press, 2000) 10: 638.

47 General Orders, 6 June 1776, *The Papers of George Washington: Revolutionary War Series*, ed. Philander D. Chase (Charlottesville: University of Virginia Press, 1991) 4: 446. General Orders, Ibid., 183. General Orders, 15 April, 1777, *The Papers of George Washington: Revolutionary War Series*, ed. Philander D. Chase (Charlottesville: University of Virginia Press, 1999) 9: 170. General Orders, 4 November 1777, *The Papers of George Washington: Revolutionary War Series*, eds. Frank E. Grizzard and David R. Hoth (Charlottesville: University of Virginia Press, 2002) 12: 113. General Orders, 20 November 1777, Ibid., 327.

48 Commissary Account of Cordials for George Washington and Other Officers, 7 August 1776 (Photostat, LGWMV).

49 Chernow, *George Washington: A Life*, 432–435, 451–457.

50 Ibid., 451–457. Benjamin Tallmadge, *Memoir of Colonel Benjamin Tallmadge* (New York: T. Holman, 1858), 63–64.

51 Memorandum on General Officers, 9 March 1792, *PGW: Revolutionary War* 10: 74–75.

52 Entry for 15 March 1758, *GWD* 1: 9–10. Entry for 16 March 1758, Ibid., 10.

53 GW to Mary Ball Washington, 15 February 1787, *The Papers of George Washington: Confederation Series*, ed., Dorothy Twohig (Charlottesville: University of Virginia Press, 1997) 5: 35. Chernow, *Washington: A Life*, 422–423, 524–526. GW to Tobias Lear, 31 July 1797, *PGW: Retirement* 1: 281.

54 Custis, *Recollections and Private Memoirs*, 169. *Quebec to Carolina*, in Lee, *Experiencing Mount Vernon*, 28. Amariah Frost, *A Day at Mount Vernon, in 1797*, ed. Hamilton B. Staples (Photostat, LGWMV), 1.

55 GW to William Pearce, 23 November 1794, *The Writings of George Washington*, ed. John C. Fitzpatrick (Washington, DC: United States Government Printing Office, 1940) 34: 41–42. GW to William Pearce, 7 December 1794, Ibid., 53.

56 Chernow, *Washington: A life*, 575–579.

57 Ibid., 575–581. For more detail on the levees and on entertaining in general at the president's residences, see John P. Riley, "Rules of Engagement: Ceremony and the First Presidential Household," *White House History* 6 (Fall 1999), 14–25.

58 Chernow, *Washington: A Life*, 718–726.

59 Slaughter, *Whiskey Rebellion*, 12–27.

60 Ibid., 71.

61 Ibid., 73, 148.

62 Ibid., 93–95.

63 Ibid., 176–189, 206.

64 Chernow, *Washington: A Life*, 718; Slaughter, *Whiskey Rebellion*, 206–212, 219.

65 Batholomew Dandridge to Henry Knox, 9 October 1794, George Washington Papers at the Library of Congress, 1741–1799: Series 2, Letterbooks, 118 (Washington, DC, Library of Congress).

CHAPTER 2

NOTES

1   Mount Vernon Farm Accounts, 1797–1798 (Photostat, LGWMV), 87–88.

2   George Washington's Last Will and Testament, Editorial Note, *PGW: Retirement* 4: 477–527. To compare the scale of Washington's business operations with his Virginia peers, see Laura Kamoie, *Irons in the Fire: The Business History of the Tayloe Family and Virginia's Gentry* (Charlottesville: University of Virginia Press, 2007). Fusonie and Fusonie, *Pioneer Farmer*, 37–49.

3   Over the next 30 years GW added another 6,000 acres of land to the Mount Vernon plantation, John H. Rhodehamel, "The Growth of Mount Vernon," *Mount Vernon Ladies' Association Annual Report for 1982* (Mount Vernon, Virginia: Mount Vernon Ladies' Association, 1983), 18–24. For an in-depth study of Washington's early business dealings and, in particular, his participation in the trans-Atlantic tobacco trade, see Bruce A. Ragsdale, "George Washington, the British Tobacco Trade, and Economic Opportunity in Prerevolutionary Virginia," *The Virginia Magazine of History and Biography* vol. 97, no. 2 (April 1989): 133–162. Allan Kulikoff, *Tobacco and Slaves: The Development of Southern Colonies in the Chesapeake, 1680–1800* (Chapel Hill: University of North Carolina Press, 1986), 47–54.

4   GW to Richard Washington, 6 December 1755, *PGW: Colonial* 2: 207. GW to Robert Cary and Company, 1 May 1759, *PGW: Colonial* 6: 315–316. Ragsdale, "British Tobacco Trade," 134–149.

5   GW to Robert Cary and Company, 1 August 1761, *PGW: Colonial* 7: 62. GW to Robert Cary and Company, 28 September 1760, *PGW: Colonial* 6: 460. Ragsdale, "British Tobacco Trade," 148.

6   Kulikoff, *Tobacco and Slaves*, 47.

7   Ragsdale, "British Tobacco Trade," 148–158.

8   Fusonie and Fusonie, *Pioneer Farmer*, 9. GW to Robert Cary and Company, 1 June 1774, *PGW: Colonial* 10: 83.

9   Lorena S. Walsh, "Slavery and Agriculture at Mount Vernon," in *Slavery at the Home of George Washington*, ed. Philip J. Schwarz (Mount Vernon, Virginia: Mount Vernon Ladies' Association, 2001), 47–77. Ragsdale, "British Tobacco Trade," 144–162.

10 A total of 55 Mount Vernon slaves were listed as tithable (subject to taxation) that year; as only individuals at least 16 years of age were considered tithable, there undoubtedly were many younger slaves also living on the plantation at the time, Memorandum List of Tithables and Taxable Land and Property, 2 July 1765, *PGW: Colonial* 7: 376–377. Fusonie and Fusonie, *Pioneer Farmer*, 37–49.

11 Dennis J. Pogue, "Blacksmithing at George Washington's Mount Vernon: 1755–1800," *Northern Neck of Virginia Historical Magazine* 46, no. 1 (December 1996): 5379–5395. For a comparative study of 18th-century blacksmith shops operating on Maryland's eastern shore, see Christine Daniels, "'Wanted: A Blacksmith Who Understands Plantation Work': Artisans in Maryland, 1700–1800," *William and Mary Quarterly*, Third Series 50, no. 4 (1993): 743–767. Pogue, "Blacksmithing at Mount Vernon," 5391.

12 Sundry Smith's Tools sold G. Washington, January 1755 (Photostat, LGWMV). Entry for 3 April 1755, Mount Vernon Ledger A (Photostat, LGWMV), 20. Pogue, "Blacksmithing at Mount Vernon," 5379–5395.

13 A slave named Peter who was listed as a smith first appeared on the Memorandum List of Tithables, May 1760, *PGW: Colonial* 6: 428, and was listed for the last time in 1770, Memorandum List of Tithables, 16 July 1770, *PGW: Colonial* 8: 356. Nat and George were listed as tithables off and on from 1764 through 1774, when the annual lists were discontinued, Pogue, "Blacksmithing at Mount Vernon," 5385. Indenture with Peter Gollatt, 19 March 1770, *The Papers of George Washington: Digital Edition*, ed. Theodore J. Crackel (Charlottesville: University of Virginia Press, Rotunda, 2007). GW recorded in his diary that Gubner began work on 20 September 1770, *GWD*: 2: 275. Nat and George were listed as smiths in the Mount Vernon Slave Census, 18

February 1786, *GWD*: 4: 278, and again in the list compiled in 1799, Negroes Belonging to George Washington in his own right and by Marriage, June 1799, *PGW: Retirement* 4: 528.

14 GW to William Peacey, 7 January 1788, *PGW: Confederation* 6: 13–14. GW to Tobias Lear, 22 November 1790, *PGW: Presidential* 6: 682. GW to Anthony Whitting, 30 December 1792, *PGW: Presidential* 11: 569. GW to Lear, 25 September 1793, *PGW: Presidential* 14: 136.

15 Pogue, "Blacksmithing at Mount Vernon," 5390–5392. Farm Accounts, 1797–1798, 9. Ibid., 48. At least two other line items in the 1797 accounting—the £969 credited to "Negro hires" and £28.17.1 for the shoemaker—also did not represent actual income, as the "hires" were debited against the respective farms and activities where their labor had been expended, as was the work of the shoemaker, Farm Accounts, 1797–1798, 87–88.

16 An Account of Weaving done by Thomas Davis &ca in the Year 1767 (Photostat, LGWMV), 3. An Account of Weaving done by Thomas Davis &ca in the Year 1768 (Photostat, LGWMV), 6. An Account of Weaving done by Thomas Davis &ca in the Year 1769 (Photostat, LGWMV), 9. An Account of Weaving done by Thomas Davis &ca in the Year 1770 (Photostat, LGWMV), 11. Ledger A, 251. Farm Accounts, 1797–1798, 87–88.

17 For a detailed study of Washington's fisheries, see Donald B. Leach, "George Washington: Waterman-Fisherman, 1760–1799," *Yearbook of the Historical Society of Fairfax County, Virginia* 28 (2001–2002), 1–28. For a description of the fishing process, see Ibid., 12–13.

18 Ibid., 19. Mount Vernon Ledger B (Photostat, LGWMV), 42. Farm Accounts, 1797–1798, 87–88.

19 Entries for 15 September through 19 October 1765, *GWD* 1: 341–343. Leach, "Waterman-Fisherman," 11–13, 15–17.

20 For Washington's agreement with Adams and the terms of the sale of the flour in Barbados, see GW to Adams, 20 July 1772, *PGW: Colonial* 9: 69–70. For an account of the subsequent events relating to the disposition of the vessel, first renamed the *Anne and Elizabeth* and then the *Farmer*, see note no. 1, Ibid., 70–71. GW to Robert McMickan, 10 May 1774, *PGW: Colonial* 10: 55–58.

21 650 barrels of herrings and 23 barrels of superfine flour were recorded

as making up the bulk of the cargo shipped on the *Farmer*, Account of Robert McMickan, 3 August 1774, Ledger B, 127. According to GW's diary, Philip Curtis, Captain of the *Farmer*, called at Mount Vernon on 1 April, 1775, just after returning from his voyage to Lisbon, *GWD*: 3, 319. According to the editors of the diaries, shipping records in London indicate that the *Farmer* carried 4,000 bushels of "Indian Corn" to Lisbon and returned with 3,000 bushels of salt from the Turk Islands, in the Caribbean, Ibid., 320. The various expenses related to the upkeep of the *Farmer* are detailed in, Accounts, Kirkpatrick and Washington, 1772–1787, 24–27. GW's sale of the *Farmer* is recorded in a letter of agreement from Thomas Contee, of Maryland, to GW, 11 April 1775, *PGW: Colonial* 10: 336. The record of payment is contained in the Cash Accounts, 1 May 1775, Ibid., 356. Records of the voyages of the *Becky* and the *George Washington* are contained in, Accounts, Kirkpatrick and Washington, 1772–1787, 54, 81, 109.

22   The most comprehensive examination of GW's campaigns of building at Mount Vernon is by Dalzell and Dalzell, *George Washington's Mount Vernon*. For a summary of GW's intentions for the two expansions of the Mansion, see Ibid., 47–53.

23   Ibid., 100–124.

24   For the influence of Langley's treatise on GW's plans, see Mac Griswold, *Washington's Gardens at Mount Vernon: Landscape of the Inner Man* (New York: Houghton Mifflin, 1999), 63–64. The best treatment of the development of the Mount Vernon landscape is by Peter Martin, *The Pleasure Gardens of Virginia: From Jamestown to Jefferson* (Princeton, New Jersey: Princeton University Press, 1991), 134–144.

25   Dalzell and Dalzell, *George Washington's Mount Vernon*, 113–124.

26   GW to George William Fairfax, 10 November 1785, *PGW: Confederation* 3: 349. For an appraisal of the impact of Young's writings on GW's agricultural innovations, see G. Terry Sharrer, "'An Undebauched Minde': Farmer Washington at Mount Vernon," *Magnolia: Bulletin of the Southern Garden History Society* XV, no. 3: 1–8.

27   GW to George William Fairfax, 30 June 1785, *PGW: Confederation* 3: 90. GW to Arthur Young, 6 August 1786, *The Papers of George Washington: Confederation Series*, eds. W.W. Abbot and Dorothy Twohig (Charlottesville: University of Virginia Press, 1995) 4: 196.

28 Sharrer, "Farmer Washington," 3–4. GW to Young, 6 August 1786, *PGW: Confederation* 4: 196.

29 Entry for 14 April 1760, *GWD*: 1: 266–267. Entry for 1 May 1760, Ibid., 275.

30 GW to Chamberline, 3 April 1788, *PGW: Confederation* 6: 190. Fusonie and Fusonie, *Pioneer Farmer*, 50–55.

31 GW to Bordley, 17 August 1788, *PGW: Confederation* 6: 450.

32 Walsh, "Slavery and Agriculture at Mount Vernon," 63–73.

33 Fusonie and Fusonie, *Pioneer Farmer*, 20–24.

34 For a survey of octagonal structures dating to this period, see Michael Olmert, *Kitchens, Smokehouses, and Privies: Outbuildings and the Architecture of Daily Life in the Eighteenth-Century Mid-Atlantic* (Ithaca, New York: Cornell University Press, 2009), 235–258.

35 GW's instructions to his farm manager to experiment with the spacing between the floor boards are contained in two letters, GW to Pearce, 16 March 1794, *The Writings of George Washington*, ed. John C. Fitzpatrick (Washington, DC: United States Government Printing Office, 1940) 33: 296, and GW to Pearce, 30 March 1794, Ibid., 308.

36 GW's plans to build another treading barn at River Farm are recorded in a letter to Pearce, 22 December 1793, Ibid., 197. GW to Thomas C. Martin, 3 October 1797, *The Writings of George Washington*, ed. John C. Fitzpatrick (Washington, DC: United States Government Printing Office, 1941) 36: 37–38. GW to Young, 1 November 1787, *PGW: Confederation* 5: 405. Young responded to GW that he had "too many doubts" about the merits of Winlaw's machine to recommend it, 1 July 1788, *PGW: Confederation* 6: 369. GW recorded his assessment of the Winlaw machine in his diary entry of 22 January 1790, *The Diaries of George Washington*, eds. Donald Jackson and Dorothy Twohig (Charlottesville: University of Virginia Press, 1979) 6: 12. GW reiterated his concern that to be effective any threshing machine "will depend absolutely upon the simplicity of construction" since it was likely to be operated by "careless Negros and ignorant Overseers," GW to Governor Henry Lee, 16 October 1793, *WGW*: 33: 132. Booker's efforts in building and later repairing the threshing machine are summarized in an editorial note for the entry for 14 August 1798, *GWD*: 6: 313. GW wrote to Booker in the spring of 1798 complaining about the performance of the

threshing machine he had built, 15 April 1798, *WGW* 36: 247. Booker's arrival at Mount Vernon to repair the threshing machine was recorded on 14 August 1798, *GWD*: 6: 313.

37 For a listing of GW's land acquisitions, see Rhodehamel, "Growth of Mount Vernon," 18–24. For Washington's plans to reorganize Union Farm, see Dennis J. Pogue, "The Domestic Architecture of Slavery at George Washington's Mount Vernon," *Winterthur Portfolio* 37, no. 1 (2002), 13–14. GW to Young, 15 November 1786, *PGW: Confederation* 4: 372. Young to GW, 1 February 1787, *PGW: Confederation* 5: 4. GW wrote to Young updating him on the progress of the barn's construction, 1 November 1787, Ibid., 403. GW to Young, 4 December 1788, *PGW: Presidential* 1: 161.

38 GW gave instructions about the construction of the proposed building in a letter to George Augustine Washington, 27 May 1787, *PGW: Confederation* 5: 197. A second letter from GW to Washington later that year indicates that construction was well underway at that time, 24 July 1787, Ibid., 270. GW to Pearce, 5 June 1796, *The Writings of George Washington*, ed. John C. Fitzpatrick (Washington, DC: United States Government Printing Office, 1940) 35: 79. Richard Peters, "Remarks on the Plan of a Stercorary," in *Memoirs of the Philadelphia Society for Promoting Agriculture* (Philadelphia: Jane Aitken, 1808), 281–285. Dennis J. Pogue, *Archaeological Investigations at the Mount Vernon Dung Repository: An Interim Report*, Mount Vernon Ladies' Association Archaeology Department, File Report No. 5 (February 1994), 6–18.

39 For an overview of GW's livestock operations, see Fusonie and Fusonie, *Pioneer Farmer*, 25–36.

40 Ibid., 32. Entry for 13 December 1785, *GWD*: 4: 249. Advice on keeping livestock was a common feature found in distilling manuals from the period, such as that by Michael Krafft, *The American Distiller, or the Theory and Practice of Distilling* (Philadelphia: Thomas Dobson, 1804), 152–157. Details of the construction of the sheds, pens, and troughs are contained in the Mount Vernon Farm Reports (Photostat, LGWMV), from 1 September to 17 November 1798.

41 Fusonie and Fusonie, *Pioneer Farmer*, 28. For example, GW wrote to his plantation manager, William Pearce, advising him to select the "best formed" ram lambs for breeding and to cull out "all the old, and

indifferent sheep from the flocks," 6 April 1794, *PGW: Presidential* 15: 523–524. GW to William Fitzhugh, 15 May 1786, *PGW: Confederation* 4: 52. GW to Arthur Young, 18 June 1792, *The Papers of George Washington: Presidential* Series, eds. Robert F. Haggard and Mark A. Mastromarino (Charlottesville: University of Virginia Press, 2002) 10: 464–465. Entry for 24 November 1785, *GWD*: 4: 240. George Washington's Last Will and Testament, Stock, 9 July 1799, *PGW: Retirement* 4: 519.

42 GW recorded his observations about the northern woolen mills in his diary on 20 October 1789, *The Diaries of George Washington,* eds. Donald Jackson and Dorothy Twohig (Charlottesville: University of Virginia Press, 1979) 5: 468. GW's letter to Governor Beverley Randolph, 22 November 1789, is printed in *GWD*: 5: 469, note no. 3. GW to John Sinclair, 20 July 1794, *WGW* 33: 439.

43 Fusonie and Fusonie, *Pioneer Farmer,* 31. Entry for 24 November 1785, *GWD*: 4: 240. Lund Washington to GW, 24 November 1775, *PGW: Revolutionary* 4: 423. The particulars of the events whereby GW received the bull from Lloyd are recorded in a letter from Gustavus Scott to GW, 16 June 1797. Niemcewicz, *Under Their Vine and Fig Tree,* in Lee, *Experiencing Mount Vernon,* 75. GW to James Anderson, 11 June 1798, *PGW: Retirement* 2: 322.

44 An Inventory of the Estate of Lawrence Washington, Subscribers the 7th and 8th of March 1753 (Photostat, LGWMV), 6. GW mentioned the dairy at the Mansion House Farm in his diary entry of 16 April 1760, *GWD*: 1: 268. Among many examples found in the plantation accounts, in 1761 GW received one Cheshire cheese weighing 60 pounds from Robert Cary and Company, Invoice, 31 March 1761, *PGW: Colonial* 7: 26; the next year GW ordered one Cheshire cheese "of about 40 lb.," Invoices to Robert Cary and Company, 15 November 1762, Ibid., 165. In 1764 GW received one Cheshire cheese weighing 29 pounds and two "dble Gloster" cheeses weighing 43 pounds, Invoice from Robert Cary and Company, 13 February 1764, Ibid., 290. GW to Lafayette, 29 January 1789, *PGW: Digital:* 264.

45 The editors of the *GWD* cite a letter from GW to Pearce, 2 November 1794, expressing his desire to establish the dairies, Introduction, *GWD*: 1: xxxiv. In a diary entry dated 28 April 1788, GW stated that the "brick work of the Dairy" had commenced, *GWD*: 5: 311. On 5 June 1788,

GW indicated that the dairy was ready to be outfitted with churns and other equipment, *GWD*: 5: 337. GW to William Pearce, 9 February 1794, *PGW: Presidential* 15: 204. Farm Accounts, 1797–1798, 15. GW to James Anderson, 13 December 1799, *PGW: Retirement* 4: 457.

46   Jefferson to Walter Jones, 2 January 1814, *The Works of Thomas Jefferson in Twelve Volumes*, ed. Paul L. Ford (New York: G.P. Putnam, 1905) 11: 376. During one particularly active period, GW hunted fox on 11 days during the month of January 1769, killing one fox, diary entries 4 to 28 January 1769, *GWD*: 1: 119–121. The horses are listed in the diary entry for 18 November 1785, *GWD*: 4: 232–233, and again on 24 November 1785, Ibid., 239. GW to Lee, 30 November 1788, *PGW: Presidential* 1: 139. Enclosure, Schedule of Property, 9 July 1799, *PGW: Retirement* 4: 519. Farm Accounts, 1797–1798, 87.

47   After many months of negotiations and careful planning, GW received word from Thomas Cushing of Boston that he had accepted shipment of "a very fine Jack Ass" that had been sent by the King of Spain as a gift for GW, 7 October 1785, *PGW: Confederation* 3: 296. GW wrote to the Marquis de Lafayette, 19 November 1786, thanking him for his efforts in sending "a Jack and two she Asses" from the Isle of Malta, *PGW: Confederation* 4: 385. The livestock inventories are included in a diary entry dated 24 November 1785, *GWD*: 4: 239–240, and in the Enclosure, Schedule of Property, 9 July 1799, *PGW: Retirement* 4: 519. Farm Accounts, 1797–1798, 87. GW to Arthur Young, 4 December 1788, *PGW: Presidential* 1: 161. Fusonie and Fusonie, *Pioneer Farmer*, 36.

48   See *GWD*: 1: 240–242 for a listing of the land parcels making up the Mount Vernon plantation, including the mill tract. GW performed his test on 8 April 1760, as recorded in his diary, Ibid., 264. GW made final payment to millwright Robert Wright on 20 October 1764, Cash Accounts, *PGW: Colonial* 7: 333. GW stated his intentions in a letter to Charles West, a neighboring land owner, 6 June 1769, *PGW: Colonial* 8: 209. On 30 December 1769, GW entered into an agreement with a millwright, John Ball of Frederick County, to build the new mill, *GWD*: 2: 204. GW noted in his diary that the mill was complete and grinding grain on 20 March 1771, *GWD*: 3, 18.

49   For the archaeological evidence indicating that the wheel was 16 feet in diameter and for much other structural information as

well, see Burson, *A Report on the George Washington Gristmill*. For a description of the workings of early American water mills, see Charles Howell and Allan Keller, *The Mill at Philipsburg Manor Upper Mills and a Brief History of Milling* (Tarrytown, New York: 1977), 31–66.

50 GW ordered "a pair of French Burr Millstones" from Robert Cary and Company, 12 August 1771, *PGW: Colonial* 8: 516, specifying that he wanted them to be "of a good and even quality" as he was entering into the merchant milling business. Invoice from Robert Cary and Company, 3 December 1771, Ibid., 565. GW purchased the pair of lower quality stones from a local supplier on 22 September 1770, *GWD*: 2: 276. Howell and Keller, *Mill at Philipsburg*, 71–73.

51 Diary entry from 27 January 1771, *GWD*: 3: 4. Lund Washington to GW, 12 May 1771, *PGW: Colonial* 8: 467–468. In his diary, GW recorded that masons began making repairs to the mill 4 September 1771, *GWD*: 3: 59. Payment to the masons is recorded in the Cash Accounts, 16 and 25 November 1771, *PGW: Colonial* 8: 531.

52 The dimensions of the race are contained in a letter from Lund Washington to GW, 2 September 1778 (Photostat, LGWMV). GW noted that work began on digging the race on 26 April 1770, *GWD* 2: 233. GW recorded his offer to the ditchers on 8 May 1770, *GWD* 2: 235. GW's last reference to digging the race dates to 11 February 1771, *GWD* 3: 7. On 20 March 1771 the water from the race was allowed to flow into the mill, Ibid., 3: 18. The slaves began work "scouring" out the race on 10 August 1772, Ibid., 3:128.

53 Diary entry, 10 August 1771, *GWD* 3: 51. Diary entry, 20 August 1771, Ibid. Diary entry, 10 September 1771, Ibid., 59. The foundation of the miller's house is indicated on a Topographic Map of Washington's Mill Property, 4 January 1932 (Photostat, LGWMV). Declaration of Assurance No. 2043, Mutual Assurance Society of Virginia, 7 April 1803 (Photostat, LGWMV). GW to Robert Lewis and Sons, 1 February 1785, *PGW: Confederation* 2: 317. Agreement of Lund Washington with William Roberts, 13 October 1770, *PGW: Colonial* 8: 395.

54 Declaration of Assurance No. 2043. GW to Robert and William Lewis, 6 September 1783, *The Writings of George Washington*, ed. John C. Fitzpatrick (Washington, DC: United States Government Printing

Office, 1938) 27: 132. Map of the Five Farms, 1793, HM 5995 (San Marion, CA, The Huntington Library).

55 Greville Bathe and Dorothy Bathe, *Oliver Evans: A Chronicle of Early American Engineering* (Philadelphia: The Historical Society of Pennsylvania, 1935), 25.

56 Eugene S. Ferguson, *Oliver Evans: Inventive Genius of the American Industrial Revolution* (Greenville, Delaware: Hagley Museum, 1980), 13– 28. GW's secretary, Tobias Lear, wrote to Oliver Evans on 29 August 1791, indicating that the millwright, William Ball, was ready to begin installing Evans's improvements; Lear also related that although the workman was fully confident of success, GW was "desirous of having it done in the most perfect manner," and thus was willing to await Evans's arrival to oversee the operation, *PGW: Presidential* 8: 463. That Oliver Evans's brother, Evan Evans, travelled to Mount Vernon to work with the millwright is indicated in GW's letter to Lear, 23 September 1791, *The Papers of George Washington*, eds. Mark A. Mastromarino and Jack D. Warren (Charlottesville: University of Virginia Press, 2000) 9: 4.

57 Ferguson, *Oliver Evans: Inventive Genius*, 19–20. Niemcewicz, *Under Their Vine and Fig Tree*, in Lee, *Experiencing Mount Vernon*, 77.

58 Lear to Evans, 26 January 1792, *PGW: Presidential* 9: 508. GW Memorandum of Work to be done, 5 November 1796, *WGW*: 35: 258.

59 Mount Vernon Mill Account Book, 1776–1785 (Photostat, LGWMV). Diary entry and accompanying note, 1 June 1771, *GWD*: 3: 36.

60 The prices paid for the different grades of flour also fluctuated with market conditions, and according to the volume sold, with higher prices generally received for smaller amounts, Farm Accounts, 1799–1800, 10, 13–14, 19, 23, 28, and 31. An entry in the flour account for 23 July 1799 listed the following prices: 44 barrels of superfine flour at $8.50, 50 barrels of fine flour at $7.66, and 12 barrels of midlings at $6.66, Ibid., 19.

61 GW to Anthony Whitting, 24 February 1793, *PGW: Presidential* 12: 213. GW to Whitting, 16 December 1792, *PGW: Presidential* 11: 520. GW to Whitting, 27 January 1793, *PGW: Presidential* 12: 54.

62 For a discussion of the mixed esteem in which millers were held in 18th-century America, see Henry Magee, *The Miller in Eighteenth-Century Virginia* (Williamsburg, Virginia: Colonial Williamsburg Foundation, 1966), 16–20.

63 See William Pearce to GW, 17 January 1796, quoted in note no. 2, *PGW: Confederation* 2: 482. On Callahan's hiring, see GW to Clement Biddle, 8 April 1798, note no. 3, *PGW: Retirement* 2: 229. For GW's assessment of Callahan, see GW to William Roberts, 17 June 1799, *PGW: Retirement* 4: 133. GW to Biddle, 8 April 1798, note no. 3, *PGW: Retirement* 2: 228–229.

64 For a summary of the sequence of events from GW's rehiring Roberts in June 1799 until his discharge on 16 November 1799, see GW to James Anderson, 8 September 1799, note no. 2, *PGW: Retirement* 4: 287. GW's description of the miller's assistant, presumably the slave, Ben, was contained in a letter sent by Lear to Evans, 26 January 1792, *PGW: Presidential* 9: 508.

65 Ten of the slaves working at the gristmill and distillery in 1799 are listed in, Negros Belonging to George Washington in his own right and by Marriage, June 1799, *PGW: Retirement* 4: 528–529; the eleventh slave is included in, A List of Negros Hired from Mrs. French, June 1799, Ibid., 540. Work on converting the cooperage is reported in the Mount Vernon Weekly Reports, 1797–1798, for January 14 and 20, and February 4, 1797 (Photostat, LGWMV). Farm Accounts, 1797–1798 and 1799–1800.

66 The transaction between GW and Robert Adam and Company is recorded in Ledger A, 326 and 341. For the shipment of 200 barrels of flour to Jamaica, see *GWD*: 3: 37, editorial note for 6 June 1771. Farm Accounts, 1797–1798, 87–88. See the flour account for the period 1 October 1797 to 1 October 1798, Ibid., 167–169. See the distillery account, Ibid., 30–33.

67 For a detailed examination of GW's experience as a western land owner, see Philander D. Chase, "A Stake in the West: George Washington as Backcountry Surveyor and Landholder," in *George Washington and the Virginia Backcountry*, ed. Warren R. Hofstra (Madison, Wisconsin: Madison House, 1998), 159–194. Posey was in dire financial difficulties, and GW recommended that he consider a fresh start in the west, GW to Posey, 24 June 1767, *PGW: Colonial* 8: 3.

68 Chase, "A Stake in the West," 160–163, 168–169, 177–179.

69 Ibid., 179. For GW's military career during the French and Indian War, see John E. Ferling, "School for Command: Young George Washington

and the Virginia Regiment," in *George Washington and the Virginia Backcountry*, 195–222. Ibid., 197; also see William M.S. Rasmussen and Robert S. Tilton, eds., *George Washington: The Man Behind the Myths*, (Charlottesville: University Press of Virginia, 1999), 37–73. Ibid., 70. On the topic of the bounty lands and GW's determined efforts to increase his share, see Douglas Southall Freeman, *Washington: An Abridgement in One Volume* (New York: Simon & Schuster, 1995), 179–190.

70 Ibid., 179–180. GW's final allotment of the bounty lands totaled 20,147 acres, Freeman, *Washington*, 190. The Schedule of Property appended to GW's will in 1799 listed more than 50,000 acres, in addition to the 8,000-acre Mount Vernon plantation, *PGW: Retirement* 4: 512–516.

71 Chase, "A Stake in the West," 182.

72 GW to James Ross, 16 June 1794, quoted in Ibid. For GW's partnership with Simpson, see diary entry dated 13 September 1784, and note no. 2, *GWD*: 4: 20–21.

73 Ibid.

74 Shreve first attempted to purchase property from Washington in 1785, but eventually agreed to rent 600 acres of the Washington's Bottom tract in 1787. GW finally agreed to sell Shreve the entire property in 1795, Shreve to GW, 22 June 1785, and accompanying notes, *PGW: Confederation* 3: 73–74. Shreve to GW, 21 December 1798, *PGW: Retirement* 3: 275. GW to Shreve, 10 January 1799, Ibid., 314. GW to Samuel Mickle Fox, 10 June 1799, see note no. 1, *PGW: Retirement* 4: 112.

75 For a detailed examination of GW's dealings with the squatters, see Achenbach, *Grand Idea*, 83–100, 144–150.

76 Ibid., GW to Thomas Smith, 7 December 1785, *PGW: Confederation* 3: 438.

77 Achenbach, *Grand Idea*, 144–150. GW to Presley Nevill, 27 November 1786, *PGW: Confederation* 4: 404.

78 Achenbach, *Grand Idea*, 111–120.

79 GW to Charles Carter, August 1754, *PGW: Colonial* 1: 197. For the history of the development of the Potomac Canal, see Achenbach, *Grand Idea*, 121–137, 213–215; also Charles Royster, *The Fabulous History of the Dismal Swamp Company* (New York: Random House, 1999), 156, 294–297, 331–332.

80 GW expressed his concerns about the future of the western settlements and registered his belief that building canals and roads was the only way to encourage trade between them and the coastal states, which he believed would ensure their continued connection with the new nation, GW to George Plater, 25 October 1784, *PGW: Confederation* 2: 108. GW recorded the findings of his 1784 trip to explore the western territory in a lengthy diary entry dated 4 October 1784, in which he expressed the hope of binding the regions together, *GWD*: 4: 66.

81 On the significance of the Mount Vernon conference, see Chernow, *Washington: A Life*, 502–503.

82 The definitive study of the Dismal Swamp Company is by Royster, *Fabulous History*. Ibid., 82–97.

83 For the details of the ultimately unsuccessful sale by GW of his shares in the Company to Lee, see Ibid., 363, 384–387, 418.

84 For the particulars of the financial considerations relating to the estate of Daniel Parke Custis, see Editorial Note, *PGW: Colonial* 6: 202–203. For the record of GW's land acquisitions, see The Growth of Mount Vernon, *GWD*: 1: 240–242. On GW's building campaigns at Mount Vernon and the crucial importance of the infusion of the Custis money to their success, see Dalzell and Dalzell, *George Washington's Mount Vernon*, 47–70.

85 Last Will and Testament, Enclosure, Schedule of Property, 9 July 1799, *PGW: Retirement* 4: 512–519. For a seriously flawed assessment that places GW at no. 59 on the list, see Michael Klepper and Robert Gunther, *The Wealthy 100* (Secaucus, New Jersey: Citadel Press, 1996), 205–207. For a much more detailed and credible analysis that places GW as one of the top 10 wealthiest Virginians during his lifetime, see Kamoie, "Three Generations of Planter-Businessmen: The Tayloes, Slave Labor, and Entrepreneurialism in Virginia, 1710–1830" (PhD diss., College of William and Mary, 1999). According to Kamoie, GW ranked as the 8th largest slave holder; he ranked only as the 38th largest land owner, but if his western lands are added to the total, his ranking would climb into the top five, Ibid., 247.

86 Chernow, *Washington: A Life*, 554.

87 Kamoie, *Irons in the Fire*, 50–61.

88 Ibid., 48–50 and 54.

89 Kamoie, "Three Generations of Planter-Businessmen," 260, 263, 287–288.

90 GW to David Humphreys, 23 March 1793, *PGW: Presidential* 12: 363; also see Ibid., for GW's reflections on accepting public service over his own "love of retirement and domestic life."

91 The best source for GW's will is the printed version found in *PGW: Retirement* 4: 477–527, to include the extensive editorial comments. The most convenient published source for examining GW's writings on slavery is Hirschfeld, *George Washington and Slavery*. The most detailed recent study of GW and slavery is by Henry Wiencek, *An Imperfect God: George Washington, His Slaves, and the Creation of America* (New York: Farrar, Straus and Giroux, 2003). For the apparent failure of GW's decision to manumit his slaves to influence others to follow his lead, see Dennis J. Pogue, "George Washington and the Politics of Slavery," *Historic Alexandria Quarterly* (Spring/Summer 2003), 8.

92 GW to Lund Washington, 15 August 1778, *The Papers of George Washington: Revolutionary War Series*, ed. David R. Hoth (Charlottesville: University of Virginia Press, 2006) 16: 315–316. Jean B. Lee, "Mount Vernon Plantation: Model for the Republic," in *Slavery at the Home of George Washington*, ed. Philip J. Schwarz (Mount Vernon, Virginia: Mount Vernon Ladies' Association, 2001), 31–38. GW to Lund Washington, 24 February 1779, quoted in Hirschfeld, *Washington and Slavery*, 28. GW to Alexander Spotswood, 23 November 1794, quoted in Dorothy Twohig, "'That Species of Property': Washington's Role in the Controversy over Slavery," ed. Donald Higginbotham, in *George Washington Reconsidered* (Charlottesville: University of Virginia Press, 2001), 128.

93 For laws regulating the activities of slaves and relating to the responsibilities of slave owners, see Philip J. Schwarz, *Twice Condemned: Slaves and the Criminal Laws of Virginia, 1705–1865* (Baton Rouge: Louisiana State University Press, 1988). On the status of the dower slaves, see Wiencek, *Imperfect God*, 81–82. GW to John Francis Mercer, 24 November 1786, *PGW: Confederation* 4: 394. GW to Robert Lewis, 17 August 1799, *PGW: Retirement* 4: 256.

94 See Joseph Ellis, *Founding Brothers: The Revolutionary Generation* (New York: Alfred A. Knopf, 2001), 81–119, for a detailed portrayal of the deliberations at the constitutional convention relating to the slavery issue.

95 GW related his intention to sell or rent portions of Mount Vernon in a letter to Arthur Young, 12 December 1793, *WGW*: 33: 174–183. The English farmer in question was Richard Parkinson, who travelled to Mount Vernon in 1798 to inspect the property, see Parkinson to GW, 28 August 1797, and editorial notes, *PGW: Retirement* 1: 323–324.

96 This sum is based on an average value of £40 per individual, a figure suggested as appropriate for the 1780s by Jackson T. Main, "The One Hundred," *The William and Mary Quarterly* 11, no. 3 (1956): 356. Farm Accounts, 1797–1798, 87–88. GW to Tobias Lear, 6 May 1794, *WGW*: 33: 357–358.

97 Ibid., 358.

98 Chase, "A Stake in the West," 183–184.

99 Chernow, *Washington: A Life*, 815.

100 GW agreed to hire Anderson on 6 October, 1796, and he began work on 1 January 1797, see Anderson to GW, 8 March 1797, and the accompanying editorial notes, *PGW: Retirement* 1: 20–22. GW to Anderson, 8 January 1797, *WGW*: 35: 353–353.

101 Farm Accounts, 1797–1798, 87–88. Before 1799 the Mount Vernon accounts were calculated using the English system of pounds, shillings, and pence; beginning in 1799 the accounts were kept using the American system of dollars and cents. According to GW's records, during this period one pound was roughly equivalent to three dollars.

CHAPTER 3

NOTES

1   Anderson's letter to GW has not been found; GW responded to Anderson, 8 January 1797, giving him permission to establish the distillery and to convert the cooper's shop to accommodate it, *WGW*: 35: 352–353. For the distillery's profits in 1799, see Farm Accounts, 1799–1800, 46.

2   For Pearce's intention to leave Mount Vernon due to "an increasing Rheumatic infection," see Anderson to GW, 8 March 1797, *PGW*: *Retirement* 1: 21–22, and editorial notes. For GW's explanation to Anderson regarding the requirements of the position, see Ibid.

3   Anderson provided a lengthy summary of his experience as a farmer in Scotland and in America in a letter to GW, 28 August 1796 (Photostat, LGWMV). John R. Hume and Michael S. Moss, *The Making of Scotch Whisky: A History of the Scotch Whisky Distilling Industry* (Edinburgh, Scotland: Canongate, 2000), 23–24.

4   Ibid. Anderson to GW, 28 August 1796 (Photostat, LGWMV).

5   Ibid.

6   See the editorial notes for a summary of the negotiations between Anderson and GW, Anderson to GW, 8 March 1797, *PGW*: *Retirement* 1: 21–22. GW to Anderson, 8 January 1797, *WGW*: 35: 352–353.

7   Anderson to GW, 22 February 1797 (Photostat, LGWMV). Farm Accounts, 1797–1798, 87. Anderson to GW, 21 June 1797, *PGW*: *Retirement* 1: 199–200.

8   GW to Fitzgerald, 12 June 1797, Ibid., 180. Fitzgerald to GW, 12 June 1797, Ibid., 181. GW to Anderson, 18 June 1797, Ibid., 193.

9   The progress of construction is recorded in the Weekly Reports, 1797–1799, 7 October 1797 through 17 March 1798.

10 GW to Davidson, 2 March 1798, *WGW*: 36: 176–177. Peter Bingle seems to have served most often as Anderson's assistant, Farm Accounts, 1797–1798, 173, and Farm Accounts, 1799–1800, 38.

11 GW to William A. Washington, 26 June 1798, *PGW: Retirement* 2: 361. GW to Washington, 24 May 1799, *PGW: Retirement* 4: 87. GW to Washington, 29 October 1799, Ibid., 379.

12 GW to Lewis, 26 January 1798, *PGW: Retirement* 2: 47.

13 GW to William Fitzhugh, 30 May 1798, Ibid., 307.

14 For the distillery account for the year 1797, see Farm Accounts, 1797–1798, 9 and 79; for the account for the year 1798, see Farm Accounts, 1797–1798, 155 and 173–175; for the account for the year 1799, see Farm Accounts, 1799–1800, 30–33 and 45–46.

15 For the listing of transactions, see the Farm Accounts, 1797–1798 and 1799–1800.

16 For Chichester's account, see Farm Accounts, 1799–1800, 10.

17 Anna C. Borden compiled the figures on the activities of the merchants; for her detailed analysis of the distillery accounts for the year 1799, see Borden, "A Study of Transition in Plantation Economy." For Gilpin's account, see Farm Accounts, 1797–1798, 99 and 143, and Farm Accounts, 1799–1800, 43–44.

18 For Hoof's account, see Farm Accounts, 1799–1800, 7.

19 Niemcewicz, *Under Their Vine and Fig Tree*, in Lee, *Experiencing Mount Vernon*, 77.

20 Michael Krafft, *The American Distiller, or, the Theory and Practice of Distilling* (Philadelphia: Archibald Bartram, 1804), 152–157. Niemcewicz, *Under Their Vine and Fig Tree*, in Lee, *Experiencing Mount Vernon*, 77.

21 The proportions of the ingredients of GW's mash bill were arrived at by tabulating the different grains which were identified as having been ground and sent to the distillery for its use, as recorded in the Mount Vernon Weekly Reports for the period from 21 April 1798 to 26 January 1799, see Esther C. White, *Distillery Research Report: Whiskey Ingredients* (Mount Vernon, Virginia: Mount Vernon Ladies' Association, 30 January 2001). Krafft, *American Distiller*, 71–72.

22 See Rorabaugh, *Alcoholic Republic*, 69–71, for a description of the distilling process. For detailed period descriptions of distilling, see

Krafft, *American Distiller*, Samuel M'Harry, *The Practical Distiller* (Harrisburg, PA: John Wyeth, 1809), and Harrison Hall, *The Distiller* (Philadelphia: J. Bioren, 1818).

23 Six men were listed as working in the distillery in 1799; see Negros Belonging to George Washington in his own Right and by Marriage, June 1799, *PGW: Retirement* 4: 529 and 540.

24 For GW's tax bills, see Farm Accounts, 1799–1800, 37 and 45. The still transaction is recorded in George McMunn's account, Farm Accounts, 1797–1798, 137. An invoice submitted by McMunn, dated 5 February 1800, includes a charge for "Leading a coffin" (Photostat, LGWMV). Coxe, *Statement of the Arts and Manufactures of the United States of America*; also reported in Rorabaugh, *Alcoholic Republic*, 225–227.

25 James Stein, distiller, Kilbagie, and John Stein, distiller, Kennetpans: goods and chattels, with schedules of distillery equipment, 1788 (Edinburgh, National Archives of Scotland).

26 For detailed information on the results of the archaeological excavations, see: www.mountvernon.org/learn/pres_arch.

27 For his directions on the type of stone to be used, see GW to Tobias Lear, 10 September 1797, *PGW: Retirement* 1: 345.

28 Weekly Reports, 1797–1799, 3 March and 10 March 1798.

29 For a list of the copper furnishings acquired for the distillery, see the account of George McMunn, Farm Accounts, 1797–1798, 137. Weekly Reports, 1797–1799, 12 May to 2 June 1798.

30 Krafft, *American Distiller*, 85.

31 For a period description of a malting kiln and of the process of malting, see M'Harry, *Practical Distiller*, 67–68 and 159–160. Weekly Reports, 1797–1799, 10 March 1798 and 17 March 1798.

32 Hall, *The Distiller*, 159.

33 See Jacques-Francois Demachy, *Descriptions de Arts et Metiers* (Geneve: Slatkine Reprints, [1773] 1984) for one illustration of a two-still set up.

34 For a description of this type of water distribution system, see Krafft, *American Distiller*, 23–28.

35 Weekly Reports, 1797–1799, 18 February to 3 March 1798.

36 For prescriptive advice on laying out the operations of a distillery, see Krafft, *American Distiller*, 18–48, and Hall, *The Distiller*, 19–45.

37 Weekly Reports, 1797–1799, 23 June and 30 June 1798, 25 February 1798.

38 An Inventory of Articles at Mount Vernon, 1800 (Photostat, LGWMV), 35.

39 Ibid., 18 and 35.

40 George Washington's Last Will and Testament, July 1799, *PGW: Retirement* 4: 489. *Alexandria Daily Advertiser*, 25 January 1804. T. Michael Miller, comp., *Artisans and Merchants of Alexandria, Virginia: 1780–1820* (Bowie, MD: Heritage Books, 1991) 1: 112. Mutual Assurance Society of Virginia (1815), Declaration of Assurance No. 1750 (Richmond: Virginia State Library and Archives).

CHAPTER 4
NOTES

1   For early efforts to brew beer and for evidence of transporting supplies of beer and wine to the New World, see, Henry R. Crowgey, *Kentucky Bourbon: The Early Years of Whiskey Making* (Lexington: University Press of Kentucky, 2008), 1–8, and Lender and Martin, *Drinking in America*, 2–6. Rorabaugh, *Alcoholic Republic*, 20–21.

2   On the history of the production and consumption of alcoholic beverages in Europe, see Fernand Braudel, *The Structures of Everyday Life: The Limits of the Possible* (New York: Harper & Row, 1985), 227–249. For the early history of whisky production in Great Britain, see Hume and Moss, *Making of Scotch Whisky*, 22–43. For more on the presumed healthful qualities of alcohol, as well as challenges in obtaining clean water, see Sarah Hand Meacham, "'They Will Be Adjudged By Their Drink, What Kinde Of Housewives They Are': Gender, Technology, and Household Cidering in England and the Chesapeake, 1690 to 1760," *The Virginia Magazine of History and Biography* III, no. 2 (2003), 120–124; also see Rorabaugh, *Alcoholic Republic*, 95–99, for more on issues with water.

3   On the decline of rum and the role of Scots-Irish immigrants in the rise of whiskey, see Rorabaugh, *Alcoholic Republic*, 61–69; also see Lender and Martin, *Drinking in America*, 30–33. On the technical issues that beset the American brewing industry, and the important role played by German immigrants in finally surmounting those obstacles, see Rorabaugh, *Alcoholic Republic*, 107–110.

4   Quoted in Meacham, "'They Will Be Adjudged By Their Drink,'" 123. Rorabaugh, *Alcoholic Republic*, 95–99.

5   Theophilus Grew, *Virginia Almanack for the Year of Our Lord 1767* (Williamsburg, VA: Purdie and Dixon, 1766), n.p; Thomas Cooper, *Some Information Respecting America Collected by Thomas Cooper, Late of Manchester* (London: 1795), 123.

6   For a study of advice relating to health found in early almanacs, see Thomas A. Horrocks, "Rules, Remedies, and Regimens: Health Advice in Early American Almanacs," in Charles E. Rosenberg, ed., *Right Living: An Anglo-American Tradition of Self-Help Medicine and Hygiene* (Baltimore, MD: Johns Hopkins University Press, 2003), 112–147. Nicholas Cresswell, *The Journal of Nicholas Cresswell, 1774–1777*, ed. Lincoln MacVeagh (New York: 1924), 22. Theophilus Grew and Joseph Royle, *Virginia Almanack for the Year of our Lord God 1764* (Williamsburg, VA: Joseph Royle and Co., 1764), n.p.; Landon Carter's diary entry is quoted in, Crowgey, *Kentucky Bourbon*, 13.

7   Rorabaugh, *Alcoholic Republic*, 113–118.

8   Increase Mather, *Wo to Drunkards* (Cambridge, MA: 1673), 4. Quoted in Crowgey, *Kentucky Bourbon*, 263.

9   William Waller Hening, comp., *The Statues at Large: Being a Collection of the Laws of Virginia, from the First Session of the Legislature, in the Year 1619* (Richmond, VA: 1819) 1: 158. Ibid., 384. In the 18th century the Quakers and the Methodists were the only significant religious denominations who openly opposed distilled spirits, Rorabaugh, *Alcoholic Republic*, 38. W.P. Strickland, ed., *The Backwoods Preacher: An Autobiography of Peter Cartwright* (London: Alexander Heylin, 1858), 119.

10 Rorabaugh, *Alcoholic Republic*, 30–31.

11 Ibid., 7–11.

12 Ibid., 25. John Bricknell, *The Natural History of North Carolina* (Dublin: James Carson, 1737), 33–34.

13 Entry for 4 March 1709, Louis B. Wright and Marion Tinling, eds., *The Secret Diary of William Byrd, 1709–1712*, (Richmond, VA: Dietz Press, 1941), 12.

14 Cooper, *Some Information Respecting America*, 123.

15 Philip Alexander Bruce, *Economic History of Virginia in the Seventeenth Century* (New York: MacMillan and Company, 1896), 2: 236. Washington County, Virginia, Will Book no. 1, 1777–1792, 118, quoted in Crowgey,

Kentucky Bourbon, 9. Cresswell, *Journal of Nicholas Creswell*, 123. Farm Accounts, 1797–1798, 46. The bequest was recorded between 1664 and 1672, Bruce, *Economic History of Virginia*, 2: 217.

16 See Rorabaugh, *Alcoholic Republic*, 152–155 for the prevalence of providing alcohol to voters. For legal efforts to discourage treating in Virginia, see Crowgey, *Kentucky Bourbon*, 17. William C. Rives, *History of the Life and Times of James Madison* (Boston: Little, Brown and Company, 1859) 1: 179–180. Irving Brant, *James Madison: The Virginia Revolutionist* (Indianapolis, IN: Bobbs-Merrill, 1941), 306. For the broader ideological significance of the reintroduction of treating during the Antebellum Era, see Lender and Martin, *Drinking in America*, 55–58.

17 On the many types of activities that were hosted by taverns in early American society, see Sharon V. Salinger, *Taverns and Drinking in Early America* (Baltimore, MD: Johns Hopkins University Press, 2002).

18 For patterns of alcohol consumption in England, and on the benefits of hopped beer over ale, see Meacham, "'They Will Be Adjudged By Their Drink,'" 118–119, and 134.

19 John Hammond, "Leah and Rachel, or, The Two Truitfull Sisters, Virginia and Maryland," in Clayton Coleman Hall, ed., *Narratives of Early Maryland, 1633–1684* (New York: Charles Scribner's Sons, 1910), 292. Meacham, "'They Will be Adjudged By Their Drink,'" 145–146.

20 Crowgey, *Kentucky Bourbon*, 5–6. On the early Dutch distillery, see J. Leander Bishop, *A History of American Manufactures from 1608 to 1860* (Philadelphia: Edward Young, 1861) 1: 250. For the 1645 legislation, see Hening, *Statues at Large*, 1: 300. The York County store inventory is included in Bruce, *Economic History of Virginia*, 2: 382. Robert Beverley, *The History of Virginia, in Four Parts* (Reprinted from the author's second revised edition, London, 1722; Richmond, VA: J.W. Randolph, 1855), 238.

21 Ann Maury, ed., *Memoirs of a Huguenot Family* (New York: 1853), quoted in Crowgey, *Kentucky Bourbon*, 4. Cooper, *Some Information Respecting America*, 121–122.

22 For the definitive study of the Madeira wine industry, see David Hancock, *Oceans of Wine: Madeira and the Emergence of American Trade*

and Taste (New Haven, CT: Yale University Press, 2009); Ibid., 394–395.

23 Ibid., 84–85.

24 Ibid., 117. For transcripts of these probate records, see Gunston Hall Plantation Probate Inventory Database, 1740–1810, www.gunstonhall. org.library/probate. The total values of the estates that included Madeira ranged from £1,515 to £6,631, with a mean of £3,368. For the types of Madeira grapes, see Hancock, *Oceans of Wine*, 51–52.

25 Lawrence Washington's estate was valued at approximately £1,600, with the spirits assessed at £43.16, Inventory of the Estate of Lawrence Washington, 1753, 7. See the inventory of the estate of Dr. Nicholas Flood, Richmond County, Virginia, Richmond County Will Book no. 7, 239–270, www.gunstonhall.org.library/probate.

26 Hancock, *Oceans of Wine*, 333–349. William M. Kelso, *Archaeology at Monticello* (Thomas Jefferson Memorial Foundation, Monticello Monograph Series, 1997), 110.

27 Rorabaugh, *Alcoholic Republic*, 29–31.

28 For a recent survey of the social history of punch, see David Wondrich, *Punch: The Delights (and Dangers) of the Flowing Bowl* (New York: Penguin Group, 2010); on the development of punch drinking in early America, and especially its prominent role in male-dominated drinking parties, see Karen Harvey, "Barbarity in a Teacup? Punch, Domesticity and Gender in the Eighteenth Century," *Journal of Design History* 21, no. 3 (2008): 205–221. On the transformative impact of the availability of cheap and strongly alcoholic rum on the drinking behavior of men in taverns, see Salinger, *Taverns and Drinking*, 121–150, and Rorabaugh, *Alcoholic Republic*, 32–35.

29 Rorabaugh, *Alcoholic Republic*, 32–35. Gunston Hall Plantation Probate Inventory Database, 1740–1810, www.gunstonhall.org.library/ probate.

30 Smith, *Caribbean Rum*, 13–27.

31 Ibid., 31. On the New London distillery, see Bishop, *History of American Manufactures*, 1: 51. On the Boston rum distillers, see Christopher R. Eck, "The Spirits of Massachusetts: Distillers and Distilling in Seventeenth- and Eighteenth-Century Boston" (master's thesis, University of Massachusetts at Boston, 1993), 73, 76.

32 On rum imports to New York City, see Ibid., 121. On the 1733 Molasses Act, see Ibid., 85–89, and Smith, *Caribbean Rum*, 64.

33 Rorabaugh, *Alcoholic Republic*, 29, 63–64.

34 Account of Dr. William Douglass, 1729, quoted in Eck, "Spirits of Massachusetts," 113. For the description of the archaeological remains, see *Data Retrieval, Quackenbush Square Parking Facility, Albany, New York* (Hartgen Archeological Associates, 2005), 223–281; for the 1784 inventory, see Ibid., 202; for the estimate of production, see Ibid., 282.

35 Cooper, *Some Information Respecting America*, 122.

36 Larry M. Neff and Frederick S. Weiser, trans. and eds., *Fredrich Heinrich Gelwicks, Shoemaker and Distiller—Accounts, 1760–1783* (Breinigsville, PA: Pennsylvania German Society, 1979).

37 For a description of the Schaeffer house, drawings depicting the evidence for the location of the two stills, and the history of the site, see Schaeffer House National Historic Landscape Nomination, n.d. (Photostat, LGWMV); for the period account, see *Brandy Wine Distilling and Wine Grade Farming in Pennsylvania*, 1804, trans. Leroy Person, excerpted in Ibid., 11–12.

38 Rorabaugh, *Alcoholic Republic*, 63–69.

39 Ibid., 69.

40 The prominent role played by Rush in laying the groundwork for the temperance movement has been portrayed by several scholars, among them are: Rorabaugh, *Alcoholic Republic*, 39–48, Lender and Martin, *Drinking in America*, 36–40, and Eric Burns, *The Spirits of America: A Social History of Alcohol* (Philadelphia: Temple University Press, 2004), 54–57.

41 Rorabaugh, *Alcoholic Republic*, 39–50, 187–220.

42 Ibid., 125–146, 187–193; Lender and Martin, *Drinking in America*, 64–72.

43 Rorabaugh, *Alcoholic Republic*, 192–202.

44 Smith, *Caribbean Rum*, 20, and Rorabaugh, *Alcoholic Republic*, 69-73. John French, *The Art of Distillation* (London: Richard Cotes, 1651); Ambrose Cooper, *The Complete Distiller* (London: P. Vaillant, 1757); Michael Krafft, *American Distiller*. Rorabaugh, *Alcoholic Republic*, 69–76.

45 For period descriptions of the distilling process, see the various manuals, such as Cooper, *Complete Distiller*, Krafft, *American*

Distiller, M'Harry, *Practical Distiller*, or Harrison Hall, *The Distiller* (Philadelphia: J. Bioren, 1818); also see Rorabaugh *Alcoholic Republic*, 69–71. On the use of paired stills, see Crowgey, *Kentucky Bourbon*, 52–53. The two stills used in the distillery described by Cooper, *Some Information Respecting America*, 122, as 115 and 60 gallons in capacity, are representative of this practice.

46 On early American still makers, see Henry J. Kauffman, *American Copper and Brass* (Camden, NJ: Thomas Nelson and Sons, 1968), 53, 102–114. One still marked "Bristol" and the date "1787" is in the collection of the Smithsonian Institution Museum of American History, Washington, DC; a second still marked "Bristol" and the date "1784" is in the collection of the Mount Vernon Ladies' Association, Mount Vernon, Virginia. For information on the export of Bristol metal products to America, see Kenneth Morgan, *Bristol and the Atlantic Trade in the Eighteenth Century* (Cambridge University Press, 1993), 97–98. A coppersmith and brazier working in Bristol in 1775 with the same last name, "Hale," that is stamped onto the second still, is listed in James Sketchley, *Sketchley's Bristol Directory* (Bristol: 1775), 40. For information on the Philadelphia stills advertised for sale, see Crowgey, *Kentucky Bourbon*, 50–51. Kauffman, *American Copper and Brass*, 113.

47 On the apparatus of the perpetual still and the benefits of steam heating, see Ibid., 111–113; also see Rorabaugh, *Alcoholic Republic*, 69–73. On the introduction and spread of steam-heated perpetual stills, see Hall, *The Distiller*, 6–7, 33–86, and Crowgey, *Kentucky Bourbon*, 54–60. For the detailed description of another design for an "improved" system of condensing chambers, see Anthony Boucherie, *The Art of Making Whiskey* (Lexington, KY: Worsley and Smith, 1819), 28–31. Hall, *The Distiller*, 34.

48 Hall, *The Distiller*, 27–32; Rorabaugh, *Alcoholic Republic*, 75–76.

49 Hume and Moss, *Scotch Whisky*, 84–85; Charles K. Cowdery, *Bourbon Straight: The Uncut and Unfiltered Story of American Whiskey* (Chicago: Made and Bottled in Kentucky, 2004), 186–187.

50 Crowgey, *Kentucky Bourbon*, 57–58; Rorabaugh, *Alcoholic Republic*, 81.

51 For the Hope Distillery, see Crowgey, *Kentucky Bourbon*, 57–58. For different mash bills, see Krafft, *American Distiller*, M'Harry,

Practical Distiller, and Hall, *The Distiller*. Hall, *The Distiller*, 14. On the continued popularity of rye whiskey in the East, see Bready, "Maryland Rye."

52 Enclosure, Invoice to Robert Cary and Company, 1 May 1759, *PGW: Colonial* 6: 463. Cooper, *Information Respecting America*, 120. Thornton to GW, 6 October 1797, *PGW: Retirement* 1: 386; GW to Thornton, 10 October 1797, Ibid., 401.

53 Cooper, *Complete Distiller*, 101–102. Crowgey, *Kentucky Bourbon*, 128–131.

54 That the prices paid for aged whiskey were higher than for new product is indicated in merchants' advertisements, such as the one quoted in Crowgey, *Kentucky Bourbon*, 122, which specified that the asking price ranged from 30 cents to one dollar per gallon, "according to age."

55 Crowgey, *Kentucky Bourbon*, 109–111. Hall, *The Distiller*, 14. Crowgey, *Kentucky Bourbon*, 111.

56 M'Harry, *Practical Distiller*, 111.

57 Ibid., 113–114.

58 On the early settlement of Kentucky and the identities of the first distillers known to operate there, see Crowgey, *Kentucky Bourbon*, 21–39. Coxe, *Arts and Manufactures of the United States*.

59 Ibid.; also see Rorabaugh, *Alcoholic Republic*, 225–227.

60 Ibid., 77–79.

61 Ibid., 84–87.

62 Ibid., 79–83.

63 Ibid., 85. For the 1810 census figures, see Coxe, *Arts and Manufactures of the United States*. For the 1850 figures, see *Statistical View of the United States: Being a Compendium of the Seventh Census* (Washington, DC: Beverley Tucker, 1854), www2.census.gov/prod2/decennial/documents/1850-06.

64 The figures for the production of New York state distilleries are printed in Rorabaugh, *Alcoholic Republic*, 87.

65 Coxe, *Arts and Manufactures of the United States. Compendium of the Seventh Census*, www.census.gov/prod/www/abs/decennial/1850.html.

66 *The Manufactures of the United States in 1860* (Washington, DC: United States Government Printing Office, 1865); *Twelfth Census of the United States, 1900, Census Reports Volume 8: Manufactures*, www.census.gov/prod/www/abs/decennial/1900.html.

67 For more on the scandals experienced by the Grant administration, see William S. McFeely, *Grant: A Biography* (New York: W.W. Norton, 1981), and C. Vann Woodward, *Responses of the Presidents to Charges of Misconduct* (New York: Delacorte, 1974), 115–140. For a detailed portrayal of the activities of the whiskey ring, see Timothy Rives, "Grant, Babcock, and the Whiskey Ring," *Prologue: Quarterly of the National Archives and Records Administration* 32, no. 3 (Fall 2000), 143–153.

68 Ibid.

69 Ibid.

70 Ibid.

71 Ernest E. East, "The Distillers' and Cattle Feeders' Trust, 1887–1895," *Journal of the Illinois State Historical Society* 45, no. 2 (Summer 1952), 101–123.

72 Staley Farm National Register of Historic Places Nomination Form, 1980 (Photostat, LGWMV).

73 For a recap of Taylor's remarkable career, see Cowdrey, *Bourbon Straight*, 169–176; for the description of the Old Taylor distillery, see Ibid., 175.

74 *Description of the O.F.C., Carlisle, and J.S. Taylor Distilleries* (Frankfort, Kentucky: 1886), 6.

75 Ibid., 10, 12, and 22.

76 Leonard Monzert, *Monzert's Practical Distiller* (Bradley, Illinois: Lindsay Publications: 1889, reprinted 1987).

77 Crowgey, *Kentucky Bourbon*, 121–122.

78 For lengthy analyses of the various "creation myths" that have been formulated for the origins of bourbon, see Ibid., 124–143, and Cowdery, *Bourbon Straight*, 22–41.

79 William Augustus Smyth, *The Publican's Guide, or, Key to the Distill-House* (London: Harrison, 1781), 2.

80 Cowdery, *Bourbon Straight*, 180.

81 Ibid., 180–181.

82 *Munsey's Magazine*, March 1895 (Photostat, LGWMV).

83 "Medicinal Alcohol and Prohibition," Rose Melnick Medical Museum, www.rosemelnickmuseum.wordpress.com. Also see Jacob Appel, "Physicians Are Not Bootleggers: The Short Particular Life of the

Medicinal Alcohol Movement," *Bulletin of the History of Medicine* 82: 355–386, and Daniel Okrent, *Last Call: The Rise and Fall of Prohibition* (New York: Simon and Schuster, 2010), 195–199.

84 Cowdery, *Bourbon Straight,* 42–46.

85 Lender and Martin, *Drinking in America,* 88–96.

86 Ibid., 106–109, 124–126. For a generally sympathetic portrayal of Nation, see Fran Grace, *Carry A. Nation: Retelling the Life* (Bloomington: Indiana University Press, 2001).

87 Lender and Martin, *Drinking in America,* 124–130. For more on the Anti-Saloon League, see Richard F. Hamm, *Shaping the 18th Amendment: Temperance, Reform, Legal Culture, and the Polity, 1880–1920* (Chapel Hill: University of North Carolina Press, 1995), and Peter Odegard, *Pressure Politics: The Story of the Anti-Saloon League* (New York: Columbia University Press, 1928). For William Wheeler's sloganeering, see George McKenna, *The Puritan Origins of American Patriotism* (New Haven: Yale University Press, 2007), 220.

88 Cowdery, *Bourbon Straight,* 81–82; for a list of the federal liquor tax rates from 1791 until the present, see Sam K. Cecil, *The Evolution of the Bourbon Whiskey Industry in Kentucky* (Paducah, KY: Turner Publishing, 1999), 20.

89 Lender and Martin, *Drinking in America,* 130–135

90 For the debate over the impact of Prohibition on the long-term rate of consumption, see Ibid., 136–147. For a thoughtful appraisal of the continuing legacy of Prohibition, see Garrett Peck, *The Prohibition Hangover: Alcohol in America from Demon Rum to Cult Cabernet* (Piscataway, New Jersey: Rutgers University Press, 2009). For the operations of the National Distillers Product Corporation, see Morris Victor Rosenbloom, *The Liquor Industry* (Braddock, Pennsylvania: Ruffsdale Distilling Company, 1937).

91 Bready, "Maryland Rye," 345–378.

92 For a perceptive assessment of recent developments in the American spirits industry, see Noah Rothbaum, *The Business of Spirits* (New York: Kaplan, 2007). For a focus on whiskey, see Cowdery, *Bourbon Straight,* 57–64.

CHAPTER 5

NOTES

1   According to an Application for a Loan from the Reconstruction
    Finance Corporation (Photostat, LGWMV), the intent was "to
    faithfully reconstruct" the distillery and several other structures
    at the site; a site Construction and Grading Plan, dated April
    1933 (Photostat, LGWMV), indicates the footprint of the
    proposed distillery reconstruction. For evidence of negative reaction
    to the reconstruction plan, see *Public Opinion*, December 1936, 20–
    22.

2   For the history of the tract and the results of the archaeological survey,
    see White and Leeson, *Washington's Mill.*

3   A Proposal for the Reconstruction of the George Washington
    Distillery at Mount Vernon, Submitted to the Brown-Forman
    Company, March 2000 (Photostat, LGWMV). Labrot & Graham's
    Old Oscar Pepper Distillery, National Historic Landmark
    Nomination, 1999 (Photostat, LGWMV).

4   "Brown-Forman Helps Restore Historic Still," *Louisville Courier-Journal,*
    12 December 2000. Linn G. Spencer, "George Washington's Stills," 21
    May 2001, www.straightbourbon.com/gwstills.

5   Stephen Dinan, "Grant to Fund Best Shot at Washington's
    Whiskey: Mount Vernon Distillery to be Rebuilt," *Washington Times,*
    6 December 2000.

6   Ibid. Prospectus: A Partnership between the American Spirits
    Industry and Historic Mount Vernon, 2005 (Photostat, LGWMV).
    In 2005 DISCUS agreed to increase its pledge of financial support
    to $2.1 million, due to the need for another year's archaeological
    excavations and the decision to increase the scope of the

distillery to include outfitting the second floor and adding to the structure to accommodate visitors' access to that space.

7   Mount Vernon was awarded a Basic Permit by the Department of the Treasury Bureau of Alcohol, Tobacco and Firearms, Registry Number DSP-VA-1797, 16 April 2001; they also received a permit to keep, store, or possess stills, from the Virginia Alcoholic Beverage Control Board, 21 May 2001. Steve Hunt, "Washington: Whiskey Pioneer," *Mount Vernon (Virginia) Gazette*, 24 May 2001.

8   The later history of the still is related in a letter from Samuel W. Thomas to the Oscar Getz Museum, 21 March 1991 (Photostat, LGWMV); also see Steven Turner, National Museum of American History, to Susannah S. Kent, 20 July 1993 (Photostat, LGWMV). For the sizes of the stills used in Washington's distillery, see Farm Accounts, 1797–98, 137, and Farm Accounts 1799–1800, 37 and 45. A second still on display in the Getz Museum, in Bardstown, Kentucky, also was purported to have been owned for a time by GW; that attribution was simply a mistake that occurred when the Smithsonian still was replaced by another vessel, and the second still was displayed with the previous label, Thomas to the Oscar Getz Museum, 21 March 1991.

9   "Who Stole H.V. Rose's Still?" *Smithfield (North Carolina) Herald*, 23 September 1958; Melvin L. Wilkins, Jr., conversation with author, Mount Vernon, VA, 25 March 2011.

10   C. Woodrow Irvin, "Auction Evokes Spirits of Mount Vernon," *Washington Post*, 17 October 2002.

11   Guy Gugliotta, "Summoning the Spirit of a Bygone Era," *Washington Post*, 21 October 2003.

12   Ibid.

13   Ibid.

14   Senator Toddy Puller sponsored the successful bill to amend the Code of Virginia, authorizing Mount Vernon to sell the spirits that were made on its premises, which was signed into law in 2007. In addition to the whiskey and rum, several craft distillers came together at Mount Vernon in October 2010 to make a 50-gallon batch of peach brandy, http://makinggeorgewashingtonswhiskey.blogspot. com.

15 For a detailed account of the entire distilling process, see "Making George Washington's Whiskey," at http://makinggeorgewashingtonswhiskey. blogspot.com/

16 Niemcewicz, *Under Their Vine and Fig Tree*, in Lee, *Experiencing Mount Vernon*, 77.

17 Jason Wilson, "George's New/Old Rye," *Washington Post*, 2 July 2010.

INDEX

E

Easter, 35
Edinburgh College of Medicine, 158
Eighteenth Amendment, 188
Elisabeth River, Virginia, 99
Elizabeth Town, New Jersey, 36
England, 3, 9, 17, 19–20, 54, 66, 68, 77, 101, 113, 133, 143, 145–48, 152,
     154, 162, 170, 197
Erie Canal, New York, 171
Erskine, David Stuart, 24
Esquire, 7
Evans, Evan, 84
Evans, Oliver, 84

F

Fairfax (brig), 63
Fairfax (family), 21, 90,
Fairfax County, Virginia, 196
Fairfax, George, 44, 68
Farmer (ship), 30, 64,
Fayette County, Pennsylvania, 92
Federal City, 78
Fitzgerald, John, 9, 115, 215
Flood, Dr. Nicholas, 151
Forrester (slave), 88
Fort Cumberland, Maryland, 96
Fort Pitt, Pennsylvania, 219
France, 19, 23, 45, 81, 149, 212
Fraunces, Samuel, 42, 219
Fraunces Tavern, 43, 219
Fredericksburg, Virginia, 113
French and Indian War, 37, 39, 41, 49, 54, 64, 90–91

G

Gadsby, John, 218
Gadsby's Tavern Museum, 218
Gazette, 162, 168
Gelwicks, Freidrich Heinrich, 156
George (slave), 59–60
George Dickel distillery, 225
Georgetown, 97, 116

Philadelphia (*Cont.*) 98, 105, 109, 114, 122, 158, 162, 164, 168, 171
Philadelphia Society for Promoting Agriculture, 75
Pickerell, David, 202, 205
Pickering, Timothy, 30
Platte Valley, 195
Pogue, Dennis, 193
Portugal, 17, 23, 54, 64, 149
Posey, John, 21, 89, 91
Potomac Canal, 97–98
Potomac River, Virginia, 33, 58, 61, 97, 126
The Practical Distiller, 168
Presbyterian Church, 94
Prohibition, 1, 7, 11, 137, 143, 166, 184–85, 187–90, 199, 217, 221–25
Public Opinion, 1
Pure Food and Drug Act, 182
Puritans, 137, 147

Q

Quakers, 1

R

Ramos, Willie, 204
Republican Party, 174–75
Richmond County, Virginia, 151
River Farm, 78, 109
Robert Adam and Company, 62
Robert Cary and Company, 27, 55
Roberts, William, 38, 83, 87
Robertson, Archibald, 24
Rorabaugh, W.J., 137
Rose, Herschel Vaughn, 198
Rover's Delight, 21
Rush, Benjamin, 158, 182
Russell, Jimmy, 202

S

Salem, Massachusetts, 154
Salvington, 113
Samuels, T. William, 222
Schaeffer, Alexander, 157
Schaeffer, Henry, 157

ABOUT THE AUTHOR

Dennis J. Pogue is an archaeologist, a museum administrator, and serves as the Vice President for Preservation at George Washington's Mount Vernon Estate, Museum, and Gardens in Virginia. As a member of the Mount Vernon staff since 1987, he has directed numerous archaeological investigations on the estate, restored several of the original outbuildings and rooms in the Mansion, and overseen the research and planning related to reconstructing a variety of 18th-century structures, including Washington's whiskey distillery.

Dr. Pogue has published extensively and lectured widely on the topics of George Washington and his Mount Vernon plantation, and on the development of American society during the 17th and 18th centuries. He holds a Master of Arts degree in American Studies from George Washington University and a PhD in anthropology, with an emphasis in historical archaeology, from The American University.